SAMUEL JOHNSON

and the Sense of History

SAMUEL JOHNSON

and the

Sense of History

JOHN A. VANCE

The University of Georgia Press

ATHENS

© 1984 by the University of Georgia Press
Athens, Georgia 30602
All rights reserved

Designed by Kathi L. Dailey
Set in 10 on 12 Linotron 202 Bembo

Printed in the United States of America

88   87   86   85   84   5   4   3   2   1

The paper in this book meets the guidelines for permanence and
durability of the Committee on Production Guidelines for
Book Longevity of the Council on Library Resources.

Library of Congress Cataloging in Publication Data

Vance, John A., 1947–
Samuel Johnson and the sense of history.

Includes bibliographical references and index.
1. Johnson, Samuel, 1709–1784—Knowledge—History.
2. History in literature. 3. History. 4. Historiography.
I. Title
PR3537.H5V36 1984   828'.609   83-18190
ISBN 0-8203-0712-2

*The portrait of Samuel Johnson on the title page is an engraving
by Cosmo Armstrong dated March 1821. The engraving was based
on a portrait of Johnson painted by Sir Joshua Reynolds.*

For Watson B. Duncan III

A teacher affects eternity;
he can never tell where his influence stops.
Henry Brooks Adams

Contents

Short Titles   ix

Acknowledgments   xi

Introduction   I

Chapter One. Learning about the Past:
The Development of Johnson's Historical Sense   5

Chapter Two. Looking at the Past: Personalities and Events   31

Chapter Three. Observing the Visual Record of History:
Johnson and Antiquarianism   62

Chapter Four. Johnson as Historian:
Looking at Literature, Lives, and the Law   84

Chapter Five. Johnson as Historian:
Looking at the Modern World in the Light of History   112

Chapter Six. Thinking about the Philosophy and Presentation
of History: Johnson on Historiography and the Historians   138

Chapter Seven. The Significance of History: Conclusions   173

Notes   181

Index   197

Short Titles

Adventurer	*The Idler and The Adventurer,* ed. W. J. Bate, J. M. Bullitt, and L. F. Powell. New Haven: Yale University Press, 1963.
DPA	*Diaries, Prayers, Annals,* ed. E. L. McAdam, Jr., with Donald and Mary Hyde. New Haven: Yale University Press, 1958.
Hawkins	Sir John Hawkins, *The Life of Samuel Johnson, LL.D.,* ed. Bertram H. Davis. New York: Macmillan Company, 1961.
Hazen	*Samuel Johnson's Prefaces and Dedications,* ed. Allen T. Hazen. New Haven: Yale University Press, 1937.
Idler	*The Idler and The Adventurer,* ed. W. J. Bate, J. M. Bullitt, and L. F. Powell. New Haven: Yale University Press, 1963.
Journey	*A Journey to the Western Islands of Scotland,* ed. Mary Lascelles. New Haven: Yale University Press, 1971.
Letters	*The Letters of Samuel Johnson,* ed. R. W. Chapman. 3 vols. Oxford: Clarendon Press, 1952.
Life	James Boswell, *The Life of Samuel Johnson, LL.D.,* ed. G. B. Hill. Revised by L. F. Powell. 6 vols. Oxford: Clarendon Press, 1934–64.
Misc	*Johnsonian Miscellanies,* ed. G. B. Hill. 2 vols. Oxford: Clarendon Press, 1897; reprinted 1966.
Poets	*Lives of the English Poets,* ed. G. B. Hill. 3 vols. Oxford: Clarendon Press, 1905.
Political Writings	*Political Writings,* ed. Donald Greene. New Haven: Yale University Press, 1977.
Rambler	*The Rambler,* ed. W. J. Bate and Albrecht Strauss. 3 vols. New Haven: Yale University Press, 1969.
Rasselas	*Rasselas,* ed. Warren Fleischauer. Woodbury: Barron's Educational Series, 1962.

Sermons	*Sermons,* ed. Jean H. Hagstrum and James Gray. New Haven: Yale University Press, 1978.
Shakespeare	*Johnson on Shakespeare,* ed. Arthur Sherbo. 2 vols. New Haven: Yale University Press, 1968.
Tour	James Boswell, *A Journal of a Tour to the Hebrides with Samuel Johnson, LL.D.,* ed. Frederick A. Pottle and Charles H. Bennett. New York: McGraw-Hill Book Company, 1961.
Works	*The Works of Samuel Johnson, LL.D.* 16 vols. in 8 bound vols. Cambridge: Harvard Cooperative Society, 1903.

Acknowledgments

I wish first to acknowledge the assistance and encouragement of Bertram H. Davis, who directed my dissertation, "Samuel Johnson and the Past." Parts of this dissertation would later be expanded and amended to form the nucleus of this book, and sections of chapters two and three were read as papers at the Northeastern ASECS, Southeastern ASECS, and SAMLA meetings in 1981 and 1982. Regarding the present form of this study, I am most grateful for the recommendations of the two readers engaged by the University of Georgia Press. They devoted much time and energy to examining the manuscript, challenged some of the conclusions and emphases, and suggested additions and stylistic alterations. I would also like to thank Paul Zimmer and the staff at the University of Georgia Press, Mary Hill, who did an excellent job of copyediting the text, Stacie Whitman, who typed an earlier version of the manuscript, Stan Lindberg, who offered advice on final revisions, and Thomas Curley, who expressed early enthusiasm for my doing a book-length study on the subject. The English Department of the University of Georgia provided research time, photocopying, and a summer grant to complete the manuscript.

I cannot fail to acknowledge my daughter Hope, who proved to me that a man can indeed make and type revisions with a four-year-old standing on the back of his chair and hanging around his neck. Finally, as always, thank you Susie.

SAMUEL JOHNSON

and the Sense of History

Introduction

Johnsonian scholars have devoted some of their best energy and writing to the refutation of long-standing impressions regarding Johnson's politics, theories of language and literature, attitude toward travel, and so on. Disheartening, then, is the knowledge that Johnson continues to carry with him into the classroom and general studies the onus of nineteenth-century pronouncements, which seems to hang on tenaciously to his reputation regardless of the many strong arms trying to pull it away. Donald Greene has noted, for instance, the profound effect of Thomas Babington Macaulay on the teaching of Johnson in our century and on the assumptions made about his political beliefs and worth as a writer.[1] With this in mind we may cite Macaulay's judgment on another important topic to which Johnson gave considerable thought: "of history he spoke with the fierce and boisterous contempt of ignorance. . . . History was, in his opinion, . . . an old almanack. . . . But it is certain that those who will not crack the shell of history will never get at the kernel. Johnson, with hasty arrogance, pronounced the kernel worthless, because he saw no value in the shell. . . . In short, the real use . . . of studying history is to keep men from being what Tom Dawson was in fiction, and Samuel Johnson in reality."[2]

Even though the pummeling of Macaulay by Johnsonians has become fashionable if not trite, his assessment of Johnson's response to history has been accepted without question by most who know Johnson casually, through Boswell or limited reading of the canon, and accepted at least in part by some who know Johnson more intimately. Joseph Wood Krutch wrote in his respected biography that to Johnson "history was meaningful only if it was social history or the biography of historical persons and he had little use for any other kind." W. K. Wimsatt thought Johnson "disdained" history, and in 1960 D. M. Low believed Johnson "was avowedly not interested in history." And even more recently, in a general study of Johnson and his world, the author maintains that Johnson regarded history as "an arrant waste of time."[3]

But an important dissenting voice was heard in 1948 with the publication of Godfrey Davies's "Dr. Johnson on History."[4] Although it too often left the impression that basically Johnson was like "professional literary men who from that day to this have tended to neglect historical writings," Davies's study analyzed for the first time some of Johnson's comments about history and criticism of the historians and challenged some of the deeply entrenched perspectives. Davies's was an important ground-breaking essay on this long-ignored and misunderstood facet of Johnson's thought. The article's influence, however, was not immediate, because over a decade passed before the publication of William R. Keast's "Johnson and Intellectual History," which offered several correctives of the old view Davies had not considered.[5] Johnson, Keast wrote, "whatever he may have thought of particular histories or particular historians, did not as a matter of fact have a low opinion of history at all." Keast argued that Johnson concerned himself with a kind of history "in which the stream of thought is deepened, a kind of history whose power, like the power of biography, lies in its applicability to the general state of human life" (p. 249). Keast's essay has easily been the best study of the subject. The efforts of Donald Greene and Thomas Curley have furthermore shed significant light on how Johnson's knowledge of history blended with his perception of politics and travel.[6] Finally, applause is owed to John Wain for calling Johnson a "passionate student of history."[7]

But often when the old views are challenged, the effort appears lukewarm or reserved at best. For example, the *Oxford Literary History* of the mid eighteenth century comments that "the benefit to be obtained from the study of history was not a topic on which [Johnson] rejoiced to concur with the common reader. He professed to 'hate historic talk.' . . . There is more to Johnson's view of history than this. . . . But undoubtedly he felt much impatience with history as it was fashionably understood."[8] In addition, Keast's fine essay only touches upon one aspect of Johnson's historical interests; there has been no attempt by critics or commentators to analyze and define the broad spectrum of Johnson's historical sense. Major biographical and critical studies on Johnson, even when they occasionally note in a sentence or two Johnson's appreciation of history, do not allow it a significant place among his intellectual priorities.[9] Whereas some specialists may agree heartily with Keast and Wain, it is doubtful they appreciate how large a role history played in Johnson's thinking and writing.

For all that was on his mind, from contemporary affairs and literature to his own personal problems, Johnson frequently took time to contemplate life in the past. Occasionally he enjoyed escaping pressing realities by conjuring images of society in and famous personalities of medieval or Elizabethan times, but, more important, he looked to history for a better perspective on how society, his nation, and the world evolved into their present states. The purpose of this book is to demonstrate that history was one of Johnson's major interests, that he was well versed in historical works, that his mind was ripe with historical analogues and personalities, that he was desirous of employing them in his writings, that he wrote often in the historical vein, that he was cognizant of current historical theory and articulate on what made for good history, and that his was one of the best historical minds of the eighteenth century. In this study I have approached Johnson's writings and philosophy from a strictly historical angle and have therefore avoided delving too deeply into his theories on politics, biography, travel, and literature, even though history often crosses through and joins with these important interests of his.[10] Nor do I wish to leave the impression that Johnson was somehow unique in his use of historical figures and events in his writings or alone among literary men and women in the appreciation of historical composition. But it is the depth as well as breadth of Johnson's understanding and employment of history and his own historical writing that elevate him far above many others who used history for literary and moral ends.

I have chosen to organize this study thematically rather than chronologically. A purely chronological arrangement would have made impossible or extremely awkward an examination of Johnson's attitudes toward the seventeenth-century British monarchs, the English Civil War, antiquarianism, and historiography, because evidence for these topics must be gathered from many of his works, written at different periods of his life. The importance of the *Journey to the Western Islands* to an understanding of Johnson's historical sense is apparent, then, throughout this book, not in a section or chapter placed in chronological sequence. But any assumptions to the effect that Johnson burst forth on the scene equipped with a strong historical sense (i.e., the "monolithic" fallacy) must be dispelled immediately; therefore, I have begun this study with a basically chronological chapter, "Learning about the Past: The Development of Johnson's Historical Sense," a look at the historical works he knew, influences on his historical vision, and his early use of history in his writings. The second chapter, "Looking at the Past: Personalities and Events," treats its subject thematically. In this chapter we discover Johnson's response to and use of historical figures and his impressions of the British monarchs from Elizabeth to Anne and the most influential event of his recent memory: the English Civil War. Chapter three examines Johnson's attitude toward antiquarianism, that frequently maligned branch of history just coming into its own in the eighteenth century. The fourth and fifth chapters are concerned with Johnson as historian, more specifically with his integration of history with literature, biography, the law, and political writings. Here we find Johnson assuming the responsibilities of the historian and composing interesting and perceptive history. Chapter six serves as a climax to the preceding chapters, for with a firm grasp of Johnson's historical sense the reader is better able to appreciate Johnson as historical theorist and accept him as one of the best historical thinkers of his age. This chapter furthermore analyzes the supposed damning evidence that has led many to believe Johnson cared little for history. The final chapter summarizes Johnson's position and considers his perspective on the progress of mankind from earlier times to his own.

My decision to quote directly from Johnson in places where simple summary or paraphrase might have sufficed was based on a desire to give the reader a strong dose of Johnson's historical sense and to emphasize his ability to translate it into an effective narrative account or analytical point. Considering that Johnson has been given little credit for appreciating history, I have justifiably included frequent quotations, especially since many of them come from little-studied works. Also, any mention of Johnson's "historical sense" is intended as a reference to an inclusive term, meaning his perception of history influenced and exemplified by a knowledge of, interest in, or enthusiasm for historical facts, personalities, events, and causation and by an intuitive understanding of the importance of history to modern life.

Students of Johnson have been right to stress his modernity and to bury forever the time-worn image of him as an inflexible, narrow-minded Tory reactionary who firmly believed the old way was best. But now Johnsonians and students of the eighteenth century should be encouraged to examine carefully and with appreciation his strong historical sense without fearing to raise specters of past reputations better left undisturbed. A man of his time concerned with present realities and the future of civilization, Johnson nevertheless saw history as one of the most accessible and crucial guides in the search for individual happiness and in the civilization of human society.

Chapter One

Learning about the Past:
The Development of Johnson's
Historical Sense

In *Rambler* 154 Samuel Johnson reminded his readers of Cicero's admonition that "not to know what has been transacted in former times is to continue always a child" (V, 57). Taking Cicero's words to heart, Johnson came to have a knowledge of history very few of his contemporaries ever equaled. Even though his absorbing mind had command of many subjects, history had a special place among his intellectual interests. History, he believed, was inherently intertwined with other subjects he often considered: biography, morality, travel/geography, and politics. To Johnson an acquaintance with the past was no idle diversion of pedants or the leisure class; it was rather a rewarding and enlightening study and a moral responsibility for anyone attempting to understand humanity and the problems and aspirations of modern society. But before examining the full range of Johnson's perception and use of history, we should first establish the foundations of his historical sense by taking a look at the books he knew, some of his early experiences with historical composition, and the historical perspective he developed from his heritage and later travels.

Samuel Johnson lived at a time when British historiography was shaking violently free from its clumsy and often immature youth and emerging confidently though still awkwardly into its young adulthood. Whether or not history actually "flowered" in the eighteenth century has been the subject of much debate, but certainly the period witnessed considerable growth and change in the study of the subject, influenced by some of the most erudite and penetrating historians ever to have written. Was history a branch of philosophy or literature, allowing free rein to theory, style, and didactic intent, or was it a science demanding meticulous research, a strict adherence to truth, and a broad view of historical periods and causes for events? Or could history accommodate a

5

marriage between the literary-philosophical and the scientific? These issues did not evolve in Johnson's day, but it was during his lifetime that more questions were asked and more answers were provided about these matters that anticipated the assumptions of modern historical thought.

Chapter six will discuss Johnson's response to these important issues, but at this point we may note that the development of Johnson's historical sense paralleled a general refinement in historical knowledge and the advancement toward a truly modern historiography. By the time of Johnson's birth in 1709 the study and composition of history in Britain had made significant progress from the medieval and Renaissance chroniclers through the ambitious attempts of Raleigh and Bacon to the influential and often controversial work of Clarendon and Burnet.[1] In addition, the effects of the English Civil War and the Glorious Revolution encouraged a flurry of historical activity, as writers sought to compare post-Revolution Britain with its past and to discover what was unique, or similar, about the era in which they lived. The several years immediately before and after Johnson's birth saw the publication of historical and antiquarian works by the likes of Clarendon, Burnet, White Kennet, Abel Boyer, Laurence Echard, John Strype, Jeremy Collier, Daniel Defoe, and John Oldmixon. And during this period the writings of the late seventeenth-century French philosophers and skeptics—Le Vayer, Saint-Evremond, Fontenelle, and Pierre Bayle—began to have considerable impact on no less a historical mind than Bolingbroke. Although this short sketch will expand in chapter six, when Johnson's positions are discussed in the context of his century's debate over historiography, we should note here how fertile the ground was for the growth and development of both an individual's and a nation's historical sense. And Johnson was one of those who garnered the fruit of what the century had to offer to anyone with an inquisitive and analytical historical mind.

An investigation of Johnson's historical knowledge commences with a tour of his library. As we begin to sort through the shelves that Donald Greene and J. D. Fleeman have reconstructed for us,[2] we notice that roughly 20 to 25 percent of the known volumes in the collection are histories or historical in nature—a fact that in itself must qualify any notion of Johnson's lack of interest in history. He possessed books on church history such as Nicephorus's "History of the Church to 610," Nicetas's "History of the Eastern Empire, 1117–1203," and Zonaras's

"Chronicles of Byzantine History to 1118." The ancient Greek historians included Thucydides and Xenophon. The ancient Romans were represented by many works, including *Historiae Augustae* (a collection of biographies of the Roman emperors from Hadrian to Carinus), Caesar's *Commentaries*, Dio Cassius's *Historiae Romanae*, Suetonius's *Lives of the Twelve Caesars*, Velleius Paterculus's "Compendium of the History of Rome," the Greek Polybius's "General History of the Early Roman Empire," and the works of Tacitus and Sallust. Later histories of Rome included Oliver Goldsmith's *Roman History*, Justus Lipsius's *Roma illustrata*, and Basil Kennett's *Antiquities of Rome*.

Because many of these classical works were included in the libraries of educated persons, one might wonder if to Johnson they were merely shelf dressing. I believe that E. L. McAdam's warning that it is "dangerous to assume that there were many books in Johnson's large library with which he was not well acquainted" (*DPA*, p. 295) is well advised. Johnson may not have read from cover to cover all these historical works written in and about antiquity, but he knew some of them well enough, for example, to criticize two of the most famous. In the "Life of Butler" he remarked that "every reader regrets the paucity of events, and complains that in the poem of *Hudibras,* as in the history of Thucydides, there is more said than done," and to Boswell he observed that Tacitus "seems to me rather to have made notes for an historical work, than to have written a history" (*Poets*, I, 211; *Life*, II, 189). Regarding Velleius Paterculus, in his first extant diary (1729) Johnson mentions his desire to read the historian along with Lucretius and Justinus, and we know that in his old age he found pleasure in perusing Suetonius's *Lives of the Twelve Caesars* (*DPA*, pp. 26, 275).

Johnson's holdings in earlier British history featured Bede's *Historia ecclesiastica*, Robert of Gloucester's *Chronicle*, Richard Grafton's completion of Hall's *Union of the Noble and Illustre Families of Lancastre and York*, John Stow's *Survey of London*, William Camden's *Britannia*, William Baxter's *Glossarium antiquitatum Britannicarum*, William Nicolson's English, Scottish, and Irish *Historical Libraries,* Henry Wharton's *Anglia sacra*, George Ridpath's *Border History of England and Scotland*, Lord Hailes's *Annals of Scotland*, and other antiquarian pieces. For the more recent periods he possessed, among other works, Gilbert Burnet's *History of His Own Times*, Gilbert Stuart's *History of Scotland*, Catharine Macaulay's *History of England*, and William Robertson's *History of Scotland*. Johnson also had volumes on the history of France, such as Louis Cousin's documents dealing with Charlemagne and the early years of the Holy Roman Empire,

François Mézeray's *Histoire de France,* the Duke of Sully's *Memoirs,* and Voltaire's *Le Siècle de Louis XIV.* In addition, he owned historical works on Ethiopia, Egypt, Sweden, Denmark, Greenland, Flanders, Spain, South America, and Antwerp, including Walter Harte's *Life of Gustavus Adolphus,* Hiob Ludolf's *A New History of Ethiopia,* and William Robertson's *History of America.* Moreover, Johnson's collection included several volumes on historical chronology, which he considered one of the "necessary preparatives and attendants" of history.[3] Among them were Eusebius's *Thesaurus temporum,* John Kennedy's *Scripture Chronology,* Lenglet du Fresnoy's *Chronology,* Benjamin Marshall's *Chronological Tables,* Isaac Newton's *Chronology of Ancient Kingdoms Amended,* and Thomas Wilson's *Classical Antiquities of the Jews, Greeks, and Romans,* which was dedicated to Johnson.

The above list, extensive though it is, comprises only a part of the historical volumes that at one time rested in Johnson's library. The original sale catalog, as Greene points out, represents only about a fourth of the nearly three thousand books owned by Johnson at his death. Although one could probably restock a part of Johnson's library shelves with historical works we know him to have owned (e.g., Holinshed's *Chronicles,* his gift to John Hawkins, and Clarendon's *History of the Rebellion,* an avowed favorite), we may safely assume that he proudly possessed during his lifetime many other important or little-known classical, British, or Continental histories of which no record remains. To dismiss the historical holdings in his library as more a reflection of gifts from friends and booksellers rather than as an indication of his interest in history would be unjust, for rarely is so large a portion of a person's private collection comprised of unwanted volumes. Johnson's library, with only a few exceptions, if any, was an extension of his literary and intellectual background and interests. To Johnson, as to most of us, displaying books in his personal library was tantamount to wearing his mind on his sleeve.

The extent of Johnson's historical knowledge cannot be limited, however, to the volumes in his library. Undoubtedly he was exposed to history from the time he was able to read. Even before he began reading on his own, Johnson must have listened to stories of medieval England, the reign of Elizabeth, and the English Civil War told by the elder sages of Lichfield. Hours might well have been spent imagining life in earlier times—the pageants, battles, coronations, castles, and mythic giants and dragons. He was never to forget the exhilarating tale of St. George and the Dragon told by his mother's maid: he later said to Hester Thrale, "Babies do not want . . . to hear about babies; they like to be told of giants and castles, and of somewhat which can stretch and stimulate their little minds" (*Misc*, I, 156). And many of the tales from history, mixed with intoxicating fantasy or even taken as unadorned fact, had the power to expand the young Johnson's imagination and vision of the past.

When Johnson began to read on his own he was exposed as we know to classical literature, and after he entered the Lichfield Grammar School he developed a facility for Latin grammar and readings from early Roman authors, moving on to Ovid, Cato, Cicero, Virgil, Horace, and such Greek writers as Hesiod, Pindar, and Theocritus as he grew older.[4] But a diversion from this concentrated study was likely a historical work or two in addition to the chivalrous romances he always loved. One can picture young Sam retiring from the labors of translation and seeking refuge in the medieval panorama depicted in a work like Holinshed's *Chronicles*. And Michael Johnson's bookshop gave Sam the opportunity to begin and then improve on his historical knowledge. Although it would be helpful to have an account of all the historical works that at one time or another found a temporary home in the elder Johnson's shop, we can imagine the number to be large; Michael Johnson's purchase in 1706 of the Earl of Derby's library of close to three thousand volumes, for instance, contained a substantial collection of histories.[5] Michael Johnson may well have entered his shop wondering why his son had failed to deliver a requested volume, only to find him standing in a corner with his eyes glued to a page of Clarendon's *History*.

In assisting his father in the shop and preparing for visits to outlying stalls, Johnson would have handled dozens of historical works, many of which he probably browsed through or at least inquired about. And we know that when he found a historical account of Lichfield Cathedral in a notebook, he took it upon himself to research the date and source of the manuscript.[6] History would also have appealed to the young Johnson because of his inability or lack of desire to concentrate for very long on schoolwork; he would have enjoyed reading a self-contained or brief unit in a large historical volume and then poring over an atlas to ascertain the location of the events about which he was learning. And history was not a formal subject of the grammar school curriculum; Johnson therefore could not have resented being forced to cultivate historical scholarship or being subjected to any unmerciful cuts from Headmaster John Hunter's rod for forgetting the dates and facts about an event like the Punic Wars.

9

Johnson's year at Stourbridge (1725–26) offered him the opportunity to add further to his historical knowledge, for during this period he was encouraged and tutored by his cousin, the accomplished Cornelius Ford. James Clifford believes Johnson discussed with Ford whatever he had been reading, a good deal of that being from Ford's own library, and Walter Jackson Bate has emphasized the profound effect the older man had on Johnson's development.[7] Ford advised his young cousin to broaden his learning to encompass the larger realms of human experience—which we trust would have included deeper immersion into history. After his return to Lichfield and before his departure to Oxford in the fall of 1728, Johnson began looking into "a great many books, which were not commonly known at the Universities" (*Life,* I, 57). Chester Chapin believes that by the time Johnson came to translate Father Lobo's *Voyage to Abyssinia* in 1733 he was already versed in ecclesiastical history and in the "major heresies and theological conflicts that form so important a part of that history," a knowledge he no doubt acquired during that period of "hard reading" preceding his Oxford residence.[8] And we cannot ignore his relationship with Gilbert Walmesley as a source of historical stimulation. Johnson later described Walmesley as a "violent Whig" with whom he "used to contend with great eagerness" (*Tour,* p. 378). We must keep in mind that in any debates between a violent Whig and a conservative thinker history had to surface as a backdrop to as well as the very subject of contention. Charles I, Cromwell, Charles II, James II, William III, Anne, Shaftesbury, Marlborough, Godolphin, Sacheverell, Harley, St. John, and Walpole were some of the names and the English Civil War, the Popish Plot, the Revolution of 1688, the War of the Spanish Succession, the Peace of Utrecht, the Jacobite Rebellion of 1715, and the South Sea Bubble some of the events the two men must have discussed and debated. Johnson's pride in his own argumentative talents may well have prompted some research of the persons and events he and Walmesley considered, but even if he did not open a book the very act of thinking about the seventeenth and early eighteenth centuries would have helped refine his historical sense and make him see the unbreakable link between the present state of affairs and the personalities and incidents of the past.

Arriving at Oxford in October 1728 Johnson brought along several works of a historic stamp; for example, volumes of Suetonius, Livy, Tacitus, and Basil Kennett's *Antiquities of Rome* (1696).[9] He told Boswell that while at Oxford he read Greek *"solidly"* but not the Greek historians (*Life,* I, 70). Perhaps not, but it is safe to assume that from time to time he dipped into the Roman historians or more contemporary historical works. In any event, it was at Oxford that he came across a French translation of Lobo's *Voyage to Abyssinia,* which included a history of the Abyssinians. Conversations with his contemporaries provided further opportunity to display his historical knowledge and analysis, well-informed talk as well as argumentative skills being expected of under-graduates. John Fludger, whom Johnson later described as a "scoundrel" and a "Whig" (*Life,* II, 444), certainly must have heard, as did Walmes-ley, Johnson's views on historical matters from the Puritan Revolution and Cromwellian Interregnum of the mid seventeenth century to the downfall of the Tory ministers at the death of Anne. Developing an impatience with loose historical talk, which characterized monarchs and events as one-dimensional representations of greatness or evil without comprehending their true signficances or complexities, Johnson would have wanted to know through further reading or hard thought the truth of the past in order to counter the arguments of those who relied on cant.

Following his departure from Oxford in December of 1729, Johnson continued his education over the next several years by further readings, and historical works were a part of his self-imposed curriculum. John Hawkins noted that in these years Johnson "applied himself to the study of the Holy Scriptures, and the evidences of religion, to the writings of the fathers and of the Greek moralists, *to ecclesiastical and civil history,* and to classical literature and philology" (Hawkins, p. 70; italics mine). As he prepared for his 1735 translation of Lobo's *Voyage to Abyssinia* he read many books on the topic such as Ludolf's *New History of Ethiopia* and Michael Geddes's *Church History of Ethiopia.*[10] And in 1736, as he was constructing his play *Irene,* he found "entertainment in turning over" Richard Knolles's *General History of the Turks* (1603), which would re-main one of his favorite historical works (Hawkins, p. 22).

The abridgment and translation of Joachim le Grand's 1728 French translation of Father Lobo's *Voyage to Abyssinia*[11] includes in its dedica-tion an important reflection of Johnson's developing historical sense: "A generous and elevated mind is distinguished by nothing more certainly than an eminent degree of curiosity; nor is that curiosity ever more agreeably or usefully employed, than in examining the laws and customs of foreign nations." As Johnson realized early in his career, an under-standing of these laws and customs was made easier by a keen awareness of history. Johnson's later writings on the law and customs support such an assertion, but, as Donald Greene has pointed out, we find as well in the translation of Lobo the spirit of scientific skepticism, the humanistic historian's belief that human nature is generally the same regardless of geographic location, and one man's criticism of colonialism and the philosophy that encourages it.[12] And, as we shall discover, these characteristics are major aspects of Johnson's historic vision, refined in later years by further readings, experience, and much serious thought, but in place, it appears, before he arrived in London and began writing for the *Gentleman's Magazine*.

When Johnson came to London and began frequenting the book stores, like Thomas Wilcox's in the Strand, he no doubt enjoyed browsing through new and unfamiliar books, perhaps some histories, which he could not afford to buy. Either at this time or a little earlier he became acquainted with Father Paul Sarpi's *History of the Council of Trent*, an important historical work on the event that marked the beginnings of the Counter-Reformation, and in July of 1737 he wrote Edward Cave about the possibility of his sponsoring a translation. Although a rival and better-supported translation caused the abandonment of the project in 1739 after some half dozen sheets were in print, it is significant that Johnson first caught the interest of Cave because of a projected translation of a historical work; his developing historical interests, which allowed him to appreciate the significance of Sarpi's book, helped win him a position with the *Gentleman's Magazine*. His letter to Cave of 12 July 1737, which proposed the translation, must have left a most positive impression: Johnson reminds his future employer that the reputation of the *History*, which had recently been translated into French, "is so much revived in England, that it is presumed, a new translation of it from the Italian, together with Le Courayer's Notes from the French, could not fail of a favourable Reception." That Nathaniel Brent had already brought out an English translation in 1620, argues Johnson, is no reason to reject a modern version, because Brent's work is difficult to read and unworthy of the *History* (*Letters*, I, 8).

Cave had to judge Johnson from this correspondence as a serious and diligent author worthy of a position with the *Gentleman's Magazine*, especially since history was becoming a more frequent interest of the periodical. Cave would have wanted someone with a good historical sense for reviews, miscellaneous writings, biographies, and, as it turned out, parliamentary reporting. Thomas Birch was enthusiastic at the prospect of a new translation of Sarpi, but he and Cave learned early of Johnson's occasional procrastination: sometime in 1738 Johnson wrote Cave, "As to Father Paul, I have not yet been just to my proposal, but have met with impediments which I hope, are now at an end, and if you find the Progress hereafter not such as you have a right to expect, you can easily stimulate a negligent Translator" (*Letters*, I, 13). Although little came of the translation, the project signaled the direction Johnson was to take in his twenty-odd years as a Grub Street writer,[13] for many of his literary efforts would reflect his knowledge, interest, and facility with respect to history. We have not adequately appreciated that whereas he was a journalist by trade Johnson was so well suited for the *Gentleman's Magazine* because he came to London with a knowledge and appreciation of history, which he strengthened in the years following 1738.

Johnson read further into history in preparation for the biographies, reviews (see chapter four), and miscellaneous writings he did for Cave in the next several years; for example, he looked into Clarendon's *History of the Rebellion*, Anthony Wood's *Athenae Oxonienses*, Bulstrode Whitlock's *Memorials of the English Affairs*, and the memoirs of Sarah Churchill. James Clifford's portrait of Johnson's work habits in the early *Gentleman's Magazine* years is worth quoting: "One can picture him sitting at his desk with a single main source before him, reading a long passage, turning it over in his mind, and then summarizing it all in a few forceful paragraphs. Occasionally he might reach for a standard historical authority, in order to check or amplify the account. . . . The few reference works he needed could have been borrowed from Birch or some other friend."[14] Both Thomas Birch and William Guthrie, Johnson's colleagues on the *Gentleman's Magazine*, were much interested and well versed in history and both published respected works in the field. Birch was the author of the *History of the Royal Society*, which Johnson reviewed, the *Memoirs of the Reign of Queen Elizabeth*, and an edition of the state papers of John Thurloe. In addition, he understood the significance of the many small pieces of historical information—documents, letters, and biographical reminiscences. Birch, Johnson later said, "knew more small particulars than anybody," and Isaac D'Israeli noted that Birch "enriched the British Museum by thousands of the most authentic documents of genuine secret history" (*Tour*, p. 218; *Life*, I, 160).

Guthrie, whom Johnson replaced as "reporter" of the debates in Parliament, was the author of *A General History of England, from the Invasion of Julius Caesar to the Revolution in 1688* (four volumes, 1744–1751) and *A General History of Scotland* (ten volumes, 1767–1768). Furthermore, he began and contributed to *A General History of the World* (twelve volumes, 1764–1767). In Boswell's estimation, Guthrie was "the first English historian who had recourse to that authentick source of information, the Parliamentary Journals"; Johnson, Boswell added, "esteemed him enough to wish that his life should be written" (*Life,* I, 117). Surely Johnson had occasion to discuss historical events and theory with these men, who must have furthered his appreciation of history as well as lent him books.

As further evidence of Johnson's enthusiasm for history at this point of his life, we may recall the historical project he proposed to Cave in the autumn of 1743:

> The first thing to be written about is our Historical Design. . . . I think the insertion of the exact dates of the most important events . . . as may enable the reader to regulate the order of facts with sufficient exactness the proper medium between a Journal which has regard only to time, and a history which ranges facts according to their dependence on each other, and postpones or anticipates according to the convenience of narration. I think our work ought to partake of the Spirit of History which is contrary to minute exactness, and of the regularity of a Journal which is inconsistent with spirit. For this reason I neither admit numbers or dates nor reject them. (*Letters,* I, 20)

One may speculate that this work was to be a history of the reign of George I (1714 to 1727) or a treatise on the transferal of power from the Stuarts to the Hanoverians; perhaps it alludes to a historical account of the English Parliament, of which Johnson seems to have completed some eighty pages, now lost. Whatever its focus, the project is a firm indication of Johnson's historical interests and his early confidence in attempting actual history.

Regarding other works of Johnson's initial literary period, we should not ignore *Marmor Norfolciense* (1739), his youthful and spirited jab at the Walpole administration. Swiftean in flavor, the pamphlet levels its satire and criticism at government, ministers, monarchs, antiquarians, and anti-intellectuals.[15] History seems also an object of the satire, seeing that the stone on which the prophecy appears is a "venerable relique of antiquity" (*Political Writings,* p. 22). The words to posterity are interpreted by a foolish antiquarian who has rapid recall of quotations from medieval writers. The antiquarian's labored consideration of whether the inscription's author was a Briton or Saxon appears to make light of the early English period as a subject fit only for the dullest of pedants, yet even within the satiric framework Johnson reflects on several important historical issues, the first being the attitudes of the foreign monarchs who have succeeded to England's throne (William III, George I, and George

II): "it has been rarely, very rarely, known that foreigners however well treated, caressed, enriched, flatter'd or exalted, have regarded this country with the least gratitude or affection" (p. 27). Based upon his knowledge of recent history, Johnson describes these rulers as having been "ready upon all occasions to prefer the petty interests of their own country, though perhaps only some desolate and worthless corner of the world." In this and the charge that English wealth has paid for foreign mercenaries and troops (the example of George I), we find not only a political propagandist for the opposition to George II and an adept satirist, but also the historian raising questions born from the past though still highly relevant to the present. The historically minded portion of Johnson's readers would have furthermore recalled the suffering inflicted on the English people when the foreigner William the Conqueror sought to solidify his monarchy in the years immediately following his victory at Hastings.

In his discussion of kingship—allowing for the exaggeration required in such political satire and ironic personae—Johnson again plays the role of historian. Instead of viewing the English monarchs as great rulers all and indulging in a colored view of the past, Johnson, after an "attentive perusal of histories, memoirs, chronicles, lives, characters, vindications, panegyricks, and epitaphs," perceives the monarchy in a less flattering but more truthful light. If the kings had talent for prophecy, he argues through his antiquarian, why have historians failed to inform us of that fact? Not far outside the confines of the satire is Johnson's assumption that many readers have failed to consult more accurate and moderate historical accounts and instead have unthinkingly uttered platitudes and party distortions about past and more recent monarchs without the slightest notion that the rulers were deficient, unwise, intemperate, violent, and occasionally immoral leaders of state. Johnson is not far removed from the truth when he sarcastically asserts that a monarch's disregard for the future health of his country "is evident from the accounts of all ages and all nations" (pp. 31–32). Throughout the first part of *Marmor* and above the shouting and laughter of the critic and satirist is a frustrated voice calling for a more sober look at history for a proper perspective on the present.

Later in the pamphlet and again through the guise of the antiquarian, Johnson mentions the treaties, alliances, agreements, and policies regarding Europe's balance of power that so reflected the course of recent history and the fact that all of these "will bear an easy and natural application to the present time." Alluding to the unstable and warlike atmosphere of contemporary European politics, Johnson points out that explanations for current problems are available in the histories of each country. Suggested here is his distress over the failure of England and Europe to understand historical precedents when they chose sides. We find, then, that the young Johnson was giving some thought to historical causation; at least he saw history able to provide some clearly defined reasons for the current strife. Although the foolish narrator is unable to interpret the inscription accurately, which makes it all the easier for the reader to do so, through him Johnson makes several interesting observations on the uses and importance of history.

In 1741 Johnson brought out, in the *Gentleman's Magazine, A Debate Between the Committee of the House of Commons and Oliver Cromwell,* an "abridgment" of the 1660 pamphlet *Monarchy Asserted.*[16] As Donald Greene notes, Johnson did not simply edit from the 1660 text; rather he extracted the essence of the speeches and "worked them up in his own words, thus composing what was virtually a new and original work" (*Political Writings,* p. 77). In this piece we find Johnson responding to the dramatic spirit of history as he captures a moment from one of England's most memorable times—a period filled with high tension and viewed with much fascination in his day. In the introduction, he sets the scene of this April 1657 confrontation between Cromwell, then solidified in his power, and the Committee from Parliament, which was supportive of a return to monarchy. The *Debate* is both interesting and unusual in its being, along with the *Parliamentary Debates,* one of the few sustained pieces of dramatic prose Johnson ever wrote—historical or otherwise. Also surprising perhaps is Johnson's depiction of Cromwell not as the incarnation of evil but rather as a dignified, rational, and intelligent head of state. In fact, Johnson's delineation of the committee, which advocates the position on established institutions that he would accept, fails to match the success of his portrait of the lord protector.

As the committee argues for the resumption of the monarchy, we sense a heightening of dramatic tension because we listen to only the committee's side of the issue for the initial nineteen paragraphs: we imagine Cromwell standing almost majestically alone before them, formulating his response to every challenge of his views. The committee cites legal cause and precedent for continuing the monarchy but sees no historical basis for the title of protector: "upon what law is it founded, and what are the limits of his authority? . . . Shall it be said that his authority is independent, despotick, and unlimited? Where then is the liberty for which the wisest and best men of this nation have been so long contending? What is the advantage of all our battles and all our victories?" (p. 86). After two days of careful thought, Cromwell finally replies that he has no strong knowledge of historical precedents but will answer based on the immediate relevance of the committee's position. Cromwell's assertion makes him more heroic in one sense as he refuses to be the slave of custom or history. Johnson nevertheless sustains the aura of historical drama with the protector's reply: "There was once a time when every office, and the title annexed to that office, was newly invented and introduced, from what did it derive its legality and its importance at its first introduction, but from general consent? The great, binding, the inviolable law, is the consent of the people; without this nothing is right, and supported by this nothing can be wrong. Antiquity adds nothing to this great sanction, nor can novelty take away its authority" (p. 91). These remarks, shaped by his handling of the choppy and ungrammatical original pamphlet, are indicative of Johnson's skill at divorcing his own bias against the Interregnum from a work he considered historical and dramatic in nature.

Invoking God as his inspiration and judge, an effective rhetorical device, Cromwell finishes his response (twenty-one paragraphs long) and waits for the committee's rebuttal. Again, the committee rests most of its case on historical precedent: "surely the prescription of many hundred years, the authority of the law, and the approbation of the people, are circumstances that will constitute the highest degree of political necessity" (p. 98). The committee adds that the "prerogative of our monarchs, and the authority of our laws, it has been already the task of several ages to regulate and ascertain" (p. 98). Antiquity must be respected because the ancient constitution has always received the "general approbation" of the people. Interestingly, after these twenty paragraphs, the protector has the final word in his shorter reply, which again has much to recommend it, although one now senses more impatience in his tone and fire in his arguments: "Such and so oppressive was the government plann'd out to us, and for our posterity, and under these calamities must we still have languish'd, had not the same army which repress'd the insolence of monarchy, relieved us with the same spirit from the tyranny of a perpetual Parliament, a tyranny which was equally illegal and oppressive" (p. 108). Johnson receives high marks in the *Debate* for his ability to capture the drama of a historical moment. Cave, Guthrie, and Birch were no doubt impressed by the dramatic skills of their colleague and confident in his ability to "report" on his own the dramatic speeches resounding through the chambers of Parliament.

As G. B. Hill observed, the *Debate* suggests the method Johnson would employ while working on the *Parliamentary Debates* for the *Gentleman's Magazine* from July 1741 through March 1744 (*Life*, I, 150). Here we find Johnson writing some contemporary history, albeit in a rather unusual form, necessitated by the laws prohibiting the straightforward reporting of the debates in Parliament. Involved with the *Debates in the Senate of Magna Lilliputia* as editor for Guthrie's early reporting, Johnson found himself proficient at shaping the actual words spoken in Parliament to fit the Swiftean framework and at capturing the basic import of the speeches and applying them to the correct speakers.[17] Johnson of course realized he was at liberty to amend, add, dramatize, and even distort what actually came from Parliament in order to make the *Debates* more readable and entertaining, but he must have sensed not only an opportunity but almost a responsibility to establish a historical framework for the benefit of his readers. Donald Greene comments that in the early months of Johnson's "reporting," when the fate of Robert Walpole was the Opposition's most pressing business, it "was an important and must have been an exciting duty for the still young and obscure hack writer to create in effect a piece of history for his contemporaries and for posterity."[18]

In the early numbers we find Johnson being his most historical. A glance at the July 1741 installment discovers him writing, "a superficial Acquaintance with History may inform us," "surely no Man who has read the History . . . of the Nations," and "If we consult History, my Lords" as he establishes the contexts for the current hostilities between Britain and her European neighbors.[19] As we learn, the war with Spain— the War of Jenkins's Ear—was not realizing those optimistic predictions about easy victory, and Frederick of Prussia's demonstrations in Silesia presaged Britain's involvement in a major European conflict. Although the matter of Walpole's dismissal is the central focus of the early debates and thus their emphasis is primarily political in nature, Johnson could not isolate the fate of Walpole from the events that would lead to a formal declaration of war in 1744, the fighting to be known as the War of the Austrian Succession. Nor would he fail to remind his readers about the nature of political power, Europe's balance of power, European history, historical precedents, motives, treaties, exploration, trade, commerce, armies, navies, military administration, and the relationship between the military and the citizenry. Johnson provides an overview of late seventeenth- and early eighteenth-century history as a way to understand the contemporary climate of war. As he asserts in the August number, "The only candid Method of Enquiry is to recur back to the State of Affairs, as it then appeared,"[20] basic and sound historical advice indeed, but at the time not generally accepted. We should remember that in his *History of England,* published in the next decade, David Hume seemed to defy the fashion and avoided judging the past solely by present standards.

Perhaps, as Benjamin Hoover argues, the *Debates* are in the main moral essays rather than attempts at political statement or historical accuracy,[21] but Johnson lived to find some of his speeches regarded as authentic and ironically incorporated into a number of historical collections and works, most notably Smollett's *History of England.*[22] On the other hand, Donald Greene contends that "[i]n a sense, Johnson in his 'Debates' is the Thucydides of the great political wars of the 1740's in Great Britain."[23] In any event, the *Debates* previewed the kind of historical writing Johnson would later compose in the *Literary Magazine* and reflected his interest in the many facets of historical inquiry and his firm belief that contemporary life could not be adequately understood and evaluated without a strong grasp of history. Although one can differ over whether Johnson imagined his "reporting" would be accepted as fact, his talent for historical writing was at least partly responsible for the manner in which the *Debates* were received.

The *Parliamentary Debates* represented a significant stage in the development of Johnson's historical sense, but the major contributor to Johnson's historical knowledge at this time was his experience cataloging the Harleian collection, which included rare books covering almost every field of British history.[24] Johnson himself said of the collection that in it were to be found, "with the ancient chronicles, and larger histories of Britain, the narratives of single reigns, and the accounts of remarkable revolutions, the topographical histories of counties, the pedigrees of families, the antiquities of churches and cities, the proceedings of parliaments, the record of monasteries, and the lives of particular men."[25] During his association with the project from 1742 to 1744, Clifford adds, Johnson "must have handled thousands of these rare books, and examined a large number in detail"[26]—an assessment I believe to be a conservative one. The collection was comprised of about forty thousand volumes, and as Johnson sorted, described, and annotated the collection along with William Oldys, he peered into an antiquarian's paradise: surveys of towns, counties, castles, churches, and other structures and accounts of rare coins, inscriptions, and remains of Roman roads and other artifacts. He also looked through many medieval histories and lives of medieval monarchs from Henry I to Edward IV. Historical works of the Renaissance and seventeenth century were well represented, and Johnson noted in his *Account,* "That memorable period of the English history, which begins with the reign of Charles the first, and ends with the Restoration, will almost furnish a library alone." In addition, Johnson examined lives of churchmen and accounts of church policy, government, and architecture; historical records of Oxford and Cambridge universities; books pertaining to England's legal history; and historical records of pageantry, heraldry, and customs. Beyond the realm of England were histories of Scotland, Wales, Ireland, France, and other European countries. Johnson moreover held in his hands copies of the Greek and Roman historians, histories of the popes, and historical works on geography, travel, military affairs, music, and literature. And we should not ignore the work he did on the "Harleian Miscellany": besides contributing the "Essay on the Origin and Importance of Small Tracts and Fugitive Pieces," Johnson had a hand in cataloging and annotating many rare pamphlets from Lord Oxford's library.[27]

With perhaps a few exceptions, Johnson did not read these books through, but he had to know them well enough to annotate or select for the catalog. He probably familiarized himself with any prefatory matter and then extracted the essence of the volume as he leafed through the text. As Boswell perceptively remarked many years later, Johnson "had a peculiar facility in seizing at once what was valuable in any book, without submitting to the labour of perusing it from beginning to end" (*Life,* I, 71)—a facility refined to a near science by his work on the Harleian collection. Johnson could not have regarded his activity as harmless drudgery; on the contrary, the perusal of these valuable books and pamphlets must have captured and sustained his imagination, even if the mechanics of cataloging were at times tedious. But as his fingers became soiled by the covers of the aged texts, his mind absorbed hundreds of years of British heritage, giving him a knowledge of history and the nature of life few could ever hope to achieve. The Harleian experience had a profound effect on Johnson's development as a scholar, thinker, and humanist; never again could he view government, the church, society, or the weaknesses of human beings from the narrow perspective of one who sees all achievements and failures as indigenous to the world of the present. Cataloging the Harleian collection, especially at this period of his life, helped to shape the author of *The Dictionary, The Vanity of Human Wishes,* the *Rambler, Rasselas,* and the *Lives of the Poets.*

The Harleian experience moreover made easier Johnson's decision to act on Robert Dodsley's suggestion that he compile an English dictionary to replace the huge and helpful but woefully inadequate publication of Nathan Bailey (1736). Johnson knew that his familiarity with history and sense of the progress made over the centuries in taste and learning were invaluable tools to the lexicographer. Even so, he must have done further historical research, renewing or beginning an acquaintance with several historical works as he searched for authors to quote. One need not read through too many letters in the *Dictionary* to detect Johnson's considerable reading in Raleigh's *History of the World,* Bacon's *History of Henry VII,* Clarendon's *History of the Rebellion,* and Richard Knolles's *History of the Turks.* Whereas these are the most frequently quoted historical works, Johnson also made use of Matthew Hale's *Primitive Origination of Mankind,* Richard Carew's *Survey of Cornwall,* Camden's *Remains,* Bacon's *War with Spain,* and Samuel Daniel's *Civil Wars,* among others. And Johnson's reading of these histories encouraged the writing of *Rambler* 122 (May 1751), his essay on the state of British historiography, in which he evaluates more specifically the works of Raleigh, Bacon, Clarendon, and Knolles.

In addition to furthering and refining his knowledge of history, the compilation of the *Dictionary* provided Johnson the occasion to think more seriously about literary history—the changes in language, literature, learning, and taste from the Elizabethan period to the end of the seventeenth century. We know, for instance, that he had once planned something along the lines of an anthology in chronological order of the examples adorning the entries. Even though he abandoned this idea owing to the sheer volume of materials with which he would have had to contend, his initial intentions suggest again the influence of his growing historical sense. One should note the following remark from the preface, reflective of Johnson's historical perspective: "But as every language has a time of rudeness antecedent to perfection, as well as of false refinement and declension, I have been cautious lest my zeal for antiquity might drive me into times too remote, and crowd my book with words now no longer understood" (*Works,* XI, 246). And the experience with the *Dictionary* reinforced Johnson's belief in the irony of historical inquiry; that is, the more one learns the more one realizes one does not know: "I saw that one inquiry only gave occasion to another, that book referred to book, that to search was not always to find, and to find was not always to be informed; and that thus to persue perfection, was, like the first inhabitants of Arcadia, to chase the sun, which, when they had reached the hill where he seemed to rest, was still beheld at the same distance from them" (251).

Near the end of the preface, Johnson, glancing at the past and then to the present, considers reasons for various alterations in the language: "Total and sudden transformations of a language seldom happen; conquests and migrations are now very rare; but there are other causes of change, which, though slow in their operation, and invisible in their progress, are, perhaps, as much superiour to human resistance, as the revolutions of the sky, or intumescence of the tide. Commerce, however necessary, however lucrative, as it depraves the manners, corrupts the language . . ." (255). These remarks speak well of Johnson's historical instincts, for he often searched into the more obscure corners of the past to determine the progress and refinement of language; he realized the answers provided by history are seldom simple. Finally, Johnson's connection of literature and history may be gleaned in his defense of the practice, though "rarely" employed in his work, of "exhibiting a genealogy of sentiments, by showing how one author copied the thoughts and diction of another: such quotations are, indeed, little more than repetitions, which might justly be censured, did they not gratify the mind, by affording a kind of intellectual history" (248).

The preparation for the *Dictionary* marks the end of a major stage in the development of Johnson's historical sense, and interestingly parallels the end of another stage in British historiography, for waiting in the wings was David Hume's *History of England (Great Britain)*, to be followed by the appearance of Robertson's and Gibbon's historical works. The remaining chapters of this book will examine Johnson's employment of and views on historical figures, events, movements, and theory, but we may complete the examination of Johnson's acquisition of historical knowledge by citing some of the works we know him to have read and used following his work on the *Dictionary*. When he came to edit Shakespeare he consulted Shakespeare's sources: Holinshed's *Chronicles*, Polydore Vergil's *Anglicae historiae*, and Edward Hall's *Union of Lancastre and York;* but he also looked into or cited Bacon's *History of Henry VII*, Camden's *Remains*, Thomas Birch's *Memoirs of the Reign of Queen Elizabeth*, Thomas More's *History of Richard III*, Plutarch's *Lives*, Peter Heylyn's *Cyprianus Anglicus*, Geoffrey of Monmouth's *Historia regum Britanniae*, and John Caius's *De ephemera Britannica*. And Johnson would have sharpened his vision of the medieval period by first reading (as he did in preparation for the *Dictionary*) and then editing Shakespeare's history plays.

Johnson's broad literary activity in the 1750s and 1760s reveals him using, reviewing, or writing prefaces for an assortment of historical works. A partial listing should illustrate his broad interest in history and growing historical knowledge: Anthony Wood's *Athenae Oxonienses*, J. F. Lafitau's *Histoire des découvertes et conquestes des Portugais*, Manuel de Faria y Sousa's *The Portugues Asia*, John Stow's *Annals*, Thomas Blackwell's *Memoirs of the Court of Augustus*, Thomas Birch's *History of the Royal Society*, John Armstrong's *History of Minorca*, Charles Aleyn's *History of Henry the Seventh*, Quintus Curtius's *History of Alexander*, Sallust's *De bello Catilinario*, De Thou's *Historiarum sui temporis*, William Tytler's *Historical and Critical Enquiry* into the "casket letters" of Mary Queen of Scots, Florus's *Epitomae bellorum*, Thucydides' *History*, John Kennedy's *Chronology*, Lenglet du Fresnoy's *Chronological Tables*, and the Duke of Sully's *Memoirs*.

In addition, in the 1770s and 1780s he cited, employed, or commented on such British histories as Clarendon's *History of the Rebellion*, Burnet's *History of His Own Times*, Lord Hailes's *Annals of Scotland* and *Remarks on the History of Scotland*, William Robertson's *History of Scotland*, Matthew Hale's *History of the Pleas of the Crown*, John Dalrymple's *Memoirs of Great Britain and Ireland*, Thomas Leland's *History of Ireland*, Hector Boece's *Scotorum historiae*, Catharine Macaulay's *History of England*, George Lyttelton's *History of Henry II*, William Temple's *Introduction to the History of England*, Kenneth Macaulay's *History of St. Kilda*, Robert Henry's *History of Great Britain*, John Macpherson's *Dissertations on . . . the Ancient Caledonians, Picts, and British and Irish Scots*, and the Scottish travel narratives of Thomas Pennant, Martin Martin, and William Sacheverell. To this list we can add such continental histories as Robertson's *History of Charles V*, Charles Henault's *Nouvel Abrégé chronologique de l'histoire de France*, Machiavelli's *History of Florence*, Charles Sheridan's *Account of the Late Revolution in Sweden*, Olof von Dalin's *Svea rikes historia*, Robert Watson's *History of Philip II*, and Nathaniel Hooke's *Roman History*, and the following accounts of the New World: Robertson's *History of America*, James Adair's *History of the American Indian*, Israel Mauduit's *Short View of the History of the Colony of Massachusetts Bay*, and Benzo's (Gerolamo Benzoni) *New History of the New World*.

We might also recall the books he recommended as important reading to Daniel Astle: Thomas Carte's *History of England*, Charles Rollin's *Ancient History*, Samuel Pufendorf's *Introduction to History*, René Vertot's *History of Knights of Malta*, Clarendon's *History of the Rebellion*, Louis Dupin's *History of the Church*, and Oliver Goldsmith's *Roman History* (*Life*, IV, 311–312). Nor should we forget his advice to students of history in the preface to the *Preceptor* (1748):

23

The Student may join with this Treatise *Le Clerc's Compendium of History,* and afterwards may, for the Historical Part of *Chronology,* procure *Helvicus's* and *Isaacson's* Tables; and if he is desirous of attaining the technical Part, may first peruse *Holder's Account of Time, Hearne's Ductor Historicus, Strauchius,* the first Part of *Petavius's Rationarium Temporum;* and at length *Scaliger de Emendatione Temporum.* And for Instruction in the Method of his Historical Studies, he may consult *Hearne's Ductor Historicus, Wheare's* Lectures, *Rawlinson's Directions for the Study of History:* and for Ecclesiastical History, *Cave* and *Dupin.* (Hazen, p. 183)

Finally we cannot ignore Johnson's knowledge of geography, which he saw along with chronology as one of history's "necessary preparatives and attendants."

All these works display Johnson's education in many facets of history—ancient, medieval, modern, British, Continental, Middle Eastern, New World, cultural, political, biographical, chronological, colonial, travel, and antiquarian. And these numerous volumes suggest Johnson's continuous accumulation of historical knowledge. For all he learned in the 1740s from the Harleian experience, he continued to discover books that had escaped him earlier in his life and to take an interest, as we shall see later in this book, in the historical studies published by his contemporaries. Reflective of his lifelong interest in history is his asking in the final months before his death for *Burton's Books,* a set of volumes comprised mainly of history.[28] The basic facts seem clear: far from being uninterested in history and far from considering it a "waste of time," Johnson's knowledge of the subject was probably excelled only by the learned historical scholars of his day. We should therefore take quite literally and seriously what he said in the summer of 1784: when Lord Eliot informed him of a work entitled "Captain Carleton's Memoirs," Johnson responded, "I did not think a *young Lord* could have mentioned to me a book in the English history that was not known to me" (*Life,* IV, 333–334).

Finally, Johnson's strong historical sense was also influenced by experiences as a youth in Lichfield and by his later travels. As Thomas Curley has written, Johnson "had few equals in his appreciation of travel for stimulating the mind. . . . He knew . . . that any ramble had an inestimable moral and intellectual significance."[29] Although the following observations hardly do justice to the importance Johnson placed on travel, we must not fail to appreciate the association he made between a place and its past. And he realized early in his life the power of place to evoke history; in Lichfield he grew up respecting the strong bond between the present and tradition. As I have noted, he would have heard innumerable tales from family, friends, and townsfolk regarding the city's recent and ancient history. Young Sam's inquisitive nature likely yearned for stories of renowned citizens and events of the fifteenth, sixteenth, and seventeenth centuries; for example, his imagination was probably titillated by the romantic story of how "Dumb" Dyott felled the Roundhead Lord Brooke in the 1640s. Lichfield's annual fair days and customs dating from ancient times—Old Fair at Shrovetide, St. George's Day, Whitsuntide, the Sheriff's Ride, the Court of Piepowder, and the Court of Array—breathed life into the distant past, and in the processions, ceremonies, games, dances, and songs Johnson would have sensed a long link from his hand back to those of boys dressed in medieval garb.[30] His later view that vigilant efforts should be made to preserve long-standing customs had its source in his boyhood days in Lichfield. The young Johnson would moreover have seen history etched on many of Lichfield's structures; as Clifford points out, "Everywhere that Sam wandered there were still traces of the disastrous Civil War of the mid-seventeenth century."[31] Even though it had been subsequently repaired, Lichfield's cathedral, the town's most impressive landmark, still bore the hideous scars of the English Civil War. Johnson would have heard the stories and then visualized the march of troops, the smashing of stone and glass, the cries of the citizens, and the smell of gunpowder drifting throughout the city.[32]

When he began traveling out from Lichfield into the countryside and to Birmingham, Stourbridge, and Oxford, Johnson moved through or near historic grounds displaying structures still proclaiming England's celebrated past. Not far from Lichfield were the famous sites of Shrewsbury, Bosworth Field, and Naseby, which once reverberated with the sounds of clashing swords, galloping horses, and the voices of Hal and Hotspur, Henry of Richmond and Richard III, Prince Rupert and Cromwell. Whether or not he actually stood on the battlefields, Johnson, having been raised near these famous sites, would have had frequent occasion to consider England's glorious yet turbulent history.[33] Southeast of Birmingham, in the vicinity of the road between Lichfield and Oxford, lay Kenilworth Castle, a twelfth-century structure that in Johnson's day still bore witness to the Civil War, as did most of the Midlands, the favorite area of iconoclasts as well as soldiers. On the path from

Lichfield to Oxford, Johnson also traveled not far from Coventry, Warwick Castle, and Banbury, three other sites evoking memories of the Civil War and a rich English heritage.

At Oxford in 1728 and 1729, and on later visits to the university, Johnson lived among several of his country's most famous and impressive landmarks such as the older colleges, New College (founded 1379), Queen's College (1341), Oriel (1326), Exeter (1314), Merton (1264), Balliol (ca. 1260), and the most ancient, University College (1249).[34] It would have been almost impossible for a young man of Johnson's sensibilities not to have imagined Oxford in medieval times when the first scholars walked the grounds. As he read or learned of the university's history and saw at first hand the structures that held some of England's greatest minds, he must have been exhilarated by the sense of history Oxford conveyed. Other sites in and around the city, however, would have painfully reminded him of destructive periods in the nation's past. The remains of the castle at Oxford stood as a grim reminder of civil war, and the ruins of numerous abbeys in the area recalled a time when they were vital and respected habitations. When Johnson returned to Oxford in the summer of 1754 he and Thomas Warton came upon the remains of Oseney and Rewley abbeys on one of their walks. Deeply affected by the sight, which could not but remind him of Henry VIII's order in 1536 to dissolve the monasteries, Johnson was silent for half an hour until he finally uttered, "I viewed them with indignation" (*Life,* I, 273). The dilapidation of a historical landmark and a tangible link to the past, combined with the reminder of man's willingness to destroy whatever opposes him, prompted Johnson's lament at the sight of the abbeys. Three years earlier he had written, "It is natural to feel grief or indignation, when any thing, necessary or useful, is wantonly wasted, or negligently destroyed" (*Rambler* 177, V, 172).[35]

Other than his many years in London, which, as Richard Schwartz rightly stresses,[36] offered him innumerable evidences of the past and many occasions to reflect on important historical events, Johnson's later travels allowed him to view many of Britain's most famous structures and to contemplate the past and its significance for the present and future. He visited the major English cathedrals between 1762 and 1783: Winchester, Exeter, Lincoln, Peterborough, Chichester, Salisbury, Chester, Ely, Norwich, and perhaps Gloucester. Other than inquiring from locals or recalling from his own reading the history of these magnificent structures, Johnson would have seen evidence of both a proud medieval and Renaissance tradition and the legacy of wanton destruction and the excesses of reform. Many of these cathedrals, and many other religious houses throughout England, still bore the wounds inflicted by the zeal of Henry VIII and the vindictiveness of the parliamentarian troops. The great castles likewise testified to both the majesty and evil of the past. Although we can name with certainty only a few of the castles Johnson visited (for instance Arundel), he no doubt gazed at or examined many of these historic structures dotting the English landscape. That his sense of history was stimulated by the old and famous cathedrals, churches, and castles he viewed is suggested in his remarks on Cowdray House, a sixteenth-century structure: "I should like to stay here four-and-twenty hours. We see here how our ancestors lived" (*Life,* IV, 160).

Johnson's trip to Wales in 1774 afforded him further glimpses at his English heritage, because many of the impressive structures were the extensions of English ingenuity, vitality, and military prowess. Edward I's great Welsh castles represented the grandeur of his reign and his country; they were edifices expected to stand the test of time as a lasting tribute to the dynamism and strength of the English people. Accordingly, Johnson no doubt found it both distressing and ironic that Carnarvon and Conway castles were in ruinous states, as were Denbigh, Rhuddlan, and Dalbaran castles. That his historical sense could be excited by the sight of a magnificent landmark is evident in his reponse to Beaumaris Castle, which he described in some detail as a "mighty pile," and especially Carnarvon, "an Edifice of stupendous magnitude and strength": "To survey this place would take much time. I did not think there had been such buildings. It surpassed my Ideas" (*DPA*, pp. 203–204). It is therefore highly unlikely he included the historic structures in the assessment he gave John Taylor: that Wales "has nothing that can much excite or gratify curiosity" (*Letters,* I, 413–414).

The trip to Scotland in the previous year, however, was the most sustained opportunity for Johnson to view historic places and landmarks and to consider their significance.[37] On his trip north through Stilton, Stamford, Grantham, Newark, Doncaster, York, Northallerton, Darlington, and Durham, Johnson traveled over more countryside reflecting the glory and violence of England's history. Near Johnson's route were Fotheringhay and Pontefract castles, the sites of Mary of Scotland's execution and Richard II's murder; Peterborough and Durham cathedrals; Stamford Bridge, where Harold defeated the Viking invaders a few weeks before destiny took him to Hastings; and Marston Moor, where Cromwell won his first major victory. As expeditiously as he progressed north and thus with little time to sightsee—although he did visit a ruined abbey in York and Durham Cathedral—Johnson would have cast his eyes to the east or west remembering the general locations of the famous sites, perhaps thinking or talking about them as he rode on. His warm feelings for Mary Queen of Scots and his frequent references to and knowledge of the Civil War strongly suggest that he would have taken several moments to reflect on history as he passed in the general vicinity of Fotheringhay Castle and Marston Moor. Johnson was never a traveler who set his eyes only in the direction of his ultimate destination; rather he drew much inspiration and philosophical insight from the terrain through and near which he moved.

After a short stay at historic Alnwick Castle, on whose walls he walked and in whose towers he climbed (*Letters*, I, 341), Johnson headed northward to Berwick, passing on the way Dunstanburgh and Bamburgh castles, the latter still showing the traces of the Wars of the Roses. Although Johnson wished to investigate "men and manners" in Scotland more than to probe for antiquities, he was looking forward to examining many of Scotland's storied landmarks. More will be said later regarding Johnson's tour of Scotland, but at this point we should remember that as he viewed the castles, churches, and cathedrals from St. Andrews to Iona, his mind recalled the ancient magnificence of the structures now in ruins, the violent reformations of John Knox, and the destruction wrought by Cromwell's cannon. Johnson's anticipation at seeing the venerable city and university of St. Andrews was met with frustration: "In the morning we rose to perambulate a city, which only history shews to have once flourished, and surveyed the ruins of ancient magnificence, of which even the ruins cannot long be visible" (*Journey*, p. 5). In this case history seems a mournful and passive memory, but, as his remarks on the dilapidated condition of the cathedral show, moments from the past could rise up vividly in his mind. He writes that the cathedral "was demolished, as is well known, in the tumult and violence of Knox's reformation," to which Boswell adds, Johnson's "veneration for the hierarchy is well known. There is no wonder, then, that he was affected with a strong indignation while he beheld the ruins of religious magnificence. I happened to ask where John Knox was buried. Dr. Johnson burst out, 'I hope in the highway. I have been looking at his reformations'" (*Journey*, p. 5; *Tour*, pp. 40–41). This famous response reveals a man for whom history speaks dramatically and poignantly. Although two hundred years dead, Knox was perceived by Johnson as a flesh-and-blood villain, whose radical philosophy continued to move many toward destructive solutions for intellectual and emotional problems. Still alive through his legacy, Knox could not be passed off as a mere figure in a history book. Influenced by his strong awareness of history, Johnson was distressed at the indifference, misguided judgment, and violent reform evidenced at St. Andrews. He wrote in frustration to Hester Thrale, "Why the place should thus fall to decay I know not" (*Letters*, I, 344).

As he and Boswell traveled on and considered the old customs, traditions, literature, buildings, and remains, Johnson was quick to articulate his knowledge of Scotland's history. He knew, for instance, that the monastery at Aberbrothick was "of great renown in the history of Scotland" and that many of the decayed and dilapidated structures of national or local prominence were the result of zealous reformation: as he remarked on some religious houses on the Isle of Col, "Two chapels were erected by their ancestors, of which I saw the skeletons, which now stand faithful witnesses of the triumph of Reformation" (*Journey*, p. 122).[38] His exploration of the Highlands and Western Islands stimulated and inspired him historically, and he heard with eagerness and wrote with enthusiasm on the clash of rival clans and a way of life now fast disappearing.

But Johnson's response to history on the Scottish tour is most wonderfully expressed in his remarks on Iona:

> We were now treading that illustrious island, which was once the luminary of the Caledonian regions, whence savage clans and roving barbarians derived the benefits of knowledge, and the blessings of religion. To abstract the mind from all local emotion would be impossible, if it were endeavoured, and would be foolish, if it were possible. Whatever withdraws us from the power of our senses; whatever makes the past, the distant, or the future predominate over the present, advances us in the dignity of thinking beings. . . . That man is little to be envied, whose patriotism would not gain force upon the plain of Marathon, or whose piety would not grow warmer among the ruins of Iona? (*Journey*, p. 148)

Walking among the ruins of Iona, Johnson visualized the land populated by barbaric settlers, violently clashing with other clans for territorial rights. He could see the fur-lined garments, the crude weaponry, and the stern and calloused appearance of the men, women, and children. But his portrait also includes the landing of Columba and the building of the famous monastery in the sixth century, which brought learning, refinement, and dignity to the region. Johnson in this passage eloquently encourages an understanding of history as a way to achieve a proper perspective about life and one's heritage and the dignity for which all human beings should strive. These impressive remarks on Iona, the product of Johnson's refined historical sense, convey well the moving emotions prompted by a keen awareness and appreciation of history as an intellectual, philosophical, and moral study. Even though the inspirational draughts of history have always been available to those raised in towns ripe with tradition, like Lichfield, and to those who have traveled to historic sites and lands, very few have taken the time to drink as often and as long as did Samuel Johnson.

Chapter Two

Looking at the Past: Personalities and Events

In *Adventurer* 95 (October 1753) Johnson argued that in his writings a moralist may "deliver his sentiments" by using "historical examples" (p. 426). Accordingly, in his writings and conversation Johnson often relied on his knowledge of history to draw a useful analogy or to illustrate a moral position. He did not make allusions to the past pedantically or perfunctorily, as did many of his contemporaries, because they were expected of educated men and women, rather he put them to specific use, and he expected his readers and friends to grasp the reference and apply it to the point addressed. But he also took much delight in recalling the famous personalities and events of the past without consciously employing them for educative or moralistic ends. This chapter will focus on Johnson's use and delight in history's famous names and on his response to the most memorable event in his recent memory: the English Civil War. Furthermore, this chapter begins—and the other chapters will continue—to explore the vigorous and skeptical nature of Johnson's historical sense; while at times charmed and excited by historical figures or memorable confrontations, Johnson could easily readjust his perspective and view these names and events from the moralist's viewpoint and, more important, in the objective historian's light.

Eighteenth-century Britons were fond of contrasting their monarchs, government, society, and national spirit with those of their past. Even though the medieval and Renaissance periods were as a result romanticized if not grossly distorted, taking liberties with historical truth was not condemned, for the point was to evoke the grandeur, martial ardor, and national pride perceived as the hallmark of earlier times in order to show that what once "was" can and should be again. Regardless of his censure of historians who romanticized history, as we shall discover in chapter six, Johnson had no objection to the poet or satirist doing so, provided the literature was enriched and the subject or theme enhanced by the inclusion of famous historical personalities glorified beyond what they were in real life. That is, Johnson was always able to separate the worlds of historical truth and literary expression and to enjoy unashamedly a romanticized look at important historical men and women without its vitiating his objective and skeptical historical perspective. As long as one made the distinction between fact and legend—as long as one could suppress the glamorous and emotional qualities of looking to the past when one sought historical truths—Johnson saw nothing wrong in indulging one's historical fancy for enjoyment or artistic purposes; he realized, as do modern historians, that often an individual or nation welcomes or needs the kind of inspiration provided only by a colored view of the past. There is no real contradiction or inconsistency, then, in Johnson's view, for when he assailed "romantic" historical composition, he was thinking specifically of those works that purported to be *objective* history.

In *London* (1738) Johnson begins his poetic career by turning to the past for inspiration and example. The poet writes that he and Thales were awed at the sight of Greenwich, the birthplace of Elizabeth: "We kneel and kiss the consecrated earth; / In pleasing dreams the blissful age renew, / And call Britannia's glories back to view" (lines 24–26).[1] Knowing of his country's love affair with the Virgin Queen, Johnson features her reign as both a recognizable and the last period of greatness with which to contrast London's present degeneration. When he alludes to England's maritime superiority, defeat of the Armada, economic prosperity, and honorable, dignified, and vigorous foreign and domestic policies, we find a poet who appreciates history's power to inspire and instruct the present. The memory of Elizabeth filled hearts with pride, made tangible the link to a rich heritage, and possibly incited some readers to the point of indignation over the changes time had wrought in government and national spirit.

Later in the poem, after Thales bristles at the thought of London as a "French metropolis," Johnson calls on another name from England's past: "Illustrious Edward! from the realms of day, / The land of heroes and of saints survey" (lines 99–100). Edward III, the fourteenth-century monarch who defeated the French at Crécy and Poitiers, was a favorite historical figure in Johnson's day. Thomson, Pope, Thomas Warton, and others evoked his memory, often in contrast to modern deficiencies. Johnson's juxtaposition of the king with the contemporary French "invasion" of London is especially effective as he recalls the English victories on French soil. Regardless of the king's administrative and fiscal shortcomings and his besotted concern for his mistress, Alice Perrers, eighteenth-century England recalled only his martial daring and prowess, typified as well by his son the Black Prince.[2] Certainly knowledgeable about Edward III's imperfections, Johnson nevertheless felt himself moved when he considered the emotional quality of the famous battles fought during the Hundred Years' War, and for literary purposes he saw nothing wrong in emphasizing only positive aspects of a monarch's personality or reign. Though dead for over 350 years Edward III could still inspire not only national pride but also a determination to rejuvenate governmental policy and modify social behavior.

Johnson, through Thales, considers another famous warrior-king:

> Ah! what avails it, that, from slav'ry far,
> I drew the breath of life in English air;
> Was early taught a Briton's right to prize,
> And lisp the tale of Henry's victories.
>
> (lines 117–120)

Like Edward, Henry V was praised by the poets for his successes in France and his general popularity, due in part to the image marvelously perpetuated by Shakespeare. Henry was perhaps the closest to being the "perfect" king in the minds of eighteenth-century Englishmen. As Johnson's verse suggests, he learned early in his life about the dashing Henry, who won battles with his sword and the hearts of his countrymen with his charm. But the most revered of the English monarchs may well have been the last one evoked by Thales: "A single jail, in Alfred's golden reign, / Could half the nation's criminals contain" (lines 248–249). Alfred's stock rose dramatically in the eighteenth century, influenced by Thomas Hearne's 1709 edition of John Spelman's *Life of King Alfred the Great* and the poetry of Thomson, Pope, and especially Thomas Warton, who portrayed the king in such pieces as *The Triumph of Isis* (1749), "Ode for Music" (1751), and "On the Marriage of the King" (1761) as an exemplar of justice, courage, patriotism, freedom, honor, and learning. In Alfred, the first recognizable English monarch, Johnson's readers would have seen the cornerstone of English greatness and a stark contrast to more recent times.

By reminding his countrymen of their illustrious heritage, Johnson hoped to trigger emotions and encourage actions to curb the debilitating habits and malaise affecting contemporary London and England. Although he had too good a historical mind to believe that Elizabeth, Edward, Henry, and Alfred were ideal or that their times were preferable to the present, he realized that as a poet he was free to exploit history's romantic side to further his artistic and political ends. To argue that he was merely following convention or the example of Juvenal in employing historical exempla dismisses too lightly the use he made of history in *London*. Placing the historical allusions strategically at the beginning, middle, and end of his poem and setting its tone in the third stanza with "In pleasing dreams the blissful age renew, / And call Britannia's glories back to view," Johnson structures *London* within a historical framework. The reader is always aware that contemporary London pales dismally in comparison with England's proud and vibrant past. The poem is an excellent illustration of Johnson's strong historical sense applied to literary creation and moral instruction.

The Vanity of Human Wishes (1749) effectively integrates history with Johnson's moral designs: "Let hist'ry tell where rival kings command, / And dubious title shakes the madded land" (lines 29–30). Once more we notice the historical framework being established early in the poem; in essence, Johnson opens up for his readers a large volume of history, turns the pages, and points out several of the hundreds of examples relative to contemporary life. He moreover contrasts unspecified periods of the past with the follies of the present: "See motly life in modern trappings dress'd, / And feed with varied fools th' eternal jest" (lines 51–52). He laments that a nobler spirit, indicative of Britain's history, lies in deep slumber: "For now no more we trace in ev'ry line / Heroic worth, benevolence divine" (lines 87–88). But far more memorable is his use of specific historical examples and the two powerful verse portraits of Wolsey and Charles of Sweden. Confident that the majority of his readers possess a fundamental knowledge of history, Johnson writes of the misfortunes that befell George Villiers (the first Duke of Buckingham), Robert Harley, Thomas Wentworth, Edward Hyde (Lord Clarendon), Galileo, Xerxes, Charles VII, Croesus, the Duke of Marlborough, Anne Vane, and Catherine Sedley. Military and political leaders, men of learning, and royal mistresses might have been portrayed as fictional characters or represented as types, but Johnson knew such depictions would have greatly diminished the strength of the poem. These men and women still lived in popular imagination, and, unlike the glorified portraits in *London,* they were presented more truthfully as well as artistically, which made them even more effective evidence of the vanity of human wishes. And Johnson chose not to restrict his examples to one era or country, as he might have done to give his poem a tighter construction; instead he broadened the scope of history as much as possible, from Croesus in the sixth century B.C. to

Anne Vane in the 1730s, as a way of emphasizing the universality of his moral and the relationship between his readers and the long history of mankind.

Johnson also refers to the warlike nature of ancient Greece and Rome as a parallel to modern Britons, who "stain with blood the Danube or the Rhine" in the War of the Austrian Succession. But these historical moments pale in comparison to the portraits of Wolsey and Charles of Sweden. Johnson obviously desired strong examples of political and military power, but why did he choose Wolsey over dozens of other qualified candidates? Both a reading of Shakespeare's *Henry VIII* and his own knowledge of Renaissance history probably influenced the choice; Johnson was likely intrigued by the wealthy and powerful cardinal who struck fear in the hearts of almost all who crossed his path—that is, according to the view of Elizabethan Protestants, perpetuated by Holinshed's *Chronicles* and John Foxe's *Acts and Monuments*. Johnson must have seen the challenge in making this austere and frightening man of fact and legend an object of the reader's pity rather than scorn. The brilliance of the portrait, then, is in his bringing Wolsey from an imposing demigod down to a humble and infirm beggar without encouraging in the reader a smile of satisfaction at the cardinal's fall—a reaction that might deter from an acceptance of the moral lesson. In the first several lines Johnson portrays Wolsey as larger than life—in "full blown dignity"—standing above all others, making the law and filling his coffers with riches given him by church and realm. (The presence of Henry VIII is not felt at this point.) He is a god in control of almost all, even the elements: "Thro him the rays of regal bounty shine, / Turn'd by his nod the stream of honour flows, / His smile alone security bestows" (lines 99–104). Wolsey is a colossus who straddles all he surveys, blocking the sun and affecting the flow of events as he so chooses. Johnson leads him to the very threshold of omnipotence:

> Still to new heights his restless wishes tow'r,
> Claim leads to claim, and pow'r advances pow'r;
> Till conquest unresisted ceas'd to please,
> And rights submitted, left him none to seize.
>
> (lines 105–108)

At this moment of high tension, with the cardinal's hand stretched toward the heavens for new gain, a mere frown from the lips of the king brings the titanic Wolsey crashing suddenly and violently to the ground. Quickly, Johnson's Wolsey decays until with "age, with cares, with maladies oppress'd, / He seeks the refuge of monastic rest" (lines 117–118). The poet's refusal to condemn overtly Wolsey's thirst for wealth and power or to relish in his fall forces the reader to witness and perhaps pity what is now merely an aged and powerless man, deserted and ignored, moving pathetically to his death. Johnson is thus able through history to touch one's humanity as well as provide a moral lesson: "Speak thou, whose thoughts at humble peace repine, / Shall Wolsey's wealth, with Wolsey's end be thine?" (lines 121–122).

Later in the poem, Johnson features the exploits of Charles XII, the "Unconquer'd lord of pleasure and of pain" (line 196), who at the height of his power was determined to take Moscow, in winter the quintessential test of military might and cunning. Unlike the devious Wolsey, Charles is admirable as well as heroic in the initial description of his character: "A frame of adamant, a soul of fire, / No dangers fright him, and no labours tire" (lines 193–194). On the other hand he seems the simple hero; the bugle blows and he dons his military habiliments and "rushes to the field." But his victories only whet his appetite for grander exploits—the conquest of Moscow and the Russian army. Again at a moment of high drama, as the reader sees Charles godlike and invincible, the great warrior becomes a pawn in destiny's game. Vanquished both by Peter the Great and the elements, Charles is left vulnerable to the cruelest of ironies. The dashing leader, always on the advance, dies in a passive and unheroic manner: his "fall was destin'd to a barren strand, / A petty fortress, and a dubious hand" (lines 219–220).[3] The final lines of the portrait speak superbly of Johnson's utilization of history: "He left the name, at which the world grew pale, / To point a moral, or adorn a tale." Johnson found Charles a most useful illustration of his theme because the Swede was a more recent figure from history and, being well publicized by Voltaire's *History of Charles XII* (1731), better known to his readers, who, as in every generation, felt more comfortable with events and personalities nearer their own time.

Charles XII had already captured Johnson's imagination before he sat down to compose *The Vanity of Human Wishes,* for in 1742 he wrote John Taylor about getting "Charles of Sweden ready for this winter," most likely an allusion to a projected drama (*Letters,* I, 23). Undoubtedly, Johnson's interest in the Swede was influenced by Voltaire's *History of Charles XII,* which Johnson called "one of the finest pieces of historical writing in the language" (*Misc,* II, 306). Voltaire's ambivalent feelings toward Charles, his spirited attack on abuses of monarchs and conquerors, and his frequent comparison of Charles with his contemporary Peter the Great not only encouraged the inclusion of the Swede in *The Vanity of Human Wishes* but also inspired *Adventurer* 99 (16 October 1753), the periodical essay that best demonstrates Johnson's use of history as a teaching device and well illustrates his belief in the uniformity of human nature regardless of period and place, his advocacy of skepticism in historical inquiry, and the strong role he assigned to chance in the determination of history.

Johnson unrolls before his readers a historical tapestry of men who designed great things: "Machiavel has justly animadverted on the different notice taken by all succeeding times, of the two great projectors Catiline and Caesar." Assured that his readers have at least some knowledge of the two men, Johnson nevertheless provides enough historical detail to insure that his point about the reputations of famous historical figures will not be missed: "Both formed the same project, and intended to raise themselves to power, by subverting the commonwealth: they persued their design, perhaps, with equal abilities, and with equal virtue; but Catiline perished in the field, and Caesar returned from Pharsalia with unlimited authority: and from that time, every monarch of the earth has thought himself honoured by a comparison with Caesar; and Catiline has been never mentioned, but that his name might be applied to traitors and incendiaries" (pp. 430–431).

Other than Johnson's command of balance and antithesis, the passage is marked by a brief though poignant tale of success and failure. Without the allusion to history, which gives the scene legitimacy and relevance to the reader, the point would have lost much of its potency. Johnson then turns to another page of history and shows his readers Xerxes, whose might filled the world with "expectation and terror" until his army and fleet were destroyed; since that time he has never been mentioned "without contempt." In contrast to the failure of Xerxes, Johnson points to another projector, "who invading Asia with a small army, . . . stormed city after city, over-ran kingdom after kingdom, fought battles only for barren victory, and invaded nations only that he might make his way through them to new invasions: but having been fortunate in the execution of his projects, he died with the name of Alexander the Great" (p. 431). This passage is effectively written for two reasons: first, Johnson adds a sense of drama and anticipation to the historical account by naming Alexander at the end of the paragraph and, second, he suggests that few historical figures of Alexander's stamp possessed the quality of inherent greatness modern readers have assumed. Rather, reputations and assessments were more often influenced not by personal courage and brilliance, but by a stroke of fortune or timing. The margin between success and failure may seem large indeed, but Johnson contends that very little prevented Xerxes from dying with the name "the Great." Therefore, in addition to his moral lesson, Johnson wished to provide his audience with a more skeptical perspective on viewing history and its famous personalities.

To those who would question the significance of recalling events two thousand years in the past, Johnson answers, "These are, indeed, events of ancient time; but human nature is always the same, and every age will afford us instances of public censures influenced by events" (p. 431). Accordingly, to supplement his classical examples, he offers an evaluation of more recent events, for example, the Crusades, which he characterizes as "a noble project" doomed by the "ardour of the European heroes": "their expeditions, therefore, have been the scoff of idleness and ignorance, their understanding and their virtue have been equally vilified, their conduct has been ridiculed, and their cause has been defamed" (p. 431). In his moral prose writings, as this assessment indicates, Johnson refused to romanticize the past, for, whereas the Crusades could easily titillate the imaginative sense of historical thinkers, Johnson was able to stop his ears and reject the voices singing the tale of a glorious Christian army fighting the barbaric infidel. Here again he offers to many of his uneducated readers a brief lesson in historical truth.

Following some commentary on Columbus and the courts that refused him aid, Johnson moves his historical survey to the modern period and the fate of Charles XII of Sweden. After his defeat at the battle of Poltawa in 1709, Johnson reminds his readers, Charles "has since been considered as a madman by those powers, who sent their ambassadors to sollicit his friendship, and their generals 'to learn under him the art of war'" (p. 432). In contrast, his contemporary Peter the Great, lacking the seeming nobility and courage of Charles, built canals and cities, murdered his subjects "with insufferable fatigues," and transplanted nations "from one corner of his dominions to another, without regretting the thousands that perished on the way." But since he achieved his goals he is "numbered by fame among the Demi-gods" (pp. 432–433). In this instance Johnson reveals the irony of history that allows one of its players the title "the Great" who rightfully stands accused of inhumanity.

That Johnson wishes to realign his readers' historical perspectives seems evident from his remarks and emphases in this essay, but to punctuate his point he adds the following:

I am far from intending to vindicate the sanguinary projects of heroes and conquerors, and would wish rather to diminish the reputation of their success, than the infamy of their miscarriages: for I cannot conceive, why he that has burnt cities, and wasted nations, and filled the world with horror and desolation, should be more kindly regarded by mankind, than he that died in the rudiments of wickedness; why he that accomplished mischief should be glorious, and he that only endeavoured it should be criminal: I would wish Caesar and Catiline, Xerxes and Alexander, Charles and Peter, huddled together in obscurity or detestation. (p. 433)

Other than marking the affinity between Johnson's and Voltaire's assessments of these conquerors, these words clearly highlight the sober, moral, and analytical side of Johnson's historical sense. The same man who could delight in the martial exploits of Charles XII, Edward III, and Henry V and use their successes and failures to enliven his poetry could also condemn the destruction and suffering caused in the name of glory and patriotism. But whereas he could easily differentiate between the fictitious and fanciful of history and the actual facts, he realized that many could not, for they had been taught only the romantic view of the past, which they tended to believe and articulate in their maturity. Much of the cant of his day related to popular though wrongheaded impressions of the glorious achievements of ancient Rome and medieval England, the necessity of the English Civil War to purge the country of a royal tyrant, and the historical authority for colonial expansion and war with France and Spain. Like a modern psychologist, Johnson believed one can do no harm by periodically indulging in fantasy; it is only when fantasy replaces rational examination that one is in danger. In addition to its moral lesson, then, *Adventurer* 99 is an antidote to the kind of historical thinking Johnson rejected. The disgust registered in the above passage is the author's way of shaking the reader's confidence in popular and romantic conclusions about the past that are applied to an "objective" examination of history. Moreover, as the essay shows, Johnson evoked history not unthinkingly, perfunctorily, or pedantically, but rather with the knowledge that historical examples were applicable to many social, personal, and political problems.

Historical figures appear elsewhere in Johnson's periodical papers. At times he simply mentions them in passing; more frequently, they are employed as were those in *Adventurer* 99. For instance, in *Rambler* 49 Johnson writes, "He that thinks himself poor, because his neighbour is richer; he that, like Caesar, would rather be the first man of a village, than the second in the capital of the world . . ." (III, 265). Not surprisingly, the majority of the historical references in the *Rambler* are from classical times, with Caesar and Alexander appearing most often, owing in large part to their popularity among even the least historically educated. Johnson also brings before the reader Pompey, Cicero, Cincinnatus, Caligula, Catiline, Nero, Pyrrhus, Constantine, Scipio, Justinian, Solon, Cleopatra, Hannibal, and others. Beyond the classical period, one finds mention of Genghis Khan, Tamerlane,[4] Alfred the Great, William I, William II, Henry VIII, Anne Boleyn, Francis Drake, Charles V, Guy Fawkes, and more.

In the *Idler* and *Adventurer* papers Johnson again calls on history to corroborate his testimony regarding the frailties and truisms of life. In addition to many of the figures mentioned above, Johnson found use for Agrippa, Xerxes, Miltiades, Elizabeth, Ferdinand, Thomas Cranmer, Cromwell, and Frederick of Prussia—a selection of famous names demonstrating once again the broad scope of Johnson's interest in history. Neither does he exclude history from his humorous pieces: in *Idler* 10, which features Tom Tempest, "steady friend to the House of Stuart," and Jack Sneaker, "hearty adherent to the present establishment," William III, Queen Anne, Charles I, the battles of Dettingen and Fontenoy, the Peace of Utrecht, and the South Sea Bubble are the topics of debate in this lively piece, reminiscent perhaps of Johnson's discussions with Gilbert Walmesley back in Lichfield. Although historical references pale in comparison to quotation and paraphrase from classical literature, in these periodical papers Johnson still finds history a useful tool to augment his other parallels and to convince his readers of the continuity of human nature from ancient civilization to the present.

Many of the historical figures and events Johnson employed in the periodical essays appear also in Boswell's *Life of Johnson,* either mentioned in passing or used to make a point. For example, while discussing courage with General Paoli in 1769, Johnson remarked that fear "is one of the passions of human nature, of which it is impossible to divest it." Searching for supportive evidence, he quickly recalled Charles V's reading on a tombstone of a Spanish nobleman, "Here lies one who never knew fear," and then responding, "Then he never snuffed a candle with his fingers" (*Life,* II, 81). In 1777 Johnson found a more poignant analogy from history as he described the seemingly joyous crowds at Ranelagh: "But, as Xerxes wept when he viewed his immense army, and considered that not one of that great multitude would be alive a hundred years afterwards, so it went to my heart to consider that there was not one in all that brilliant circle, that was not afraid to go home and think; but that the thoughts of each individual there, would be distressing when alone" (*Life,* III, 199).

At times Johnson liked to draw from historical fact and vivid historical anecdote to comment on contemporary situations: "The House of Commons was originally not a privilege of the people, but a check for the Crown on the House of Lords. I remember Henry the Eighth wanted them to do something; they hesitated in the morning, but did it in the afternoon. He told them 'It is well you did; or half your heads should have been upon Temple-bar.' But the House of Commons is now no longer under the power of the crown, and therefore must be bribed" (*Life,* III, 408). Johnson also broadened his scope of history in his conversation to include the earliest periods of known history. Feeling himself and his society an extension of ancient civilization, he remarked in 1776, "The grand object of travelling is to see the shores of the Mediterranean. On those shores were the four great Empires of the world; the Assyrian, the Persian, the Grecian, and the Roman.—All our religion, almost all our law, almost all our arts, almost all that sets us above savages, has come to us from the shores of the Mediterranean" (*Life,* III, 36).[5] This eloquent passage wonderfully conveys Johnson's affection for history; he was frequently invigorated by the noble spirit of the past, which he was adept at articulating for those in his company.

As implied earlier, Johnson was also curious about, if not fascinated by, military figures from history. In April of 1778 he remarked, "Every man thinks meanly of himself for not having been a soldier, or not having been at sea; . . . were Socrates and Charles the Twelfth of Sweden both present in any company, and Socrates to say, 'Follow me, and hear a lecture in philosophy'; and Charles, laying his hand on his sword, to say 'Follow me, and dethrone the Czar'; a man would be ashamed to follow Socrates" (*Life,* III, 265–266). Although he assumed with ease the historian's or moralist's stance and evaluated generals and soldiers for what they actually were, as *Adventurer* 99 amply illustrates, and dispassionately used them as examples of success, pride, or corruption, he took pleasure, even in his old age, in the romantic spirit of a good battle. For example, he once asked to hear James Oglethorpe's account of the siege of Belgrade in 1717, to which he listened "with the closest attention" (*Life,* II, 181).

41

From Johnson's writings on the Seven Years' War we sense a man opposed to war in general, and yet when we consider his response to the exploits of men like Oglethorpe and Charles XII, the discussions of warfare in several of his writings, his plans to write a history of a war, a military dictionary, and a biography of Cromwell,[6] and his often favorable allusions to the likes of Alexander, Caesar, Darius, Scipio, Pompey, Hannibal, Tamerlane, Catiline, Peter the Great, Marlborough, and Frederick of Prussia,[7] we discover one of the elements that make history such a rewarding and pleasurable study. As argued earlier, even those who look to the past with sober and analytical minds may also delight in the romantic aspects of history—the near mythical qualities of a leader, the successful battle against impossible odds, the trappings of pageantry, and so on. Few historians lose the spark of imagination that first encouraged an interest in history, and neither did Samuel Johnson.

But Johnson could also look to ancient and English history and utter disparaging comments such as "Men in ancient times dared to stand forth with a degree of ignorance with which nobody would dare now to stand forth" and "Our present heraldry, it may be said, is suited to the barbarous times in which it had its origin. It is chiefly founded upon ferocious merit, upon military excellence" (*Life,* IV, 217; I, 492). Hardly as eloquent as the passage on the four great empires of the Mediterranean, these comments nevertheless accentuate the vigorous aspect of Johnson's historical sense that responded negatively to an infatuation with the past based solely on cosmetic considerations. As he knew, history often entices through its charm and appearance, thereby preventing the reader from ever looking beneath the surface to discover the more important qualities that add subtance to the attractive demeanor. Many of his often-quoted disparaging remarks about history are in direct response to attitudes toward and assumptions about the past that tend to diminish the progress government and society have made over the years and to reject the intellectual superiority of modern times.

Even so, a reading of Boswell's *Life* shows Johnson's vulnerability to the sweet charms and melodious song of history. Topham Beauclerk's resemblance to Charles II, Boswell informs us, "contributed, in Johnson's imagination, to throw a lustre upon his other qualities."[8] He was moreover "not the less ready to love [Bennet] Langton, for his being of a very ancient family"; Johnson said with pleasure that the family Langton had "a grant of free warren from Henry the Second; and Cardinal Stephen Langton; in King John's reign, was of this family" (*Life,* I, 248–249). From such comments we can assume Johnson would have allowed

himself to revel in a work like Scott's *Ivanhoe,* for he had the capacity to
set aside willingly his historical skepticism and critical stance and flow
imaginatively and childlike through scenes of chivalry, court life, and
military splendor. And representative of this quality is his writing, at
sixty-nine, to young Queeney Thrale regarding her visit to a military
camp (24 October 1778). Johnson hopes she will appreciate surveying
"perhaps the most important scene of human existence, the real scene of
heroick life." If she feels bored with or unimpressed by the day-to-day
activities of soldiers safe from the battle, "reflect," he writes, "what a
camp must be surrounded by enemies in a wasted or a hostile country."
He goes on to remark that Sir Robert Cotton does not stand "on even
ground with Alexander and Darius; Caesar and Pompey, Tamerlane and
Bajazet; Charles, Peter, and Augustus. These and many more like these,
have lived in a camp like Sir Robert Cotton" (*Letters,* II, 260–261).[9] One
cannot fail to detect Johnson's still youthful vitality, sparked in large part
by his response to history, a vitality assuredly stimulated by his visit to
Warley Camp several months earlier. As Langton recalled, Johnson,
even though in poor health, brightened to the sights and sounds of
military life. He sat "with a patient degree of attention" while observing
a regimental court-martial; accompanied at eleven o'clock at night an
officer on his rounds; "took occasion to converse at times on military
topicks, such as weaponry and ammunition"; and walked among the
tents "observing the difference between those of the officers and private
men" (*Life,* III, 360–362).

Any supposition that Johnson disdained history certainly fails under
the emotional weight of his final letter to Hester Thrale in the summer of
1784, five months before his death. For all who know him well, this
letter cannot be read without some pain, for the reader shares Johnson's
anguish and helplessness as he tries to keep the new Mrs. Piozzi from
leaving England. After providing her with logical reasons for remaining,
Johnson, in a moment of desperation, turns once more to history for the
most poignant analogy possible to touch her heart and make her realize
the significance of her decision.

When Queen Mary [of Scots] took the resolution of sheltering herself in England, the Archbishop of St. Andrew's attempting to dis-
suade her, attended on her journey and when they came to the
irremeable stream that separated the two kingdoms, walked by her
side into the water, in the middle of which he seized her bridle, and
with earnestness proportioned to her danger and his own affection,

pressed her to return. The Queen went forward.—If the parallel reaches thus far; may it go no further. The tears stand in my eyes. (*Letters*, III, 178)[10]

Few passages summarize so well the depth and emotional quality of Johnson's historical sense; he saw that history could help to articulate and perhaps comfort even the most intimate feelings of personal anguish.

An examination of Johnson's two major poems, his periodical papers, letters, and conversation has shed light on his use of many historical figures from antiquity to the early eighteenth century. But there was another group of important names from the past for whom he had a special interest: the English monarchs of the modern era, those rulers of Great Britain from Elizabeth through Anne. Because these kings and queens were topics of contemporary thought and debate, their policies, successes, and failures having helped to shape the turbulent epoch of the seventeenth century and the course of modern British life, Johnson wished to perceive clearly these monarchs and their reigns without being clouded by the mists of romanticism through which they were usually viewed. And, as he was well aware, the reputations of the monarchs were the most powerful weapons wielded in the battle between the partisan historians—the Whigs in general condemning the constitutional abuses of Charles I and the other Stuarts, justifying the rebellion of the mid seventeenth century and reveling in the Glorious Revolution and in the reign of William III, while the Tories were defending the legality of Charles I's actions, decrying the Interregnum, and harshly criticizing the policies of William and the power accorded such military leaders as the Duke of Marlborough. Unfortunately, too many readers and commentators have long assumed Johnson's perspective was blinded by his romantic and political prejudice, certainly a gross misunderstanding of his position on these rulers.

As I have noted, eighteenth-century England fondly recalled the reign of Elizabeth (1558 to 1603) as a time of great national achievement: it was easy to take pride in the age that produced Drake and Hawkins, Spenser and Shakespeare. To many in the eighteenth century, Elizabeth stood for all worth preserving of England's heritage. The queen was, as romanticized figure as well as monarch, equal in esteem to Alfred, Edward III, and Henry V. And Samuel Johnson realized that her reign was "the favourite period of English greatness"; as he wrote in 1760, it "has now been fashionable, for near half a century . . . to exalt and magnify" the queen's forty-five years on the throne.[11] Without question he saw much in Elizabeth to justify the fashion: she had "learning enough to have given dignity to a bishop"; her policies allowed England to extend her trade and discover new regions; and her ships destroyed the dreaded Armada, thus putting "a stop, and almost an end, to the naval power of the Spaniards." He also observed that under the queen "Liberty again began to flourish" after the turbulent reigns of Henry VIII, Edward VI, and Bloody Mary.[12] When he so chose, as *London* also informs us, Johnson could relish in his English heritage by marveling at the queen's accomplishments and extolling the symbolism of her monarchy.

But unlike many of his contemporaries, Johnson was able to see Elizabeth's other side. In the *Life of Ascham* (1763), he reflects on the queen's unforgiving nature, which manifested itself when Ascham left his teaching post without her consent: "and, as those who are not accustomed to disrespect cannot easily forgive it, he probably felt the effects of his imprudence to his death." Johnson also points to Elizabeth's parsimony: the queen, he writes, "was not naturally bountiful" (*Works*, XV, 104, 109). Colonial expansion during her reign, he adds elsewhere, was based upon "no very just principles of policy."[13] But his major criticism of Elizabeth is directed at her treatment of Mary Queen of Scots.

Of all the important figures of history, no woman captured Johnson's fancy as much as Mary Stuart (1542 to 1587), whose tragic story continues to elicit the sympathies of modern readers. The degree of his affection for her is evident in his reply to Boswell's lament that the Scots were no longer independent: "Sir, never talk of your independency, who could let your Queen remain twenty years in captivity and then be put to death without even a pretence of justice, without your ever attempting to rescue her; and such a Queen, too!—as every man of any gallantry of spirit would have sacrificed his life for" (*Tour*, p. 24). Evident once more is the romantic side of Johnson's historical sense, for there is much medieval flavor in the comment. He could imagine himself galloping up and rescuing the lovely queen from the clutches of Elizabeth's guards.

His romantic impressions notwithstanding, Johnson's 1760 review of William Tytler's *Historical and Critical Enquiry* into the famous "casket letters" of Mary Queen of Scots is indicative of his sober historical perspective. Although he is reviewing Tytler's vindication of Mary, Johnson obviously shares the author's view that the letters implicating the Queen of Scots in the murder of her husband, Lord Darnley, were forgeries and that her reputation has been unfairly maligned. While recounting the events leading up to the trial, he considers Elizabeth's reaction to the evidence implicating Mary: "Elizabeth, indeed, was easily satisfied; she declared herself ready to receive the proofs against Mary, and absolutely refused Mary the liberty of confronting her accusers, and making her defence. Before such a judge, a very little proof would be sufficient." The Bishop of Ross, Johnson tells us, called spurious the confession of Nicholas Hubert, which implicated Mary, but Ross's writings were "suppressed by Elizabeth." Finally, in summarizing Mary's ordeal, Johnson points out that she was never allowed to see the evidence against her: "She demanded to be heard, in person, by Elizabeth, before the nobles of England and the ambassadours of other princes, and was refused" (*Works,* XIII, 265, 271).

Johnson's commentary in the review and elsewhere indicates his strong disapproval not only of the English queen's unjust and immoral treatment of Mary Queen of Scots but also Elizabeth's frigid manner, obstinate temperament, and lack of compassion. Willing to credit the queen with all due respect for what she had accomplished, Johnson realized that she, like any other monarch, was fallible in matters of state and morality. And discovering the defects of revered figures goes far beyond his delight in argument for argument's sake, for as a historical thinker he knew it was his responsibility to shape in his mind a more accurate picture of the past, regardless of how it might contradict popular views. His objective sense of history prevented his ever embracing with unbridled enthusiasm the memory of the time-honored Elizabeth—and her successors, the Stuarts.

While dining at Tom Davies's on 6 April 1775, Johnson, Boswell, Thomas Hickey, and John Moody were discussing gentility and morality when Davies happened to mention Charles II as a man who was "immoral with exteriour grace." As Boswell recorded the conversation, Johnson, "taking fire at any attack upon that Prince, for whom he had an extraordinary partiality," forcefully argued that even though Charles might have been licentious in his practices he always maintained a "reverence for what was good." Gathering steam, Johnson forged ahead to stress that Charles "knew his people, and rewarded merit": "The Church was at no time better filled than in his reign. He was the best King we have had from his time till the reign of his present majesty [George III], except James the Second. . . . He took money, indeed, from France: but he did not betray those over whom he ruled: he did not let the French fleet pass ours." To punctuate his remarks Johnson contrasted to

Charles's reign that of William III, whom he described as "one of the most worthless scoundrels that ever existed" (*Life,* II, 341–342).[14]

The above passage, one of the most memorable in the *Life of Johnson* and reflective of a partisan "Tory" historian, is largely responsible for the belief that Johnson had an affection for the House of Stuart and especially for Charles II. After all, did not Johnson once lament that the Stuarts "have found few apologists"?[15] Although, as Donald Greene has pointed out, Johnson could express a "low opinion" of the Stuart rulers,[16] we only find how misleading the passage from Boswell is when we look at what Johnson wrote about the individual Stuart monarchs during his long career. A careful investigation reveals that he looked upon these rulers with the historian's, not the partisan's, eye and that he was far more often a detractor than an admirer of the Stuarts. In addition, Johnson's estimations are all the more interesting and significant considering that partisan assessments of seventeenth-century history allowed for little independence of thought: one either attacked the Stuarts without reservation or defended them similarly; there were very few who deviated from party lines.

Whereas Johnson seemed almost infatuated with Mary Queen of Scots, his fondness did not pass on to her son, James I of England, who reigned from 1603 to 1625. Even though he appreciated the king's knowledge of books and theology and refused to hold him responsible for initiating the doctrine known popularly as the "divine right of Kings,"[17] Johnson realized in 1756 that James, who he felt had "no practical wisdom," sacrificed "upon all occasions" the "true interest of himself, his kingdom, and his posterity." James, Johnson adds, was "so conscious of his own knowledge and abilities, that he would not suffer a minister to govern, and so lax of attention, and timorous of opposition, that he was not able to govern for himself." Johnson was especially critical of the king's personal habits because they reflected themselves in foreign policy, which was to Johnson a major criterion by which to judge seventeenth-century monarchs: "With this character," he writes, "James quietly saw the Dutch invade our commerce; the French grew every day stronger and stronger and the protestant interest, of which he boasted himself the head, was oppressed on every side, while he writ, and hunted, and dispatched ambassadors."[18] Although, as Johnson argues, the union between England and Scotland was necessary to check the power of France, James I added neither dignity nor glory to the throne. At best, Johnson considered him the lesser of possible evils.[19]

These impressions hardly reveal a staunch defender of the House of Stuart; rather they are the beliefs of an impartial historian unaffected by emotional ties to the past. Although he was a king, James's stature is considered only in just proportion to his policies, his time, and his personal weaknesses and strengths.

In 1783 Boswell mentioned Thomas Sheridan's belief that Johnson hated the Scots because they turned Charles I over to a hostile Parliament. Johnson responded, "Then, Sir, old Mr. Sheridan has found out a very good reason" (*Life*, IV, 169). The response was of course tailored to Johnson's "anti-Scots" pose, but it also suggests a man sensitive about and protective of the memory of Charles I, who reigned from 1625 to 1649. Johnson's seemingly sympathetic view of Charles was not, however, based on an admiration for the man or his policies, for he was always cognizant of the king's limitations. Charles, Johnson wrote in 1756, "had seen the errors of his father, without being able to prevent them," and he observed over twenty years later in the "Life of Waller" that the king's judgment "too frequently yielded to importunity."[20] Instead, his estimation of Charles was for the most part colored by the king's role in one of England's darkest hours. When he and Boswell stopped at Colchester in the summer of 1763, Johnson "talked of that town with veneration, for having stood a siege for Charles the First" (*Life*, I, 466). Johnson displays here his fine historical sense, which allowed him to draw inspiration and the glow of patriotism from historical sites; but, more important, his words suggest that in certain instances history assumed a symbolism he could not ignore, regardless of his analytical and objective perspective on the past. This symbolism went beyond a romantic evocation of Edward III or Henry V; it carried with it important lessons to the present. That is, Johnson did not have in mind Charles the man or ruler when he praised the courage of Colchester; rather he pictured Charles as the symbol of order and stability. He at no time depicts Charles as an ideal or even a good king, but king he was, and there was not justification for his execution, which he termed "murder of the most atrocious kind" (Sermon 23, *Sermons,* pp. 246–247). Although he could easily pity the "unhappy Charles," it was his perception of the king as something larger than himself that prevented a totally emotionless consideration of Charles's responsibility for the Civil War and its aftermath. We find, then, that in this instance the philosopher and moralist in Johnson pushed to the background the historian. He may have spared Charles I the scrutiny he gave other Stuart monarchs, but his lack of criticism cannot be linked to any affection for the house itself. Had the reigning king in 1649 been Plantagenet, Tudor, or Hanoverian, Johnson's reaction would have been the same.

Recalling the remarks Johnson made at Davies's in the spring of 1775, one could certainly credit the defense of Charles II, who reigned from 1660 to 1685, to the enthusiasm of a strong Stuart loyalist. And elsewhere Boswell records his friend's praise of Charles's charisma and social graces: he was, according to Johnson, the "last King of England who was a man of parts" (*Life*, I, 442). But evidence outside the confines of Boswell's biography reveals a far different evaluation of the king. Initially, Johnson's statement that Charles "rewarded merit" is not supported by several passages in the *Lives of the Poets*. He mentions, for instance, Cowley's failure to receive benefit at the Restoration and doubts the report that Charles gave Samuel Butler three hundred guineas in appreciation of *Hudibras*. Johnson adds, "To write without reward is sufficiently unpleasing" (*Poets*, I, 13, 205–206). Even his acknowledgment of Denham's good fortune underscores his belief that the king was close-fisted about monetary gifts: Denham, Johnson writes, obtained "that which many missed, the reward of his loyalty" (*Poets*, I, 74). As one who worked slavishly on Grub Street for many years, Johnson could not have dismissed lightly Charles's lack of generosity.

Whereas at Davies's he quickly passed over Charles's licentiousness, Johnson was unable to ignore the "many frailties and vices" that marked the king's character.[21] On several occasions he describes the Restoration years as a time "when fancy and gaiety were the most powerful recommendations to regard," when young men of high rank indulged in "riotous and licentious pleasures," and when "Vice always found a sympathetick friend." Johnson believed Charles set the tone for his time, and it was thus to his discredit, owing in part to his example, that his wits had "seldom more than slight and superficial views."[22] Although the romantic side of his historical perspective brightened when envisaging the general appearance and style of Charles, the sober Johnson saw the king's moral laxity as detrimental to his reputation. As he noted in *Rambler* 4 (1750), "Vice . . . should always disgust; nor should the graces of gaiety, or the dignity of courage, be so united with it, as to reconcile it to the mind" (III, 24). It is not difficult to imagine Johnson thinking of Charles II as well as Tom Jones when he penned these words.

In his *Review of the Account of the Conduct of the Duchess of Marlborough* (1742), Johnson states unhesitatingly that Charles "betrayed and sold" his country (*Works*, XIII, 167). His reference is obviously to the king's overtures to France and the financial benefits derived from what the nineteenth century would discover as the infamous Treaty of Dover. In regard to his position at Davies's that Charles did not allow the French fleet to "pass" the English, Johnson writes in the *Introduction to the Political State of Great Britain* (1756) that the king watched the growth of French power "with very little uneasiness." Even though public opinion forced him on occasion to oppose France, Charles "never persevered long in acting against her, nor ever acted with much vigour"; as a result of his "feeble resistance, he rather raised her confidence, than hindered her designs." Johnson does not qualify his remarks, nor does he suggest anything else but the king's partial responsibility for a precarious shift in Europe's balance of power. Louis XIV and his chief minister, Jean-Baptiste Colbert, might have steered France's course, but Charles acted as one of the navigators. Because of the king's "fondness of ease and pleasure, the struggles of faction, which he could not suppress, and his inclination to the friendship of absolute monarchy," he had little power or desire "to repress" the increasing naval power of France (*Political Writings,* pp. 139–142). Sincere in his praise of the king's social graces and refusal to indulge in revenge upon assuming the throne,[23] Johnson nevertheless wrote nothing to support the view that he had an "extraordinary partiality" for Charles II.

Johnson also argued at Davies's that Charles II was the best king England had until George III, "except James the Second, who was a very good King." The remark is consistent with the view of a Stuart loyalist, but it is also a contradiction of everything else Johnson had to say about James, who reigned from 1685 to 1688. The kindest observation, perhaps, is in the *Introduction to the Political State of Great Britain,* but even that is tempered with criticism: "He was not ignorant of the real interest of his country; he desired its power and its happiness, and thought rightly, that there is no happiness without religion; but he thought very erroneously and absurdly, that there is no religion without popery" (*Political Writings,* p. 142). In the *Introduction* and some twenty-five years later in the *Lives of the Poets,* Johnson criticizes or condemns James for his disregard for literature, his "dangerous bigotry," the "violence of his innovations," and the "contentious turbulence" of his reign (*Political Writings,* p. 342; *Poets,* I, 233–234, 305, 384).

Johnson told James Oglethorpe in 1783, "What we did at the Revolution was necessary: but it broke our constitution" (*Life,* IV, 170–171). The first part of this famous quotation deserves as much emphasis as the second, for James's "holy war," as Johnson phrases it, left his country no alternative but to force him from the throne; it was simply a matter of "self-preservation" (*Poets,* I, 275; *Political Writings,* p. 142). Johnson believed James could blame no one but himself for the loss of his kingdom. One has to wonder, therefore, at the impression Boswell leaves. Perhaps Johnson's other biographer, John Hawkins, was closer to the truth when he wrote that Johnson "condemned the conduct of James the second during his short reign; and, had he been a subject of that weak and infatuated monarch, would, I am persuaded, have resisted any invasion of his right or unwarrantable exertion of power" (Hawkins, pp. 223–224). At any rate, the commentary on the reign of James II demonstrates the vigorous and blunt analysis reflective of Johnson's strong historical sense. Even English monarchs could not expect to escape censure when censure was due; Johnson would not allow feelings of patriotism or reverence to institutions to compromise his probing historical mind.

Johnson's calling William III, who reigned from 1689 to 1702,[24] "one of the most worthless scoundrels that ever existed" once again suggests a Tory historical bias and a fondness for the House of Stuart, and one is tempted, based on the conversation at Davies's, to attribute Johnson's seeming disdain simply to William's being the one who supplanted "good" King James. Although he called William over the years an "arbitrary, insolent, gloomy, rapacious, and brutal" king as well as a "scoundrel,"[25] Johnson's emphases, on the other hand, can only in part be explained by his perception of the man and his policies. As Johnson well knew, William was viewed by many in 1688 as a deliverer, a reputation that took on added luster in the years that followed. The eighteenth century, and especially the Whig historians, frequently saw him, as David Ogg informs us, directing "the path of Englishmen upwards to that Ark of the Covenant, known as the British Constitution."[26] But Johnson's natural inclination was to struggle against the tide of opinion if he had any doubt about its historical validity. He wrote in 1760, "there remains, still, among us, not wholly extinguished, a zeal for truth, a desire of establishing right, in opposition to fashion."[27] His instinctive skepticism in political and historical matters (more on this subject in chapter six) and pride in his argumentative talents, I believe, had at least some effect on his assessing William less enthusiastically than many of his contemporaries and emphasizing more vigorously his negative side. He was no doubt angered when the king was invoked unthinkingly by men or women whose political views were different from his own. If, as Donald Greene has argued, Johnson could defend the Stuarts because an "unthinking contempt" for them was fashionable,[28] then there is reason to feel he stepped up his attack on William in part because defending and praising him was just as fashionable.

But Johnson's historical perspective prevented him from ignoring the king's strengths. In the *Introduction to the Political State of Great Britain* (1756), Johnson questions William's motives but applauds him nonetheless for acting against France, whose might had "become dangerous to Europe": "if her incroachments were suffered a little longer," he continues, "resistance would be too late" (*Political Writings*, p. 143). Because he placed much significance on the handling of foreign affairs, in this very important regard he considered William more effective in his kingship than were James I, Charles II, and James II. Second, we should remember that in the review of Sarah Churchill's memoirs (1742), when Johnson wrote that Charles II "betrayed and sold" his nation, he also noted that for all his "insolence and brutality" William "protected and enriched" his people (*Works*, XIII, 167). Finally, we cannot ignore Johnson's sincere appraisal of the king's character in the "Life of Prior": "His whole life had been action, and none ever denied him the resplendent qualities of steady resolution and personal courage" (*Poets*, II, 185). These comments are not as well known as those in Boswell's *Life of Johnson,* but they can be trusted as the remarks of an objective historical commentator, not the emotional rhetoric of a lively debater. And even though he cannot be considered an admirer of the king, Johnson judged William to be a far better monarch than James II and, in several important respects, even preferable to Charles II.

Whereas we might expect Johnson to recall with affection the memory of Queen Anne, who reigned from 1702 to 1714, for having touched him for the King's Evil, he never displayed warmth for either Anne or her reign. When he reviewed Sarah Churchill's memoirs he observed that the queen revealed an anxious and impatient temperament, a "helpless dependance on the affection of others, and a weak desire of moving compassion." Lacking the skill or determination to curb the power of the Whigs, Anne was little more than "the slave of the Marlborough family" (*Works,* XIII, 168–169). Although he could sympathize with her for having to deal with "insolent" ministers, Johnson knew Anne was an ineffective monarch because she was not intellectually or emotionally equipped to rule. The queen "was probably slow" to effect change and to promote sound policy, Johnson writes near the end of his life, "because she was afraid" (*Poets*, III, 17). That she was romantically viewed by some as the last "English" monarch before the arrival of the crude Hanoverians mattered little to his perception of her. Johnson thus parted company with the Tom Tempests, who smiled paternally on the memory of Anne and pointed out that she "meant well" (*Idler* 10, p. 34).[29]

Johnson's assessments of and observations on the Stuart monarchs in his writings clearly prove that he looked to the past far more objectively than one might assume from a reading of Boswell's *Life of Johnson* and, more significantly, that he was among the very few who were totally independent of the two major lines of partisan historical thinking. Both Whig and Tory camps would have found in Johnson's remarks much to praise and much to denounce. Interestingly, he spoke most critically of the Stuarts in the 1740s and 1750s during the reign of George II, whom we know Johnson to have disliked, and thus during a period when he might be more inclined to champion those who ruled before the Hanoverians. But even after the accession of George III, a king Johnson was quick to defend, his depiction of the Stuarts did not appreciably alter, to which comments in the *Lives of the Poets* attest. One cannot therefore assume that by the time he spoke up at Tom Davies's he had rethought his position on the Stuart monarchs. If Boswell's record of Johnson's conversation on that April evening is accurate, we can only assume he was "talking for victory" rather than stating his sincere beliefs. Johnson's independent nature prevented him from shaping his perception of the past from political prejudices or loyalty to an idealized family of rulers.

As the remarks on the Stuarts demonstrate, Johnson took considerable interest in the historical events of the seventeenth century. The struggle between England and France, the relationship between the kings and their parliaments, the machinations of ministers, the conflict over religious beliefs, and the bloodless revolution of 1688 all have their place in Johnson's writings and conversation. But of all the historical periods he considered, none was more memorable or influential in the shaping of his philosophy than the English Civil War. As we have seen, his knowledge of those years[30] was substantial; he read many works on the war (e.g., Clarendon, Burnet, and the many books he examined while cataloging the Harleian collection)[31] and he referred frequently to it in print. And from his boyhood in Lichfield and his later travels he came to realize that no other historical event so permanently marked the landscape of eighteenth-century England. Johnson would well understand the tenor of Gilbert Burnet's observation thirty years after the event: the "mischiefs of civil wars are so great and lasting" that they reach far beyond their allotted places in history to affect subsequent generations. The war, Burnet added, left among Englishmen "many seeds of lasting feuds and animosities."[32] Although others have established that the English Civil War made a significant impression on Johnson's formative years and political beliefs,[33] we have not appreciated enough the way in which this historical event captured and sustained his imagination. Different from the many who looked back upon the Civil War as an evil deserving of oblivion, Johnson believed the event should be kept fresh in the minds of his contemporaries, not relegated to the history books, for it remained a powerful teaching device, the proper understanding of which could lessen greatly the odds that similar chaos would occur again.

Although it would be inaccurate to suggest an insensitivity to the famous battles of the Civil War (Edgehill, Newbury, Marston Moor, and Naseby), Johnson's thoughts turned principally to the effect the struggle had on English society and the implications of the war to his age and the future. His fear of political instability, which became more pronounced as he grew older, was nourished by his contemplation of the mid seventeenth century, a time, he believed, when stability was maintained by the threat of force, not by justice and law: "the system of extemporary government, which had been held together only by force, naturally fell into fragments when that force was taken away"—that is, at the death of Cromwell.[34] The splinter groups of the 1640s—the Levellers, Diggers, Fifth Monarchists, Seekers, and Ranters, who seemed to delight in novelty and sweeping reform—might certainly have been on his mind as supporting evidence when he wrote John Taylor in 1783, "To change the constituent parts of Government must be always dangerous, for who can tell where changes will stop. A new representation will want the reverence of antiquity, and the firmness of Establishment" (*Letters*, III, 5). Johnson would recommend that his age recall the violence and disorder brought about by the those groups caught up in a general mood of iconoclasm and reform. Regardless of some solid arguments to the contrary, Johnson refused to look upon the instability of the Civil War years as in any way a step toward political progress: as he wrote in his sermon commemorating the execution of Charles I, "This 'strife,' as we all know, ended in 'confusion.' Our laws were over-ruled, our rights were abolished" (Sermon 23, *Sermons*, p. 247).

We cannot underestimate the significance of this observation, in which Johnson asserts that the "freedom" from monarchal rule resulted in suppressive measures detrimental to the public good. When he heard his contemporaries considering and advocating sweeping change or reform, he must have been both angered and frustrated at those who could not extract precedent and wisdom from the English Civil War. Johnson, as Donald Greene points out, realized and deplored the premium totalitarian regimes placed on "falsification and suppression of fact" and "subjection of the rational intelligence to canting propaganda."[35] His deep respect for the truth in historical as well as political matters furthered his negative conception of those who, from his perspective, destroyed the continuity of government and disdained Britain's heritage. To him these reformers appealed, not to the truth, but to prejudice, superstition, ignorance, and the base desire for power.

Symbolizing the political and social disorder of the mid seventeenth century was the image of Charles I baring his neck for the executioner's ax, an act Johnson termed a murder of the most "atrocious" kind. Accordingly, when Boswell mentioned in 1772 the motion made in the House of Commons to abolish the commemoration of the event on 30 January, Johnson argued that terminating it now "would be declaring it was wrong to establish it" (*Life,* II, 151–152).[36] This comment suggests both his belief in the symbolic importance of the event and the war's continuing significance for the present. In his mind, England would be wise to recall periodically the bloody business conducted in January 1649, for whatever political stability it enjoyed in 1772 might easily be shattered by a return to the philosophy that led to the murder of a lawful king. To Johnson the warning was clear: England had fortunately repaired "the ruins" of its constitution after Cromwell's death,[37] but there was no guarantee it could do it again. Although, as I have said, he was among many men and women of his time who condemned the Civil War, Johnson's perception of the event as a teaching device worthy of contemplation elevates him from the company of those who agreed with his basic assessment of the conflict and its immediate effects.

When Johnson thought of the Civil War years he also recalled how "the fanatick rushed into the church" (Sermon 23, *Sermons,* p. 247). As a boy in Lichfield he would certainly have heard of Roundhead troops relishing in sacrilegious acts, from hunting a cat with hounds in the cathedral to damaging the altar, stained glass, and exterior. The sacrileges suffered by other English cathedrals and churches he had seen or known of indicated to him that wanton destruction was too often the rule rather than the exception. In 1641 the House of Commons ordered the removal or destruction of all "images, altars, or tables turned altarwise, crucifixes, superstitious pictures," and other relics, to which were added over the next three years crosses, portraits, railings, screens, and organs.[38] Many of those carrying out the orders further desecrated England's finest religious structures by smashing glass and stabling horses in the naves. The impressive castles, many dating from medieval times, crumbled under intense bombardment or "slighting." Winchester Cathedral, which Johnson visited in 1762, suffered the indignity of having parliamentarian troops ride in, kick over the altar, and destroy tombs, images, and glass. And such havoc was more than the natural result of a soldier's anger and frustration; as John Phillips argues, it was "*de facto*" an "attempt to destroy that which the object symbolized religiously, which in turn was inseparable from the fabric and basis of the political state."[39]

Extreme iconoclasm of the mid seventeenth century manifested itself in the prosecution of ministers considered scandalous by the Puritans, the burning of Bibles by religious zealots, and the flaunting of atheistic rhetoric and philosophy.[40] Johnson seems not to have considered to any large extent the many devout and rational men and women who supported Parliament's and Cromwell's cause, which shows that his normal historical objectivity was not always operative when he thought of the Civil War; but his perception of the extremists—those, for example, who held that Christ was a bastard—as being representative of the religious chaos characteristic of the period only underscores his belief that, regardless of their size, the radical element had the power to enact unhealthy change. The moderate voices were then and could be again drowned out by a small but powerful chorus of zealots.

In the *Life of Cheynel* (1751) Johnson recalls the time when the representatives of Parliament took to the pulpits of Oxford to effect change and were heard "with very little veneration": "Those who had been accustomed to the preachers of Oxford, and the liturgy of the church of England, were offended at the emptiness of their discourses, which were noisy and unmeaning; at the unusual gestures, the wild distortions, and the uncouth tone with which they were delivered; . . . and at, what was surely not to be remarked without indignation, their omission of the Lord's Prayer" (*Works*, XIV, 353). To Johnson these reformers could be laughable as well as dangerous creatures, but more to the point is the remark he made some twenty-two years later when he said that "permitting men to preach any opinion contrary to the doctrine of the established church, tends, in a certain degree, to lessen the authority of the church, and, consequently, to lessen the influence of religion" (*Life*, II, 254). Even though this comment has helped to reinforce the stereotype of Johnson as a narrow-minded and inflexible conservative, we should remember that at the back of his mind was the example of the mid seventeenth century.

Johnson's most emphatic statement against innovation in religious matters, however, is found in Sermon 7, a piece easily evoking the memory of the English Civil War as well as the Reformation: "That no change in religion has been made with that calmness, caution, and moderation, which religion itself requires, and which common prudence shews to be necessary in the transaction of any important affair, every nation of the earth can sufficiently attest. Rage has been called in to the assistance of zeal, and destruction joined with reformation. Resolved not to stop short, men have generally gone too far, and, in lopping superfluities, have wounded essentials." The privilege of individual judgment, Johnson continues, may be given too much freedom when reform captivates the minds and energies of both zealots and the well-intentioned: "it may be exercised without knowledge or discretion, 'till errour be entangled with errour, 'till divisions be multiplied by endless subdivisions, 'till the bond of peace be entirely broken, and the church become a scene of confusion, and chaos of discordant forms of worship, and inconsistent systems of faith" (Sermon 7, *Sermons*, pp. 76–77). Whereas Johnson could point to Henry VIII's reforming zeal in England and that of John Knox in Scotland as examples supporting his assertions, it was the English Civil War, due to its proximity in the more recent past and its still visible legacy, that provided him with the most effective and irrefutable corroborating evidence for the arguments advanced in the sermon. He was not so much opposed to what he termed the "sour solemnity, the sullen superstition, the gloomy moroseness, and the stubborn scruples" of the ancient Puritans[41] as he was to their desire to destroy the fabric of established religion.

Other than affecting the religious realm, the radical seventeenth-century reformers sought to eradicate as much of England's history as they could. Johnson wrote in his remarks on Shakespeare's *Henry V*: "Late events obliterate the former: the civil wars have left this nation scarcely any tradition of more ancient history" (*Shakespeare*, II, 557). His statement may be exaggerated but it nevertheless illustrates his awareness that the English Civil War undermined England's heritage. More to the point is his observation in the "Life of Butler": "What can be concluded of the lower classes of the people when in one of the parliaments summoned by Cromwell it was seriously proposed that all records in the Tower should be burnt, that all memory of things past should be effaced, and that the whole system of life should commence anew?" (*Poets*, I, 215). Johnson was both angered and amazed at powerful and misguided men who attempted to sever England's link with its past, therefore scoffing at the process that over the centuries brought their country to its deserved place in the world. But again, Johnson did not view such concepts as locked within the dusty confines of history. He knew that the "presumptuous confidence in private judgment" if left unchecked could once more manifest itself in proposals similar to the one made by Cromwell's Parliament.

Johnson realized his own age could learn to avoid similar chaos if it heeded the warnings of history; therefore, he would not allow his readers to forget the disastrous tenor of life during the Civil War years. In the "Life of Butler" he writes, "It is scarcely possible, in the regularity and composure of the present time, to image the tumult of absurdity and clamour of contradiction which perplexed doctrine, disordered practice, and disturbed both publick and private quiet in that age, when subordination was broken and awe was hissed away; when any unsettled innovator who could hatch a half-formed notion produced it to the publick; when every man might become a preacher, and almost every preacher could collect a congregation" (*Poets,* I , 214–215).[42] In Sermon 23 Johnson similarly characterizes the period, but in this piece he stresses the significance of the event to the present: the "power of the faction, commenced by clamour, was prompted by rebellion, and established by murder." It was a time, he continues, "in which the lowest and basest of the people were encouraged by men a little higher than themselves" to rise up against lawful religious and secular authorities. Rather than sweeping social, political, and religious reform, the new regime brought only chaos: "usurpers gave way to other usurpers" and the people "heard nothing from their teachers but varieties of errour." But above all, Johnson wishes to impress on the listener an understanding that the same tumult awaits England if she is not careful: "Such evils surely we have too much reason to fear again, for we have no right to charge our ancestors with having provoked them by crimes greater than our own. *Let us therefore be warned by the calamities of past ages*" (Sermon 23, *Sermons,* pp. 246–247; italics mine). No other passage sums up as well Johnson's view that the English Civil War (and history in general) had relevance for contemporary life.

Often a figure from history embodies in the minds of subsequent generations the particular characteristics for which an age is known. Genghis Khan, Charles II, and Robespierre, for instance, stand as representatives of their times. History has thrust Oliver Cromwell into a similar role; as Christopher Hill has written, "In folk memory, so apt to embody causes in individuals, Oliver Cromwell came to personify the English Revolution, particularly its more destructive and violent aspects."[43] The hundred or so years following his death testified to England's interest in the Civil War's most famous personality. Sketches by Edmund Ludlow, Algernon

Sidney, Nathaniel Crouch, Lucy Hutchinson, Gilbert Burnet, James Heath, Isaac Kimber, Laurence Echard, John Banks, David Hume, Catharine Macaulay, and Clarendon varied in their evaluation of the lord protector; some were favorable, some were almost vengeful, and others, like Clarendon's, were mixed: "In a word, as he had all the wickedness against which damnation is denounced, and for which hell-fire is prepared, so he had some virtues which have caused the memory of some men in all ages to be celebrated; and he will be looked upon by posterity as a brave bad man."[44] Like Clarendon's, Johnson's opinion of Cromwell was balanced, although the scales ultimately tipped toward the unfavorable side.

Evidence that Johnson did not consider Cromwell merely as the embodiment of his period may be found in the *Life of Blake* and in the *Introduction to the Political State of Great Britain;* in both pieces he deals with the protector as would an objective historian. Of more note is Johnson's portrait in the *Debate Between the Committee . . . and Oliver Cromwell,* in which he portrays the protector in a dignified, polished, and intellectual manner. As we have seen, in his argument against monarchy, Cromwell exhibits an awareness of and a respect for his opponent's position and presents his own view with logic and conviction. In addition, one can easily admire Cromwell's apparent modesty as Johnson depicts it: he did not aspire to the title of protector, he says; he only assumed responsibility of the position to obliterate the evils "impending over the nation, and to prevent the revival of those disputes in which so much blood had been already shed" (*Political Writings,* pp. 91–92).

Boswell records William Bowles's recollection that Johnson once considered writing Cromwell's life: "he thought it must be highly curious to trace his extraordinary rise to the supreme power, from so obscure a beginning" (*Life,* IV, 235). Other than his fascination with Cromwell's rise from relative obscurity, due perhaps in large part to his own humble beginnings, Johnson was also intrigued by Cromwell's prowess on the battlefield and dominance over the powerful men who stood in his way. In the first instance the romantic side of Johnson's historical sense was intensified by the thought of Cromwell's military exploits, as it was by those of Alexander, Caesar, and Charles XII. In the second, Johnson knew that Cromwell, as a complex man in a turbulent time, would make a fascinating biographical and historical study. Johnson furthermore gave Cromwell credit for bringing some stability to the Scots: "he civilized them by conquests, and introduced by useful violence the arts of peace" (*Journey,* p. 27). And in his biography of Frederick of Prussia, he noted Cromwell's talent for survival and manipulation within the political sphere: "I have always thought that what Cromwell had more than our lawful kings, he owed to the private condition in which he first entered the world, and in which he long continued: in that state he learned his art of secret transaction, and the knowledge by which he was able to oppose zeal to zeal, and make one enthusiast destroy another" (*Works*, XV, 7).

But the historian in Johnson enabled him to look beneath the success, power, and charisma of Cromwell and discover less admirable qualities. In the "Life of Waller," Johnson criticizes the poet's failure to present in his 1654 Panegyrick an accurate picture of the protector: "there is . . . no mention of the rebel or the regicide. . . . The act of violence by which he obtained the supreme power is lightly treated, and decently justified. It was certainly to be desired that the detestable band [the Long Parliament] should be dissolved which had destroyed the church, murdered the King, and filled the nation with tumult and oppression; yet Cromwell had not the right of dissolving them" (*Poets*, I, 269). Here Johnson evaluates Cromwell not only as a man and leader of his faction, but also as a symbol of the disorder that marked his age.

In *Idler* 45, Johnson suggests a worthy subject for a painter: the dissolution of Parliament by Cromwell. Indicative of the sense of drama he drew from history and his negative feelings for the protector, Johnson writes that the point of time should be "when Cromwell, looking round the pandaemonium with contempt, ordered the bauble to be taken away; and [Thomas] Harrison laid hands on the Speaker to drag him from the chair." Johnson advises the painter to capture the "ferocious insolence" of the main figure of the piece (p. 142). And in the "Life of Milton," he reminds his readers that Cromwell dismissed Parliament "by the authority of which he had destroyed monarchy." It was appropriate, Johnson adds, that "rebellion should end in slavery: that [Milton], who had justified the murder of his king . . . should now sell his services and his flatteries to a tyrant, of whom it was evident that he could do nothing lawful" (*Poets*, I, 115–116). Johnson's opinion of Cromwell was shaped by his strong knowledge of mid seventeenth-century history, the effects the period had on English society, and the significance of those times to contemporary life. There was much he found attractive about Cromwell, but to set the historical record correctly Johnson was forced to portray the protector first as a lawless tyrant, a man fittingly reflective of the violence and instability of his day.

As Johnson wrote in his *Account* of the Harleian collection, the mid seventeenth century was a "memorable" period, one he recalled frequently in his writings and in his thoughts. Even though he praised individual Puritans like Robert Blake and Richard Baxter, Johnson saw the destruction of property, the suppression of rights, the uncontrollable zeal for innovation, the penchant for iconoclasm, and the disregard for tradition as the real legacies of the English Civil War. In sum, he held that "rebellions and civil wars are the greatest evils that can happen to a people."[45] These evils, he furthermore believed, were not the exclusive province of history; without a clear understanding of the causes of rebellion and civil war, such violence could again rise up to plague his country. Regardless of his comment in the "Life of Butler" that present times were marked by "regularity and composure," Johnson was painfully aware of the radical element and riotous disturbances affecting London from the 1760s to the end of his life.[46] We must keep in mind his assessment, probably written in the 1760s, that the "prevailing spirit of the present age seems to be the spirit of scepticism and captiousness, of suspicion and distrust, a contempt of all authority, and a presumptuous confidence in private judgement; a dislike of all established forms merely because they are established, and of old paths, because they are old" (Sermon 7, *Sermons,* p. 77). In January 1783 he must have felt tensions mounting toward a climactic stage, as he wrote to John Taylor, "this is not a time for innovation. I am afraid of a civil war" (*Letters,* III, 5–6).[47] To Johnson the English Civil War was far more than a fascinating and frightening moment in history, for the event still spoke clearly and ominously as a symbol of all that could go wrong in a society. Therefore, he saw the occasional need of bringing the period into sharp focus both as a warning to the present and as a provision for the future. He could not always view those years as an objective or disinterested historian, although much of what he writes corrects romantic impressions, because the English Civil War affected him too much emotionally, philosophically, and morally.

Chapter Three

Observing the Visual Record
of History:
Johnson and Antiquarianism

In the eighteenth century the rise of historiography was paralleled, though less glamorously, by a growth of interest in antiquities. The efforts of William Dugdale, Anthony à Wood, George Hickes, White Kennett, Henry Wharton, and Thomas Hearne in the late seventeenth and early eighteenth centuries gave antiquarianism a credibility among scholars and learned people. Johnson's century evinced an almost boundless enthusiasm for antiquity; the discoveries of Herculaneum (1719) and Pompeii (1748), for example, stimulated an interest in excavating ancient lands. Greek and Roman architecture, ancient inscriptions, rare coins, armorial remains, costumes, weapons, handicrafts; the histories of towns, counties, houses, abbeys, churches, and monuments; the ruins of castles and religious houses dotting the countryside; and other aspects of pre-seventeenth-century culture were all the province of the antiquarians. In England several antiquarian societies sprang up to accommodate the growing interest in the past, the most significant being the London Society of Antiquaries, led by its guiding spirit William Stukeley, which first met informally in 1707 and was founded officially in 1717.

Regardless of their positive contributions to knowledge, which encouraged and paved the way for much nineteenth- and twentieth-century research, the antiquarians became the object of considerable laughter and criticism. Pope's *Dunciad* and Foote's *The Nabob* are only two of the many works and squibs that ridiculed the antiquarians and their efforts. Portrayed as bumbling pedants oblivious to the world around them, hands stained by the moldy volumes they lovingly caressed, the antiquarians certainly had those in their midst who fit the portrait (they in fact laughed at the excesses of their own kind), but such a depiction is a gross distortion of the typical antiquarian of the eighteenth century. In an attempt to counter the prevailing view, Thomas Warton published in

1777 "Written in a Blank Leaf of Dugdale's Monasticon," a sonnet in defense of the antiquarian and his research: "Think'st thou the warbling Muses never smil'd / On his lone hours? . . . / Nor rough, nor barren, are the winding ways / Of hoar Antiquity, but strown with flowers."

To the uninitiated, however, antiquarianism was little appreciated and therefore looked upon as a waste of time or, at worst, a refuge from present realities for unimaginative or eccentric minds. The resulting satires were thus a quite normal response to what few adequately understood. And some of the most memorable lampoons and criticism directed against the antiquarians came from the pen of Samuel Johnson. In *Marmor Norfolciense* (1739) Johnson assumed the role of a ridiculous and vacuous antiquarian, a staunch Walpolite, to help emphasize the government's mishandling of current affairs. In *Rambler* 161 (1751) he wrote that "to rouse the zeal of a true antiquary little more is necessary than to mention a name which mankind have conspired to forget; he will make his way to remote scenes of action thro' obscurity and contradiction, as Tully sought amidst bushes and brambles the tomb of Archimedes" (V, 90). Earlier, in *Rambler* 82, Johnson had given his readers Quisquilius (which means "rubbish man"), who collected such items as ancient marble and porphyry, "three letters broken off by a learned traveller from the monuments at Persepolis; a piece of stone which paved the Areopagus of Athens, . . . a plate without figures or characters, which was found at Corinth, . . . sand gathered out of the Granicus; a fragment of Trajan's bridge over the Danube; some of the mortar which cemented the water-course of Tarquin; a horse shoe broken on the Flaminian way; and a turf with five daisies dug from the field of Pharsalia." And Quisquilius did not limit his searches to the continent; he found many valuable properties at home: "a lock of Cromwell's hair . . . sand scraped from the coffin of King Richard . . . a commission signed by Henry the Seventh . . . the ruff of Elizabeth and the shoe of Mary of Scotland . . . a stirrup of King James . . . and a thimble of Queen Mary" (IV, 68–69).

Even acknowledging the portrait of Quisquilius to include the kind of exaggeration necessary in good satire, one easily senses that Johnson had little respect for antiquarians and that he considered antiquarianism, as have many from his day to our own, to be the black sheep of the historical family. But whereas Johnson judged some of their activity useless and pedantic if not downright absurd, he approved of much of the antiquarians' work, enjoyed the friendship and respected the scholarship of many of them, and showed an interest himself in preserving and commenting on aspects of the past the antiquarians held dear. First of all, he was fully aware of the Society of Antiquaries and their activities. It appears, for instance, that he was directly satirizing them in *Rambler* 177.[1] The number of his friends and acquaintances who had an active interest in antiquities suggests that Johnson did not shy away from the antiquarian world.[2] Initially, we may point to William Oldys, with whom he worked on the Harleian collection in the 1740s. One of the century's most prominent antiquarians, Oldys certainly had some positive influence on the struggling young journalist, who could not help viewing the older man as a serious scholar. Johnson knew at various periods of his life such antiquarians as Thomas Birch, Michael Lort,[3] Thomas Coxeter, Thomas Astle, William Tasker, who submitted two of his translations for Johnson's revision, Edward Lye, whose *Dictionarium Saxonico-et Gothico-Latinum* greatly interested him, and Charles O'Connor, the Irish antiquary to whom he wrote urging the composition of an early history of Ireland (*Letters*, II, 172–173). We find furthermore that in the last year of his life Johnson broke bread with the antiquarians Jacob Bryant, Colonel Charles Vallancey, and John Pinkerton (*Life*, IV, 272–273, 278, 330).

More immediate friends included such Fellows of the Society of Antiquaries as Joshua Reynolds; Sir William Chambers; George Steevens; Richard Farmer, the noted antiquarian of Cambridge University; and Daines Barrington, who was also an Essex Head Club member. Barrington is of special note, for besides being actively involved in the society, where he gave papers and exhibits, he was one of the few men on whom Johnson ever waited (*Life*, III, 314). Johnson also had a high regard for the antiquarian interests of his friend Robert Chambers, with whom he worked on the Vinerian law lectures in the late 1760s. As Thomas Curley has written, "Chambers's fascination with British antiquities would have heightened Johnson's interest in the early history of the realm and the gradual evolution of a more sophisticated and unified body politic."[4] Another member of the Essex Head Club and a good friend during Johnson's last years was the prolific antiquary John Nichols, the editor of the *Gentleman's Magazine* and, as Edward Hart sees it, the "center of the antiquarian and anecdotal movement" in the late eighteenth century.[5] The two men were in frequent correspondence during the making of the *Lives of the Poets,* and Nichols supplied Johnson with information used in at least six of the lives.[6] In October 1784, Johnson demonstrated in a letter to Nichols a respect and even an enthusiasm for an aspect of antiquarianism when he wrote regarding Lichfield, "I should certainly have been very glad to give so skilful a Lover of Antiquities any information about my native place, of which however I know not much, and have reason to believe that not much is known" (*Letters,* III, 238).

There was also Johnson's friendship with Thomas Percy, the editor of the *Reliques of Ancient English Poetry* and noted scholar and antiquarian. As Bertram Davis has informed us, in their early meetings of the late 1750s Percy "discussed his folio manuscript of old ballads and romances with Johnson, who encouraged its publication, and by 4 October 1760, Johnson was advising Percy on the terms offered by Robert Dodsley for an edition of the ballads."[7] That Johnson learned firsthand of the hard work, dedication, and erudition characteristic of serious antiquarianism is apparent when we recall that Percy spent a good amount of time with his friend in London and that from June to August of 1764 Johnson stayed with him at Easton Mauduit. Johnson knew Percy's *Reliques* well, aided him in the preparation of the work, and wrote its dedication to the Countess of Northumberland. "Percy's attention to poetry," he wrote Boswell, "has given grace and splendour to his studies of antiquity" (*Letters,* II, 247).[8] These remarks are significant because they reveal Johnson's belief that, for all the useless and ridiculous activity of which the antiquarians were capable, the subject could rise to the level of dignity and "splendour" in the right hands.

Johnson's favorite among his antiquarian friends, at least during his middle years, was Thomas Warton, poet, literary critic, Oxford don, Fellow of the Society of Antiquaries, and author of the *History of English Poetry* and other works of an antiquarian stamp. Johnson cemented his relationship with Warton during his five-week stay at Oxford in the summer of 1754, at which time the two men walked and surveyed the antiquities in the vicinity of the city (*Life,* I, 273). Although he could poke fun at his friend's "antiquated" verse, Johnson always respected Warton's scholarship and literary projects, as is evident in his praise of the younger man's *Observations on the Fairy Queen of Spenser* (1754), "You have shown to all who shall hereafter attempt the study of our ancient authours the way to success, by directing them to the perusal of the books which those authours had read," and in his appreciation of the *History of English Poetry,* which he felt set a "noble example" (*Letters,* I, 56, 405). We should not underestimate the importance of Johnson's friendships, especially with Warton, Chambers, Percy, and Nichols, for they made it impossible for him to view antiquarianism as the province of foolish and unimaginative pedants. Because of his circle of friends, whom he sincerely respected, Johnson could not help developing more of an appreciation of antiquarianism as he got older. When he laughed at the excesses of the study he would have had to stop and remind himself that some of the brightest and most dedicated scholars and writers were also turning out respectable work in the field.[9]

Other than his knowledge and use of antiquarian volumes, many of which he became familar with while cataloging the Harleian collection,[10] letters to Thomas Patten and Thomas Astle written in 1781 indicate Johnson's willingness to take antiquarian concerns quite seriously. He wrote Patten concerning Thomas Wilson's *Archaelogical Dictionary,* published in 1782 and dedicated to Johnson: "If I had been consulted about this Lexicon of Antiquities while it was yet only a design, I should have recommended rather a division of Hebrew, Greek and Roman particulars, into three volumes, than a combination in one" (*Letters,* II, 435). He desires to see the work done correctly, so that the reader can more easily draw from it the material needed. There is no sense here of Johnson's shrugging his shoulders at an unimportant work; he later wrote Wilson that the study was needed, "for no man has so much skill in ancient rites and practices as not to want it" (*Letters,* II, 526). To Thomas Astle he wrote, "to see a man so skilful in the Antiquities of my Country, is an Opportunity of improvement not willingly to be missed." He then went on to discuss Astle's book, published seven years later, and to reflect his own interest in the subject: "Your Notes on Alfred appear to me very judicious and accurate, but they are too few. . . . Had the Saxons any gold Coin? . . . I have much curiosity after the Manners and Transactions of the Middle Ages, but have wanted either Diligence or Opportunity or both" (*Letters,* II, 432).

These remarks to Patten, Wilson, and Astle suggest how far Johnson may have come in his appreciation of antiquarianism from the satire and criticism of the 1750s to the last years of his life. Warton, Percy, and Nichols would have been proud of their friend for the enthusiasm he showed in these later letters. And the final comment in the Astle letter also reveals that he was not insensitive to the medieval period. Although many of his contemporaries followed Bolingbroke's advice to ignore pre-sixteenth-century history, others began to be stricken by a growing epidemic of "medieval fever." Johnson, as we have seen, thought it appropriate to employ figures from the Middle Ages (Alfred, Edward, Henry) for artistic purposes, but he also disdained the habit of some to glamorize the period in historically oriented prose pieces and conversations by somehow arguing that society, learning, and literature were superior in an earlier time.[11] As we shall later discover, Johnson demonstrated a strong knowledge of the medieval period in parts of the Vinerian law lectures he probably wrote with Robert Chambers, but suffice it to say here that he let very few opportunities go by in the lectures without emphasizing the "prejudice and ignorance" and "ferocious barbarity" of the period as compared with the present.

Johnson was thus in general agreement with Thomas Warton, who scorned the superstition, manners, and lack of intellectual refinement characteristic of the Middle Ages, while at the same time championing medieval trappings as most conducive for imaginative verse. He would appreciate that an intelligent man like Warton could indulge himself in the delights of the medieval panorama, as Warton often did in his poetry, but still step back at any time and realize the superiority of modern times. Johnson resisted the lure of a period that no doubt could stimulate his imagination when the boundaries between artistry and objectivity were blurred by eighteenth-century medieval enthusiasts. Even so, with all his other activities and interests, Johnson, near the end of his life, harbored a desire to explore the rich texture of pre-sixteenth-century history. Stripped of its romanticism, the medieval period would inform him of how the English institutions evolved, how they stood severe tests, and how personalities helped shape the course of events. As it was, Johnson knew a good deal about the period from his reading, but his historical sense, which was strong at the end of his life, made him want to know more.

Other examples of Johnson's interest in antiquarianism would be his writing an essay on epitaphs in 1740 ("If our prejudices in favour of antiquity deserve to have any part in the regulation of our studies, epitaphs seem entitled to more than common regard, as they are, probably, of the same age with the art of writing")[12] and his encouraging Boswell to study ancient tenures and laws and Charles O'Connor to publish on Irish antiquities (*Letters*, I, 280; II, 172). And although he satirized the antiquarian "collector," Johnson was fascinated by collections of old books. Here was an area of antiquarianism about which he could be unashamedly enthusiastic. Developing an appreciation of old and rare volumes as a boy in Lichfield, where he discovered that dirty and tattered books written a hundred or more years earlier could still delight and inform, he would have sensed a continuity from the past, not so much from reading the words of ancient authors in modern translations or editions, but from actually holding in his hands the very books read by his ancestors in the scholarly and intellectual community. The cracked bindings and blemished pages would not obscure the knowledge that these books were historical artifacts worthy of deep respect. Accordingly, Johnson took special enjoyment in visiting the English libraries when he could, and his trips to Scotland and France in 1773 and 1775 included satisfying visits to the Library of Marischal College at Aberdeen, the Library of St. Germain de Prés, and the Bibliothèque du Roi in the Rue Richelieu, where he again saw a Gutenberg Bible. His sense of history must have been warmly aroused as he viewed this famous work, recalling his first experience with it when cataloging the Harleian collection. As E. L. McAdam has written, when Johnson toured the libraries he asked at each one "what early or remarkable" volumes the library possessed and then, "with great interest, examined those which were handed him."[13]

Sounding like a serious antiquary, Johnson in 1768 wrote about book collecting to Frederick Augusta Barnard, the king's librarian. He spoke of the transferal of books from one country's libraries to another's, the availability of rare books, and the importance of knowing where to find works of distinctive subject matter and emphases: "English Literature you will not seek in any place but England. Classical Learning is diffused everywhere and is not except by accident more copious in one part of the polite world than in another. . . . in Italy you may expect to meet with Canonists and Scholastic Divines, in Germany with Writers of the feudal Law, and in Holland with Civilians" (*Letters,* I, 215–216). Johnson's advice is a further reflection of his historical vision: he understood so well the significance of books as records of and as tangible links to the past. But not merely fascinated with old books because they were of ancient vintage, Johnson was able to distinguish among works appealing to a sense of history, beauty, or utility: "a royal Library should have at least the most curious Edition, the most splendid, and the most useful. The most curious Edition is commonly the first and the most useful may be expected among the last. . . . The most splendid the eye will discover" (I, 216). Johnson furthermore recommends acquiring a strong collection of geographical documents: "Many Countries have been very exactly surveyed, but it must not be expected that the exactness of actual mensuration will be preserved when the Maps are reduced by a contracted scale, and incorporated into a general System" (I, 217).

Johnson then writes of the "great ornaments" of a library as the first editions and goes on to discuss typography, mentioning that the "annals of typography" began with the Codex of 1458 but acknowledging that there may be "in obscure corners books printed before it." Also of interest to him were the editions of the Bible: "There prevails among typographical antiquaries a vague opinion that the Bible had been printed three times before the edition of 1462. . . . One of these editions has been lately discovered in a Convent, and transplanted into the french King's Library. Another copy likewise has been found but I know not whether of the same impression or of another. These discoveries are sufficient to raise hope and instigate enquiry." One cannot fail to notice the facility with which Johnson speaks of the history of old books; he truly enjoyed writing on antiquarian matters if the subject were of a serious nature. Convinced that rare volumes must be found and preserved, Johnson advised that they be "diligently sought" and wisely purchased: "In the purchase of old books let me recommend to you to examine with great caution whether they are perfect. In the first editions the loss of a leaf is not easily observed. You remember how near we both were to purchasing a mutilated Missal at a high price" (I, 218–219).[14]

Although his trip to Scotland in 1773 was not intended as a purely antiquarian mission, Johnson looked at and commented on inscriptions, tombstones, and even arrowheads and reflected philosophically on searching for graves of prominent men: "A large space of ground about these consecrated edifices is covered with grave-stones, few of which have any inscription. He that surveys it, attended by an insular antiquary, may be told where the kings of many nations are buried, and if he loves to sooth his imagination with the thoughts that naturally rise in places where the great and the powerful lie mingled with the dust, let him listen in submissive silence; for if he asks any questions, his delight is at an end" (*Journey*, p. 151). Elsewhere he comments on another aspect of the past interesting to most antiquarians: tradition, which he defined in the *Dictionary* as "any thing delivered orally from age to age," rather than the modern usage of "a long-established custom or practice that has the effect of an unwritten law." Johnson believed tradition was at best an interesting reflection of the past but at worst a distortion of the truth: tradition was "but a meteor, which, if once it falls, cannot be rekindled" (*Journey*, p. 111). Revering the truth in all historical accounts, he knew that with oral tradition each generation could add or subtract what it desired, leaving future generations an unclear history and unwarranted superstitions. Besides, as he argued, "one generation of ignorance effaces the whole series of unwritten history" (*Journey*, p. 111). One notes the similarity between Johnson's position and David Hume's: "the history of past events is immediately lost or disfigured when entrusted to memory and oral tradition" (*History*, I, 1–2).

Even though Johnson saw the traditions of the clan wars as interesting and deserving of the traveler's notice, "because they are the only records

of a nation that has no historians, and afford the most genuine representation of the life and character of the ancient Highlanders," he understood that one had to view them with suspicion: "The traditions of an
ignorant and savage people have been for ages negligently heard, and
unskilfully related. Distant events must have been mingled together, and
the actions of one man given to another" (*Journey,* pp. 50–51). Johnson
certainly did not disdain hearing oral history: recalling perhaps the stories
he was told as a boy in Lichfield, he could easily allow his imagination to
capture the spirit of an earlier and more primitive society; he could also
envisage from these accounts the clans locked in combat across a wild
landscape. But when it came to accepting the stories as historical truth he
quickly laid aside his romanticism, however appealing the traditions
were, and coldly rejected them as evidence of a nation's history. Because
Johnson was so forceful in his position, Boswell was compelled to admit
that his friend had "weakened" his belief in "remote tradition" (*Tour,*
p. 186).

But Johnson did not have to qualify his love of the ancient Scottish
customs, which he delighted in witnessing, discussing, and understanding. He talked, for instance, of the custom of fosterage, which was
"passing fast away," and regretted the loss of prize fighting; he said that
"every art should be preserved." He also had whiskey in a clamshell
"according to the ancient Highland custom," discussed the ancient custom of dress ("What we have long used we naturally like, and therefore
the Highlanders were unwilling to lay aside their plaid"), and remarked
on the continuation of the *mercheta mulierum,* "a fine in old times due to
the laird at the marriage of a virgin. . . . It is pleasant to find ancient
customs in old families."[15] Influenced in his view by the rich heritage he
experienced as a youth in Lichfield, Johnson took pleasure in these customs, and customs in general, because they were the only way he and
others could live historical moments. One could, of course, stand upon a
famous battle site, touch an archaeological relic, or read an ancient volume or manuscript, but these experiences cannot provide the same sense
of a living continuity with the past. Johnson's sipping whiskey out of a
clamshell was an animate act allowing him to drink not only with his
hosts but with Scots of earlier centuries. The taste of the liquid would
have warmed his historical sense as well as his body and spirits. He
would have appreciated the modern "founders day" celebrations, complete with period customs, recipes, and activities, for such observances
keep the spirit of history alive and encourage citizens to appreciate and
take part in their heritage. Always a man of his times, Johnson did not

revel in these customs as a temporary escape from the harshness of present strife; rather as a man of his times he nevertheless realized that he and his contemporaries were products of their nation's history. Taking part in seemingly archaic or harmless rituals kept this thought firmly in his mind.

Johnson deemed as well that customs were not the result of caprice, which by some mindless stroke of fortune had endured over the years. Instead, national customs were the products of "general agreement," not imposed "but chosen" and continued "only by the continuance of their cause" (*Idler* 11, p. 37). Therefore, a rejection of established practice implied a rejection of "common opinion, a defiance of common censure, and an appeal from general laws to private judgment" (*Adventurer* 131, pp. 485–486). Such remarks naturally helped spawn the impression that he fought progress by clinging tenaciously to established doctrines and practices, but Johnson always allowed for the breaking of a longstanding custom or practice if society would thereby benefit. That slavery had a long history in many societies made it no less abhorrent to him. "It is vain," he wrote, "to continue an institution, which experience shews to be ineffectual" (*Idler* 22, p. 71). And he saw the "tyranny of custom" as detrimental to both individuals and society.[16] Even so, he stressed vigorously that customs "are not to be changed *but for better*. Let those who desire to reform us shew the benefits of the change proposed" (*Idler* 90, p. 279; italics mine).

Although not an unqualified supporter of long-respected customs, Johnson believed they aided in constituting a firm line of defense against the disruption of society, for continuing at least some of the practices established in earlier centuries helped curtail the kind of uncontrollable change he associated with the mid seventeenth century. Because he saw history as a block-by-block process, with each generation building upon the success and failure of the past, to break from one's heritage meant undermining the foundation laid by the hard labor and wisdom of many preceding generations. With no foundation, Johnson argued, the structure of society could easily crumble into chaos. It therefore troubled him deeply that many of his contemporaries rejected established forms simply because they were established: in modern times, he once noted, an "overfondness for novelty, a desire of striking out new paths to peace and happiness, and a neglect of following the precept in the text of asking for the old paths, where is the good way, and walking therein" are part of the accepted philosophy (Sermon 7, *Sermons*, p. 78). Johnson's famous comment to Boswell that most schemes for political improvement are "very laughable things" has also been viewed as evidence of a conservative's reaction to change, but his laughter is at the expense of those who refuse to see the past as a cornucopia of wisdom, overflowing with the fruits of examples, precedents, and lessons for the present and future. Johnson possessed none of the arrogance so typical of those who believe that experience means little and that only new ideas can work.

Although one would assume he championed customs more vigorously as he grew older, his position was probably firmly in place by his early thirties. In the *Debate Between the Committee of the House of Commons and Oliver Cromwell* (1741) he writes in the guise of the committee that old institutions are preferable to new plans because most people judge only from custom; it will be long "before new titles attract their regard, esteem and veneration." The continuation of "any practice which might have been altered or disused at pleasure," the committee adds, demonstrates its worthiness of being retained, for a custom "not in itself detrimental becomes every day better established." As to the practical advantages of custom, the committee says that changing practices that are reverenced because they have long endured is to be avoided for the most part, for the "real usefulness is always the same, and the accidental esteem of them is always increasing." Change must be balanced "by some equivalent advantage," because if amendments become the fashion men will "go on from change to change" and thus "remove one evil by introducing another" (*Political Writings,* pp. 88, 98, 99, 101).[17]

Accordingly, whether the custom was political, social, or religious, Johnson viewed it with respect; he had little patience for those who disdained the examples, lessons, customs, and in many cases even the artifacts of the past: "A contempt of the monuments, and the wisdom of antiquity, may justly be reckoned one of the reigning follies of these days. . . . The study of antiquity is laborious, and to despise what we cannot, or will not understand, is a much more expeditious way to reputation" (Sermon 7, *Sermons,* p. 82). It is simply not enough to argue that he would naturally have had an affinity for customs because there was much tradition in eighteenth-century life, for very few who enjoy the delights and practices of even our own assortment of holidays take time to consider as Johnson did their symbolism and significance.

Finally, because he delighted in customs and saw their symbolic value, Johnson was disappointed in not finding in Scotland more evidence of past cultures: "There was perhaps never any change of national manners so quick, so great, and so general, as that which has operated in the Highlands, by the last conquest, and the subsequent laws. We came

72

thither too late to see what we expected, a people of peculiar appearance, and a system of antiquated life" (*Journey*, p. 57). He regretted not being able to wander through a living museum of the past, where he could examine more of the domestic and cultural ceremonies and practices steeped deeply in antiquity. And, although he was sensitive to the necessity and inevitability of change, he was also, as Thomas Curley points out, sympathetic to clan tradition: "Johnson sought a compromise solution that would permit the survival of the old life-style upon a more stable economic base of modern commerce."[18] He felt moreover a sense of loss at the passage of a rich, vibrant, and unique culture, which would in all probability never come again. He knew custom could survive welcomed and inevitable progress, and in this case was dismayed that it had not.

Johnson's interest in the history and customs of the Highlanders reflects the growth in the later eighteenth century of local histories as a respected branch of antiquarianism. Johnson seems not to have been an enthusiast of most of these efforts, but he certainly judged some of them worthy of the reader's attention. For instance, he wrote Barnard in 1768 that local histories of Continental towns or villages "may be generally neglected," but he went on to state that some are deserving of attention because of the "celebrity of the place, the eminence of the authour, or the beauty of the Sculptures" (*Letters*, I, 217). And when Edmond Malone came upon Johnson reading the *History of Birmingham* he mentioned that local histories "were generally dull." Johnson agreed but was interested nonetheless in the Birmingham account (*Life*, IV, 218). We have already seen his enthusiastic response to John Nichols's study of Lichfield, and in regard to his birthplace he "often lamented," according to Nichols, that "no city of equal antiquity and worth has been so destitute of a native to record its fame, and transmit its history to posterity" (*Misc*, II, 410). This evidence demonstrates that if the subject were worthy of a detailed account, Johnson advocated its being written as an important contribution to historical scholarship. Having read at least several of the local histories, he knew the listing and describing of every building and landmark was of little use to the reader, but when the author devoted his time to the customs of the people and the histories of important structures the work took on special interest and value.

At any rate, Johnson enjoyed and drew inspiration and philosophical insight from the many historical structures he visited in his lifetime.

Other than the cathedrals, castles, and churches of Britain, he was curious enough to examine the Druid remains in Scotland but appeared little impressed with them. After viewing a Druid temple above Inverness, he observed that "to go and see one is only to see that it is nothing, for there is neither art nor power in it, and seeing one is as much as one would wish" (*Tour,* p. 99). His remark is significant because his position on antiquities was that although collections of coins, fragments, clothing, and other artifacts (such as those gathered by Quisquilius) might be interesting historical remains, they quickly lose effectiveness and importance when they merely lie silently as relics without any sense of "art or power." To Johnson, the treasured remains must move the viewer to historical or philosophical contemplation; they must draw forth the spirit of history and make the viewer a part of an illustrious past, thereby conveying a sense of change and cultural progress. This is why Stonehenge did not leave him cold; as he wrote Hester Thrale in 1783, it was a "hard task to make an adequate description": "Salisbury Cathedral and its Neighbour Stonehenge, are two eminent monuments of art and rudeness, and may show the first essay, and the last perfection in architecture" (*Letters,* III, 86).

Another aspect of antiquity that stimulated Johnson's historical sense and philosophical reflection was the many ruins scattered across the Scottish landscape. Ruins had already captured the fancy of antiquarians of the late seventeenth and early eighteenth centuries, and it was fashionable to visit the ruined sites in Britain, Rome, and Greece and bring back fragments of stone. But Johnson's considerable interest in ruins was not simply the result of their being the historic remains of once-important structures or the visual proof of the transitory way of the world, as was many an antiquarian's view, rather he found them significant because they were representative of a far more serious decay. A ruined structure was to Johnson a metaphor of deeper ills, diseases that left unchecked could destroy the very fabric of society. And although he saw the ruins as a reflection on Scotland he also recognized in them danger signals his own country could not afford to ignore.

His indignation over the ruins of Oseney and Rewley near Oxford in the summer of 1754 is evidence that Johnson came to Scotland in the summer of 1773 with an understanding of what decay symbolized. Taking also into consideration the connection he made as a youth in Lichfield between the dilapidated, damaged, or ruined state of a building and the violence and disorder brought about by zealous reform and political instability, we can see why Imlac responded negatively to young Rasselas's insistence that nothing important could be gained from surveying "piles of stone" (*Rasselas*, p. 117). Far from being reluctant to explore ruins, Johnson was more likely looking forward to viewing Scotland's crumbling edifices; as Boswell mentioned, Johnson was "abundantly desirous" of surveying the old buildings of St. Andrews (*Tour*, p. 40).

Johnson first of all examined many of the crumbling structures along the route of his journey, from the ruined fort on Inch Keith to the ruins at Auchinleck, "which afford striking images of ancient life" (*Journey*, p. 161). Boswell on several occasions informs the reader that his friend viewed the ruins with "much attention" or with "wonderful eagerness" (*Tour*, pp. 36, 266). For all his years and general state of his health, Johnson took great interest in moving about the ruins, measuring distances and hypothesizing on what must have stood where. Certainly he shared the enthusiasm of many antiquarians in trying to reconstruct the history of the area he visited, but, more notably, because they were important to him philosophically he wanted to experience physically as much of the ruins as he could. He wished to draw forth by standing within the shell of a church or castle all the artistry and power the ruins could evoke. He was thus quite different from those of his century who saw something stylish in decayed buildings. One need only recall the trend toward artificial ruins in gardens and parks and the debate over "Gothic" as opposed to "Greek" ruins: Lord Kames, for one, arguing that Gothic ruins—time conquering strength—should always be chosen over Greek—barbarism conquering good taste. Even though Johnson could share with writers like Thomas Warton a sensitivity for the sheer impressiveness of medieval edifices (his diary of the Welsh trip in 1774 tells us so) and a regret that society has allowed these historical monuments to decay, he was not one who would, for aesthetic gratification, willingly sit "Beneath yon ruin'd abbey's moss-grown piles" (Warton's *The Pleasures of Melancholy*).[19] The "Gothic Revival," then, appears to have had little effect on his reaction to ruins.

On the opening page of his *Journey to the Western Islands* Johnson comments on a ruined fort on Inch Keith, just to the north of Edinburgh. And it was more than a perfunctory glance, for Boswell records that his friend examined it in a way befitting a serious traveler (*Tour*, p. 36). We have already noted in chapter one Johnson's disappointment in the condition of St. Andrews. Gazing at "the ruins of ancient magnificence," he remarked that even the crumbling stones will soon bear no trace of their former state "unless some care be taken to preserve them; and where is the pleasure of preserving such mournful memorials?" (*Journey*, p. 5)—

words evincing the emotion he could feel when contemplating ruins. As he would do several times in the *Journey,* he expressed a "mournful" reaction to the decayed structures around him. But his lament at the condition of St. Andrews goes beyond a reflection of life's impermanence: he observes that the cathedral, "of which the foundations may be still traced, . . . appears to have been a spacious and majestick building, not unsuitable to the primacy of the kingdom. Of the architecture, the poor remains can hardly exhibit, even to an artist, a sufficient specimen" (p. 5). His ability to envisage the majesty of the structure in early sixteenth-century Scotland and to understand the importance of the cathedral to the religious and secular heritage of a proud people provoked his anger at what John Knox had wrought while attempting to forward his "reformations."

Whereas Johnson frequently evinced an antipathy for Scottish Presbyterianism, his remarks on St. Andrews seem to provide just cause. Because of what he sees as a Presbyterian disregard for tradition, a great cathedral was now lying in ruination. The equation was thus drawn between the ruins and religious and political chaos. In Johnson's mind, Knox, along with Henry VIII and Cromwell, sought to efface a way of life and a rich tradition, thereby leaving many historical landmarks in the condition of St. Andrews's cathedral. One would be wrong, however, to attribute Johnson's indignation over Knox's legacy merely to his high-church bias, for although he reacted most violently to a ruined cathedral or church, he knew that the effects of neglect and destruction do not limit themselves to the spiritual realm; as he writes, St. Andrews, "when it had lost its archiepiscopal preeminence, gradually decayed" (*Journey,* p. 6). And one of the secular structures most affected was the university, the magnificence of which was marred by the decay of one of its three major colleges, St. Leonard's. Of the plan to convert the ruins into a kind of greenhouse, Johnson remarks in frustration, "To what use it will next be put I have no pleasure in conjecturing. It is something that its present state is at least not ostentatiously displayed. Where there is yet shame, there may in time be virtue" (*Journey,* p. 7). His final comment deserves special emphasis, for if a society realizes how disgraceful is its neglect of such buildings, it may begin the virtuous act of arresting the decay. The *Journey,* then, helps raise to the level of consciousness the shame England as well as Scotland should feel at the dilapidation of its religious and secular structures. Even though Johnson was quick to satirize those who had a fashionable attachment to ruins and the past,[20] he placed a high premium on preserving important buildings that served as symbols of a proud heritage and a promise of future growth.

His concluding observation on St. Leonard's College casts further blame at the present government for neglecting its responsibilities: "It is surely not without just reproach, that a nation . . . denies any participation of its prosperity to its literary societies; and while its merchants or its nobles are raising palaces, suffers its universities to moulder into dust" (*Journey*, p. 7). Here is an excellent illustration of Johnson's use of ruins as a tangible symbol of a deeper decay; he stresses the incongruity of investing wealth into structures important only to their inhabitants at the expense of a vital university or college having symbolic as well as practical significance. He visited St. Andrews with the intention of viewing its antiquities, but it shocked and saddened him that a city with such an illustrious history was now in disrepair. And his distress was magnified because he realized that if decay could affect a major city like St. Andrews, one would have to assume there was no commitment to preserving tradition or pursuing the future.

Before leaving the city Johnson gives his readers a rather "mournful" impression: "But whoever surveys the world must see many things that give him pain. The kindness of the professors did not contribute to abate the uneasy remembrance of a university declining, a college alienated, and a church profaned and hastening to the ground. . . . St. Andrews indeed has formerly suffered more atrocious ravages and more extensive destruction, but recent evils affect with greater force. We were reconciled to the sight of archiepiscopal ruins. The distance of a calamity from the present time seems to preclude the mind from contact or sympathy. . . . Had the university been destroyed two centuries ago, we should not have regretted it; but to see it pining in decay and struggling for life, fills the mind with mournful images and ineffectual wishes" (*Journey*, p. 9). Johnson's point, however generally true and artistically put, misleads us as to his own view, for his indignation at the ruined abbeys near Oxford and his anger over Knox's "reformations" two centuries earlier prove that his mind was not precluded from "contact or sympathy" with events long past. Regardless of its age, as long as a ruined structure had a living symbolism, he could not dismiss it as a mere historical curiosity.

After leaving St. Andrews, Johnson viewed the remains of the monastery at Aberbrothick, which seem to have impressed him greatly: "I should scarcely have regretted my journey, had it afforded nothing more than the sight of Aberbrothick" (*Journey*, p. 11). And then, after passing through Aberdeen, he and Boswell arrived in Elgin. Even though it was raining, Johnson stood in the downpour and examined the ruins of Elgin Cathedral with a "most patient attention" (*Tour*, p. 82). He comments further on the significance he attached to such sights: "The ruins of the cathedral of Elgin afforded us another proof of the waste of reformation. There is enough yet remaining to shew, that it was once magnificent." Although there are parts still preserved, "the body of the church is a mass of fragments" (*Journey*, p. 23). And who had allowed the cathedral to fall into decay? "The church of Elgin had, in the intestine tumults of the barbarous ages, been laid waste by the irruption of a highland chief, whom the bishop had offended; but it was gradually restored to the state, of which the traces may be now discerned, and was at last not destroyed by the tumultuous violence of Knox, but more shamefully suffered to dilapidate by deliberate robbery and frigid indifference" (*Journey*, p. 23). The history of Elgin Cathedral was particularly distressing to Johnson, because it had been restored after its destruction in less civilized times and then left to decay by those who had respect for neither the grandeur of the past nor the importance of the structure.

At this point he recalls that the lead from this cathedral and the one at Aberdeen was once removed for sale and shipment to Holland. Fortunately, Johnson feels, the plan went awry: "I hope every reader will rejoice that this cargo of sacrilege was lost at sea" (*Journey*, p. 24). He next addresses his English audience: "Let us not however make too much haste to despise our neighbours. Our own cathedrals are mouldering by unregarded dilapidation. It seems to be part of the despicable philosophy of the time to despise monuments of sacred magnificence, and we are in danger of doing that deliberately, which the Scots did not do but in the unsettled state of an imperfect constitution" (*Journey*, p. 24).[21] Johnson's words reflect clearly the indignation he could feel over ruins and his belief that England was as guilty as the Scots of neglecting its heritage. He could not have been pleased, for example, when viewing the scars from the English Civil War on the cathedrals of Winchester, Exeter, Ely, and Norwich, which he visited before going to Scotland. And in *"O.N." On the Fireworks for the Peace of Aix-la-Chapelle* (1749), almost assuredly by Johnson, the author laments "so many" English churches "sinking into ruins" (*Political Writings*, p. 115). In fact, few in Johnson's day could have been unaware of the deplorable state into which many of the magnificent religious and secular structures had fallen. (One need only have looked into the drawings of Samuel Buck.) Johnson's beginning the above passage with "Let us" suggests his intention to educate his readers as to the implications of Scotland's decay. The English could not afford to look upon Scotland's ruins as a local problem, for the symbolic properties had significance for their country as well. Johnson is expressing more than indignation as to what transpired in the past; he is also displaying a fear of what may happen in the future.

Upon landing on Raasay in the Western Islands, Boswell observed "a cross, or rather the ruins of one"—an apt symbol for the decay into which so many of the religious houses had fallen (*Tour*, p. 132). On the island, Johnson summarized after examining a dilapidated chapel, "Of the destruction of churches, the decay of religion must in time be the consequence" (*Journey*, p. 65). Few statements articulate as well his belief in the associative value of ruins. But the examination of Scotland's decayed structures reached its climax at Iona, a historic site well known to Johnson through his reading of Thomas Pennant, Martin Martin, and William Sacheverell. Boswell describes his emotions as they landed at the "venerable place": "Indeed, the seeing of Mr. Samuel Johnson at Icolmkill was what I had often imaged as a very venerable scene. . . . What an addition was it to Icolmkill to have the Rambler upon the spot!" (*Tour*, p. 331). As noted in chapter one, Johnson's account is characteristically more philosophical: "Whatever withdraws us from the power of our senses; whatever makes the past, the distant, or the future predominate over the present, advances us in the dignity of thinking beings. . . . That man is little to be envied, whose patriotism would not gain force upon the plain of Marathon, or whose piety would not grow warmer among the ruins of Iona?" (*Journey*, p. 148).

The following morning Johnson "took a very accurate inspection of all the ruins," entering the cathedral that he might "attentively view and even measure" the decayed structure (*Tour*, pp. 332–333, 336–337). After his examination, he portrayed those who live among the dilapidated edifices: "The inhabitants are remarkably gross, and remarkably neglected: I know not if they are visited by any minister. The island, which was once the metropolis of learning and piety, has now no school for education, nor temple for worship" (*Journey*, p. 152). He saw quite clearly, as he wanted his readers to see, the connection between the ruins and the intellectual and religious decay of the society. Iona was to Johnson the example par excellence of this correlation: due to neglect, indifference, and superstition it had become a desolate curiosity. He concludes with a pious wish: "Perhaps, in the revolutions of the world, Iona may be sometime again the instructress of the Western Regions" (*Journey*, p. 153). Whatever its future, Johnson would see that Iona could be an instructor in its present ruinous state, for if societies could learn to prevent the causes of such decay, Iona would indeed teach an important lesson. Much like a clergyman dwelling on the destruction of Sodom and Gomorrah as the inevitable result of immoral and perverse behavior, Johnson places before his readers the crumbling remains of once proud and vital structures for the purpose of awakening moral sensibilities and warning the insensitive to grim possibilities.

We can agree with Thomas Curley when he writes that Johnson's *Journey to the Western Islands* "chronicles a cumulative *memento mori* of a culture's demise and a people's degradation with much of the artistic and moral force of *Rasselas.*"[22] But Johnson wanted his readers to see beyond the borders of Scotland. The ruins he described in the north had their counterparts in the south and were representative of what he despised and feared most: disrespect for tradition, indifference, neglect, wanton destruction, and chaos. By understanding the *symbolic* properties of decayed churches and castles, England itself stood to gain much from Johnson's depiction of Scotland's ruins. As he wrote in 1760, "He only is a useful traveller who brings home something by which his country may be benefited" (*Idler* 97, p. 300).

If the evidence in this chapter suggests that Johnson took quite seriously the pursuits of the antiquarians and that aspects of antiquarianism were important to him symbolically, how then do we reconcile it to his explicit statements deriding the antiquarians and their work? Certainly, we cannot pass off all of these remarks as gratuitous satire. The problem, as R. W. Ketton-Cremer points out, was that the "distinction between the genuine antiquary and the fashionable virtuoso was never clearly defined."[23] Because Johnson deeply respected serious scholarship and knew there were so many pedants and faddists engaged in antiquarian studies, he was forced to maintain an ambivalent attitude about antiquarianism as a whole; he was never able, regardless of the friends who showed him the best side of such work, to embrace enthusiastically all efforts at recalling and studying the past. A revealing passage on this matter lies at the beginning of the preface to *Shakespeare:* "Antiquity, like every other quality that attracts the notice of mankind, has undoubtedly votaries that reverence it, not from reason, but from prejudice. Some seem to admire indiscriminately whatever has been long preserved, without considering that time has sometimes co-operated with chance; all perhaps are more willing to honour past than present excellence; and the mind contemplates genius through the shades of age, as the eye surveys the sun through artificial opacity" (*Shakespeare,* I, 59).

Although Johnson uses these comments to introduce a literary topic, they are totally relevant to his perception of antiquarianism. It is doubtful he was ever insensitive to touching or viewing a relic of antiquity—whether coin, garment, weapon, or stone—but he could not bring himself to share the enthusiasm of those who marveled at the object because it was Roman, medieval English, or once the possession of a famous name from the past. Unless the relic stirred his historical sense or sustained a symbolic meaning or other significance, Johnson would not have taken much pleasure in handling an eleventh-century arrowhead found at Hastings. More important, he refused to support the philosophy of those who believed in the superiority of the past, those who admired "indiscriminately whatever has been long preserved." Unfortunately, he was never able to divorce that philosophy from the image of the typical antiquarian, even though he knew, especially as he grew older, that such a generalization was an unfair and limiting one. Much like a man in the political arena who, although knowing that most in his party advocate his own positions and stand for integrity and compassion, is nevertheless forced to change sides because of the large excesses and repugnant philosophy of a vocal and influential minority, Johnson had to remain apart from the antiquarianism of his day.

His ambivalence and sense of conflict are nowhere better evident than in *Rambler* 83, written in 1751 but representative of his position throughout his mature years. In the essay he reveals both his disgust with pursuits "which seem but remotely allied to useful knowledge, and of little importance to happiness or virtue," and his deep-rooted respect for intellectual endeavor. He remarks that "utensils, arms, or dresses" of foreign countries, which constitute the bulk of many collections, are of no importance when one treasures them only because they are foreign. "Yet," he continues, "they are not all equally useless, nor can it be always safely determined, which should be rejected or retained; for they may sometimes unexpectedly contribute to the illustration of history, and to the knowledge of the natural commodities of its inhabitants." Johnson goes on to discuss other subjects of the antiquarian's interest that seem of little value, but once more he cannot bring himself to condemn them outright. Regarding those "fragments" of antiquity—urns,[24] pieces of pavement, armor of prominent persons—Johnson writes that the "loss or preservation of these seems to be a thing indifferent, nor can I perceive why the possession of them should be coveted. Yet, perhaps, even this curiosity is implanted by nature; and when I find Tully confessing of himself, that he could not forbear at Athens to visit the walks and houses which the old philosophers had frequented or inhabited, . . . I am afraid to declare against the general voice of mankind, and am inclined to believe, that this regard, which we involuntarily pay to the meanest relique of a man great and illustrious, is intended as an incitement to labour, and an encouragement to expect the same renown, if it be sought by the same virtues" (IV, 73–74).

Rarely do we find Johnson so tentative in his observations; he appears torn between the undaunted critic and the timid friend of all learning. But Johnson was indeed betwixt and between on this matter: he refused to allow a fashionable and unthinking delight in antiquities to escape censure and yet he sought to justify in his mind another reason for the hours spent in tracking down, preserving, and displaying relics of a bygone age. He could not dismiss out of hand any work that might "unexpectedly contribute to the illustration of history." And there was also his innate desire to accumulate new information of whatever kind: as he said at another time, "All knowledge is of itself of some value. There is nothing so minute or inconsiderable, that I would not rather know it than not" (*Life*, II, 357). Johnson does, however, arrive at a compromise by the end of *Rambler* 83, one that satisfies both his critical and historical sides: "The virtuoso therefore cannot be said to be wholly useless; but perhaps he may be sometimes culpable for confining himself to business below his genius, and losing in petty speculations, those hours by which if he had spent them in nobler studies, he might have given new light to the intellectual world" (IV, 74–75).[25] Johnson could not forgive the cheapening of history by the faddist or the misapplication of research by a talented scholar. Because lists of stone fragments or collections of tarnished coins would never provide contemporary society with much information relevant to its own problems or aspirations, they must always remain minor attainments. As he noted earlier in *Rambler* 71, "It is lamented by Hearne, the learned antiquary of Oxford, that this general forgetfulness of the fragility of life, has remarkably infected the students of monuments and records; as their employment consists first in collecting and afterwards in arranging or abstracting what libraries afford them, . . . but when they have undertaken a work, they go on searching and transcribing, call for new supplies, when they are already overburdened, and at last leave their work unfinished" (IV, 10). Perhaps Johnson regretted most of all the sheer waste of time and talent characteristic of many antiquarian efforts. His conclusions were by and large those of

Edward Gibbon, who saw both the immense value of much antiquarian research and the utter foolishness of those falling victim to antiquarian zeal.[26]

"A mere antiquarian," he wrote in 1778, "is a rugged being" (*Letters,* II, 247); but the important thing to remember is that to Johnson he is not the *only* kind of antiquarian. Regardless of their many fruitless searches into antiquity, Johnson had respect for the useful work of which the antiquarians were capable; he knew that there were a good number "whose labors cannot without ingratitude be depreciated."[27] For all his satire against the collector of ancient artifacts, he believed the study of antiquities was no laughing matter, but rather a serious and rewarding pursuit if approached in a true historical spirit of inquiry and application to the present. He wrote in his dedication to Percy's *Reliques,* "No active or comprehensive mind can forbear some attention to the reliques of antiquity: It is prompted by natural curiosity to survey the progress of life and manners, and to inquire by what gradations barbarity was civilized, grossness refined, and ignorance instructed" (Hazen, p. 167). In the final analysis, Johnson wanted his contemporaries to share the feelings of Nekayah, who, after accepting the wisdom of Imlac, said she would "rejoice to learn something of the manners of antiquity" (*Rasselas,* p. 119). When we weigh such comments along with the other evidence, we find it less surprising, as we learn from Percy, that at one time Johnson planned a "Dictionary of English or British Antiquities."[28]

Chapter Four

Johnson as Historian: Looking at Literature, Lives, and the Law

The previous chapters in this study have focused on the development of Johnson's historical sense, his perceptions of historical personalities and the English Civil War, and his response to antiquarianism. Even though these chapters have demonstrated the effect of Johnson's historical sense on his writings, we may now look more directly—in this and in the following chapter—at the large role history played in his compositions. This chapter will examine works of a more purely literary nature, the biographical writings, and the possible contributions Johnson made to the Vinerian law lectures of Robert Chambers in order to determine more fully the considerable influence of his historical sense, the manner in which history illuminated and embellished his writings, and the occasions on which he leaves the realms of the strictly biographical and steps enthusiastically into the province of the historian.

A number of the reviews Johnson wrote from 1742 to 1760 clearly reflected his strong historical interests. First of all there were reviews of historical works: Thomas Birch's *History of the Royal Society,* Patrick Browne's *History of Jamaica,* and William Borlase's *History of the Isles of Sicily,* all done in 1756. Here we might also recall his dedications to Charlotte Lennox's *Sully's Memoirs* (1755), John Lindsay's *Evangelical History* (1757), John Kennedy's *Chronology* (1763), and Percy's *Reliques* (1765), and his prefaces to Du Fresnoy's *Chronological Tables* (1762) and Alexander Macbean's *Dictionary of Ancient Geography* (1773). But most significant are the reviews of Sarah Churchill's memoirs, William Tytler's *Historical and Critical Enquiry* into the "casket letters" of Mary Queen of Scots, and Thomas Blackwell's *Memoirs of the Court of Augustus.*

In 1742 Johnson reviewed in the *Gentleman's Magazine* Sarah Churchill's memoirs in the *Account of the Conduct of the Duchess of Marlborough.* He found exceedingly valuable for historical research in the late seventeenth and early eighteenth centuries those accounts written by actual participants in the events. We have already ascertained some of Johnson's impressions of Charles II, William III, and Queen Anne from his reading of the memoirs, but as a historical work, Johnson moreover argues, the Duchess's account allows the reader to have "an intimate acquaintance with the characters of those whose names have crowded the latest histories, and discover the relation between their minds and their actions" (*Works*, XIII, 165). Such a work furthermore provides the historian a glimpse at the inner workings of political decisions and the operations of household government. Public transactions, speeches, and journalistic accounts can only go so far toward an understanding of the period, because the door to the monarch's chamber is barred to almost all. But Sarah Churchill used her key to open that door and usher the reader into the intimate affairs of state.

In Johnson's mind, the duchess's inclusion of letters to augment her collection only strengthens the work as an important historical document: "we have a more exact knowledge than can be expected from general histories, because we see them in their private apartments, in their careless hours, and observe those actions in which they indulged their own inclinations, without any regard to censure or applause" (p. 166). Johnson does more in this piece than merely perform the task of describing the contents of a work, quoting several of its parts, and remarking on style and organization. More important, he offers many clues regarding his conception of good historical composition and demonstrates a keen awareness of the complexity in searching for historical truth. Although more space will be allotted to these matters in chapter six, we may say here that whereas many of his contemporaries—and many educated persons since—would base their assumptions and arguments only on the writings of historians, Johnson realized, as a mature historical mind must, that period studies are simply not enough. One must consult as well those works approaching events and personalities subjectively and at times emotionally—diaries, reminiscences, journals—in order to grasp a fuller knowledge and the subtle nuances of history. Johnson understood that historians who furnish an overview of a large period of time or a major event cannot adequately assess, even if they have the materials, the domestic activity or idiosyncrasies of important persons because to do so would deter from the grand design of the history. And yet, as Johnson also knew, these everyday activities or personal quirks may have had considerable effect on the way a nation was governed. Today this is all basic historical theory, but in the early 1740s and therefore before the "flowering" of British historiography such knowledge could hardly be considered commonplace. It is therefore to Johnson's credit, especially at this early stage of his career, that he sensed and articulated so well the significance of a work like the memoirs of Sarah Churchill.

In the 1760 review of William Tytler's *Historical and Critical Enquiry*, Johnson begins by characterizing his time as one that delights in talk of liberty, independence, and private judgment: "little more is to be desired, except that one should talk of [liberty] less, and use it better" (*Works*, XIII, 260). This comment leads to one of his most profound observations, in this or in any other work, which too often gets overlooked because it appears in a minor piece: "When an opinion has once become popular, very few are willing to oppose it. Idleness is more willing to credit than inquire; cowardice is afraid of controversy, and vanity of answer" (p. 260). Few bits of Johnsonian wisdom express as well the philosophy behind his historical outlook: in order to be a good historian, one must reject popular interpretations of events, no matter how widely accepted, and make the effort to question the validity of a view and then search for contrary evidence. Johnson perceived that the kind of independence and skepticism required of the historian is hard to come by; too many have been satisfied with handy or facile assessments of history. His words could serve handsomely as the historian's credo.

From this introduction Johnson turns to the historical subject of the review, but feels the need to punctuate what he has already argued: "It has now been fashionable, for near half a century, to defame and vilify the house of Stuart, and to exalt and magnify the reign of Elizabeth. The Stuarts have found few apologists, for the dead cannot pay for praise; and who will, without reward, oppose the tide of popularity? yet there remains, still, among us, not wholly extinguished, a zeal for truth, a desire of establishing right, in opposition to fashion" (p. 261). The commentary on the Stuart rulers in chapter two should place these remarks on the House in their proper perspective and explain why he could defend with fervor the reputation of Mary, but his enthusiasm for Tytler's vindication of the queen goes much deeper. In the review, Johnson champions a vigorous examination of historical facts as the only way to peer beneath the murky waters of fashion. He is not so much angered at the Stuarts' failure to receive any just credit as he is disappointed that the romantic aspects of history, which were in large part responsible for the impression of Elizabeth and her times, had the weight of historical truth. That misconceptions about the past, stemming from an innocent desire to think well of one's heritage, were applied in a *historical* rather than an artistic context to contemporary social and political matters made them even more objectionable to Johnson. He was able to enjoy an occasional intoxicating draught of historical romanticism without overindulging or depending on it, but he knew that too many of his contemporaries were not as temperate.

In paraphrasing Tytler's arguments, Johnson demonstrates a facility for historical narration mixed with analysis as he presents the evidence implicating Mary in the murder of Lord Darnley and Elizabeth's reaction to that evidence. His commentary is judicious, yet one senses with ease the drama of the event. Although he did not condone, except in poetry and satire, turning history into romance by ignoring or modifying the truth, Johnson, like the majority of historians before and after his time, saw the record of any nation or civilization as ripe with dramatic moments the reader must sense and respond to if the historical work is to be enjoyable and significant. Quoting passages from Tytler and several observations of David Hume and William Robertson,[1] Johnson neatly summarizes Tytler's evidence and concludes in the final sentence: "That the letters were forged, is now made so probable, that, perhaps, they will never more be cited as testimonies" (p. 271). In stark contrast to what he wrote in the review of Blackwell's *Memoirs,* Johnson has nothing negative to say about Tytler's handling of his materials or his prose style; Johnson is preoccupied with the historical issue at hand, influenced, no doubt, by his interest in Mary Queen of Scots. Regardless, Johnson makes a case for more intense historical scrutiny, and reading over the concluding sentence of the review must have given him great satisfaction, for in advertising Tytler's *Enquiry*—and the review is by and large an advertisement—he struck a blow against fashionable approaches to the past and another for historical skepticism and truth.

The most interesting of these major reviews, however, may be the 1756 assessment of Blackwell's *Memoirs of the Court of Augustus,* because more than a criticism of the author's book the review is important to our understanding of Johnson's impressions of ancient Rome. As we have seen, Johnson often used examples from antiquity to illustrate his moral lessons or color his arguments, and he realized his readers probably had more familiarity with Roman history than with any other period; it was, after all, fashionable to *claim* a knowledge of Roman events, leaders, and artifacts, if nothing else. (Johnson once remarked to Boswell, "Why . . . we know very little about the Romans.")[2] Julius Caesar appears to have stimulated the full range of Johnson's historical sense, for he could as a good historian both censure and assess the great Roman objectively and place him along with other great figures from history into the world of historical fancy. In the preface to *Shakespeare* he writes that if the playgoer can be persuaded "his old acquaintances are Alexander and Caesar . . . he is in a state of elevation above the reach of reason, or of truth" (*Shakespeare*, I, 77). Although Johnson is arguing against a strict adherence to the dramatic unities in this passage, it still reflects the kind of enjoyment he on occasion allowed himself when contemplating the mighty Caesar and men like him. And his summation of Shakespeare's play suggests his artistic preference for a more magnificent Caesar: "I have never been strongly agitated in perusing it, and think it somewhat cold and unaffecting, compared with some other of Shakespeare's plays; his adherence to the real story, and to Roman manners, seems to have impeded the natural vigour of his genius" (*Shakespeare*, II, 836). Disappointed in the play's emphasis on the lesser figures Anthony, Brutus, and Cassius, Johnson believed Shakespeare wasted a golden opportunity to concentrate primarily on the most famous ruler in the history of Western civilization.

But Johnson was quick to take the skeptical historian's view of Rome when he heard his contemporaries praising the virtues of Roman government, stoicism, and commonwealth at the expense of modern times. When Boswell sought in 1777 to admire the Roman Senate as being "composed of men sincerely desirous to resolve what they should think best for their country," unlike the British Parliament, which was corrupt, Johnson "would allow no such character to the Roman Senate" (*Life*, III, 206). John Robert Moore has written that too often the example of Rome suggested to Johnson "a radical approach to reform" and "*regicide* to end political and *suicide* to end private woes."[3] The best source of his attitude toward Rome, though, remains the review of Blackwell's *Memoirs of the Court of Augustus*. Here Johnson hints at his century's knowledge of Roman particulars when he criticizes Blackwell for providing nothing but what has long "furnished employment to the studious, and amusement to the idle." As he begins his summary of the book, Johnson immediately reveals impatience with the popular views of Rome: "These were surely very dismal times to those who suffered; but I know not, why any one but a school boy, in his declamation, should whine over the commonwealth of Rome, which grew great only by the misery of the rest of mankind. The Romans, like others, as soon as they grew rich, grew corrupt, and, in their corruption, sold the lives and freedoms of themselves, and of one another" (*Works*, XIII, 171). That he saw in the review a chance to criticize contemporary political notions as well as Blackwell's literary shortcomings is furthermore apparent in the following: "Among other affectations of this writer, is a furious and unnecessary zeal for liberty; or rather, for one form of government as preferable to another" (p. 173). Johnson adds that political institutions can suffer change provided laws are obeyed and the change is not advanced for mere novelty's sake, but "who can bear the hardy champion who ventures nothing? who, in full security, undertakes the defence of the assassination of Caesar, and declares his resolution *to speak plain?*" (p. 173).

Johnson's anger is impossible to overlook in this review, and although he spends considerable time outlining Blackwell's stylistic faults, it is the author's depiction of Rome that most clearly infuriates the reviewer. Johnson accuses him of stabbing Caesar "every day and night in his sleeping or waking dreams" and coming "too late into the world with his fury for freedom, with his Brutus and Cassius" (p. 174). The attack on the two major conspirators helps to explain further his coolness toward Shakespeare's play, but more than this, the assassination of a lawful ruler, however dangerous, could not but remind him of the patriotic zeal surrounding the execution of Charles I in 1649. That Johnson deplored the fanaticism of the mob and the subversion by individuals or groups of established laws and religious practices is clear, but it moreover distressed him that the lessons of history were obviously ignored by many of his contemporaries, who spouted platitudes about Rome and its system of government.

Now fully submerged in historical argument, Johnson mentions the difficulty of suppressing his laughter at those honoring a people who, "while they were poor, robbed mankind, and, as soon as they became rich, robbed one another" (p. 175). He blames Blackwell for illustrating only the evils perpetrated by Caesar's party and refusing to condemn his opposition: "every act is sanctified by the name of a patriot"—a remark quite relevant to his own time. Johnson's theme in many of these historical pieces is that modern citizens are too easily misled about their history by emotional allegiances to causes or an unthinking and unequivocal support of the government's or the opposition's distortions of historical facts. As a good historian, he offered his readers a caveat concerning the manner in which history is interpreted. Any event or person despicable to the penetrating eye of history, he realized, may be cleverly disguised in the beautiful garments of patriotism, whether the time be 44 B.C. or 1756. This and the other major reviews are excellent illustrations of Johnson's willingness to engage with important historical questions, challenge existing conceptions, and offer alternative methods of historical inquiry. In short, these reviews were excellent vehicles for displaying Johnson's historical mind.

In addition to the writings discussed in the first chapter, we should not ignore the *Miscellaneous Observations on Macbeth* (1745), in which Johnson provides a short history of witchcraft in England, later repeated in the notes to the play in the 1765 Shakespeare edition. Remarking that the height of this "credulity" came during the Crusades, when the Christians "imputed all their defeats to enchantments or diabolical opposition," Johnson devotes several paragraphs to this background material, and in places is conscious of adding literary and dramatic flair to his account: "The Reformation did not immediately arrive at its meridian, and tho' day was gradually encreasing upon us, the goblins of witchcraft still continued to hover in the twilight" (*Shakespeare*, I, 5). We learn furthermore of James I's interest in the subject, his examination of an accused witch, his writings on witchcraft, and the laws directed against the practice: "Thus, in the time of Shakespeare, was the doctrine of witchcraft at once established by law and by the fashion . . ." (p. 6). As commentator and editor Johnson would be expected to inform his readers of relevant matter pertaining to the play, but one can argue whether he needed to write as much as he did on witchcraft for a better understanding of *Macbeth's* first scene. Johnson's sense of history, then, expanded what might have been a few sentences of remarks to an interesting historical account. He delighted in these specifics of history as well as in the larger events and questions; as a historian he took pleasure in marking the streaks of the tulip.

When he came to edit Shakespeare in the period 1756 to 1765, Johnson had accumulated a substantial historical knowledge, and not just from a reading of Shakespeare's major sources, Holinshed, Vergil, and Hall. And in some of the notes to the plays we find him flexing his historical muscles by going slightly beyond what one would expect from a good editor of Shakespeare. For instance, in his discussion of heirs in *3 Henry VI* (IV.i, 51–64), Johnson adds, "It must be remembered, that till the Restoration the heiresses of great estates were in the wardship of the king, who in their minority gave them up to plunder, and afterwards matched them to his favourites. I know not when liberty gained more than by the abolition of the Court of Wards" (*Shakespeare*, II, 606). Similarly, regarding Henry IV's promise to amend his errors by committing to a crusade, Johnson considers the "lawfulness and justice" of the holy wars. He believes there may exist a principle on which to settle the debate over the propriety of the Crusades: since the "Mahometans" considered the destruction of all other religions a holy objective, then "it is, by law of self-defence, lawful for men of every other religion, and for Christians among others, to make war upon Mahometans, simply as Mahometans . . ." (I, 455). Although one might differ with Johnson's conclusions, we cannot fail to notice that he enjoys commenting on historical questions, even those five hundred years old.

More significantly, however, Johnson's historical sense made him a better editor of Shakespeare, as it did a better lexicographer. Reading the preface to the edition and the notes, one is confident the editor has a strong command not only of Elizabethan literature but also of the philosophies, events, and personalities that helped to shape Shakespeare's art. As literary historian Johnson establishes with ease and with a sense of importance the literary and historical context in which Shakespeare wrote as one way to diffuse the explosive strictures coming from the likes of Thomas Rymer, John Dennis, and Voltaire: "Shakespeare engaged in dramatick poetry with the world open before him; the rules of the ancients were yet known to few; the publick judgment was unformed; he had no example of such fame as might force him upon imitation, nor criticks of such authority as might restrain his extravagance" (preface, *Shakespeare*, I, 69). And yet Johnson is always able to transcend when appropriate the historical context: Shakespeare "sacrifices virtue to convenience, and is so much more careful to please than to instruct, that he seems to write without any moral purpose. . . . This fault the barbarity of his age cannot extenuate; for it is always a writer's duty to make the world better, and justice is a virtue independant on time and place" (p. 71). As literary critic and moralist, Johnson saw an *unqualified* historical method of criticism at times detrimental to an accurate assessment of a writer's worth. Johnson was not so blinded by his historical vision that his evaluations of earlier authors could not transcend the rigid confines of the times in which they lived.

And yet arguing that fully to understand and appreciate Shakespeare one must be aware of the social and political forces at work in Elizabethan times, Johnson occasionally finds some of the historical questions difficult to answer: "Whether he represented the real conversation of his time is not easy to determine; the reign of Elizabeth is commonly supposed to have been a time of stateliness, formality, and reserve, yet perhaps the relaxations of that severity were not very elegant. There must, however, have been always some modes of gayety preferable to others, and a writer ought to chuse the best" (p. 72). At one point Johnson seems to pause—apparently for effect—and states uncategorically: "Every man's performances, to be rightly estimated, must be compared with the state of the age in which he lived, and with his own particular opportunities" (p. 81). Given the qualification to this position mentioned above—that a writer may be judged by universal standards transcending time and place—Johnson endorses the historical method of criticism and the notion of literary history forwarded by his friend Thomas Warton's *Observations on the Fairy Queen of Spenser* (1754; 2nd edition, 1762), later reinforced in Warton's *History of English Poetry* (1774–1781), and by Richard Hurd in *Moral and Political Dialogues* (1759) and *Letters on Chivalry* (1762).

Curiosity, Johnson continues in the preface, "is always busy to discover the instruments, as well as to survey the workmanship." And to illustrate his point regarding the importance of grasping historical particulars of any author's age, Johnson draws forth another historical analogy: "The palaces of Peru or Mexico were certainly mean and incommodious habitations, if compared to the houses of European monarchs; yet who could forbear to view them with astonishment, who remembered that they were built without the use of iron?" (p. 81). History provided Johnson a knowledge of those instruments that shaped the poet's art—a knowledge he believed crucial enough to share with his readers. Johnson then punctuates his argument with a brief historical overview of learning and taste in the sixteenth century: "The English nation, in the time of Shakespeare, was yet struggling to emerge from barbarity. . . . The publick was gross and dark; and to be able to read and write, was an accomplishment still valued for its rarity" (pp. 81–82). Johnson considers Shakespeare's development and the influences on him in a clearly articulated historical context: "Those to whom our authour's labours were exhibited had more skill in pomps or processions than in poetical language" (p. 83). It should therefore come as no surprise that Johnson later praised Warton's *History of English Poetry*, for Warton's work approaches early English poetry from the very historical perspective Johnson advances in the edition of Shakespeare: Warton would place considerable emphasis on the "barbarity" of the times and the medieval and Renaissance interest in the trappings of custom and ceremony.[4] One cannot overstress the significance of Johnson's historical sense on his editing and criticism of Shakespeare.

These observations may be applied equally to the *Lives of the Poets*, in which Johnson's knowledge and interest in history influences both the literary criticism and the biographical writing. We have long agreed that, because of his command of seventeenth- and early eighteenth-century literature, his impressive recall of classical and Renaissance authors, and his facility with biographical compositions, few were as qualified as Johnson to write these critical and biographical prefaces to the works of the English poets. But we have not emphasized enough the importance of his historical sense to the molding and ultimate success of the *Lives.* By the late 1770s his knowledge of historical facts, movements, personalities, issues, and conflicts was substantial; he was therefore prepared to set correctly the major authors in their historical contexts and demonstrate how the literature reflected or was affected by the events of the mid to late seventeenth and early eighteenth centuries.

Johnson furthermore understood, from his readings and experience with the *Dictionary* and edition of Shakespeare, the progress of language and literature from the "barbarity" of former times to the refinement of his own century. He knew as well that literary expression, although reflective of its time, often led the way out of the relative darkness of the period's learning and taste. Johnson could characterize much of medieval and Renaissance life as unrefined and yet praise the talents and universality of Chaucer and Shakespeare. These authors, and others of lesser note, affected the culture of their and subsequent times, for the respect accorded to Chaucer or Shakespeare helped to influence the taste of monarchs and persons of political and social significance. In the gradual progress of civilization, frequently literature was a harbinger of advancement in general learning and taste. Accordingly, Johnson, as we have noted, would not allow any author immunity from criticism, regardless of the rudeness of his age, because he believed it the responsibility of a Shakespeare to pull free on occasion from the historical forces at work and, through his art, help refine intellectually and morally his and immediate generations.

Considering further Johnson's designs in the *Lives of the Poets,* Jean Hagstrum has spoken for many by arguing that Johnson was "undeniably opposed to many . . . points of view associated with historical investigation" of literature and that he was "extremely chary of expressing in his own works any philosophy of literary history."[5] Far more willing to accept Johnson in some ways as a literary historian, Leopold Damrosch, Jr., writes that Johnson's "real interest in literary history was not in the evolution of form and technique but in the creative leaps of genius."[6] It is not the intent of this study to claim for Johnson a theory of literary history and then consider its significance in detail, for the issue is a complex one, worthy of a book-length study. But in addition to the commentary on the edition of Shakespeare above, one should pay heed to the judicious study of a recent critic, Maximillian Novak, who has properly emphasized Johnson's knowledge of history as it may apply to a work as important as the "Life of Dryden."[7] Although, as Novak reminds us, Johnson commented in the "Life," "To adjust the minute events of literary history is tedious and troublesome; it requires indeed no great force of understanding . . . ," he also wrote, "To judge rightly of an author, we must transport ourselves to his time, and examine what were the wants of his contemporaries, and what were his means of supplying them" (*Poets*, I, 368, 411). In an attempt to reconcile both passages, Novak comments, "Johnson, of course, acknowledged [in the former remark] that he did not always have the materials available that would have made" possible a "scientific" approach to literary history. In addition, Johnson's observation is directly related to his misunderstood estimation of historical facts, which will be discussed in chapter six; Johnson does not disdain the "minute events" or the very conception of literary history but rather objects to delving too minutely into factual matter at the expense of failing to analyze carefully the important literary activity of an earlier period. For all his praise of Warton's *History of English Poetry,* Johnson would have found most "tedious and troublesome" Warton's method of scouring the literary landscape for anything that explains, illuminates, or relates to the poetry of the Middle Ages or Renaissance. "Transporting" ourselves to an author's time was one thing to Johnson; burrowing about in literary minutiae, as Warton did, was quite another. We must keep in mind that when Johnson wrote about the "tedious and troublesome" nature of adjusting "the minute events of literary history" he had the first two volumes of Warton's *History of English Poetry* before him, serving as an ample illustration of what "literary history" demanded of the author.[8]

That we cannot divorce a *modern* conception of literary history from the *Lives of the Poets* should be apparent, and Novak's conclusions about the "Life of Dryden" deserve careful attention: "Johnson writes well on Dryden because his literary history is infused with an understanding that there can be no history of poetry or the drama that is separated from ordinary existence." In the "Life of Dryden," Johnson's "real task was literary history, and his reading of Dryden against the Restoration milieu produced what may be the most masterful of his poets' 'lives.' "[9]

As the *Lives of the Poets* moreover illustrates, biography and history should be linked in a harmonious marriage, with one partner assisting and flattering the other. But biographers, particularly in short accounts, make their own decision as to how much historical fact to include. When they choose to incorporate details, historical digressions, or historical analysis that, if removed, would not deter significantly from an understanding of the subject's life, then biographers become historians interested in revealing information and commenting on events and persons not always related directly to an understanding of one individual's life. Robert Folkenflik has considered Johnson's perception of biography as different from historical writing,[10] but for the purposes of this study we should investigate more fully those sections of his early biographies and the *Lives of the Poets* in which he allows the historian to supplement and at times dominate the biographer.[11]

We know that in general Johnson did no major historical research for his biographies, although his readings in history—from his younger days through the Harleian experience—certainly kept him well informed of the events and personalities dominating the period in which the subject of his biography lived. And one would do Johnson a gross disservice to suggest that he merely copied from one or two biographical sources without opening up other historical volumes to supplement the primary works he used or what was already etched on his mind. There is little doubt that he took pleasure in commenting on historical as well as biographical matters, and, as a good historian should be, he was adept at ordering events in narrative form for their most significant impact. Effective historical narration, we must remember, was not a universal characteristic of historians in Johnson's day. He moreover analyzed for the benefit of the readers the historical details he chose to include in his account. Even though several of the lives (Burman, Morin, Sydenham, and Boerhaave) are for the most part devoid of historical matter because the subject was not involved with memorable events or famous persons, a good many of the early lives strongly evinced Johnson's historical interests.

In the middle of the *Life of Sarpi* (1738), Johnson points to the pivotal period of his subject's life as beginning around 1605, when a frustrated Pope Paul V, angered over political opposition from the Venetian Senate, imposed an interdict on the entire state. At this point Johnson the biographer might have condensed the event and its aftermath while stressing its seriousness, and then commented on Sarpi's reaction to the pope's order. But he senses the high drama and historical importance of the occasion and devotes several paragraphs to an analysis of the conflict involving the pope, the Jesuits, and the state. Sarpi assumes a secondary

role in the biography as Johnson outlines the arguments for papal infalli-
bility, which he labels "maxims equally shocking, weak, pernicious, and
absurd; which did not require the abilities or learning of father Paul, to
demonstrate their falsehood, and destructive tendency" (*Works,* XIV,
151). Johnson furthermore informs us that the pope settled matters by
signing a treaty with Henry IV of France and that the "defenders of
Venetian rights" suffered for their principles. Father Sarpi then re-
emerges as the primary subject of the piece. Clearly, one better understands through the narrative the period in which Sarpi lived, but again
Johnson was not directed by any rule of biographical writing regarding
the amount of historical background to include, and it is no mere coinci-
dence that the strongest section of the *Life of Sarpi* is the one in which
Johnson assumes the role of historian.[12]

The lives of Robert Blake and Francis Drake—undeniably more history than biography—appearing in the *Gentleman's Magazine* for 1740
exploited the feelings of patriotism and martial ardor made manifest by
England's war with Spain. Even so, we detect no artificial imposition of
historical detail in these lives, and Johnson's growing knowledge and
enthusiasm for history made him an excellent choice to provide these
biographical/historical accounts. Drawing primarily from an anony-
mous biography and observations of Clarendon and Whitlock,[13] Johnson
begins the *Life of Blake* by mentioning quickly the events of the admiral's
life up to the outbreak of civil war in 1642. Now Johnson unfurls the
historical panorama of the mid seventeenth century: the committed soldier and sailor, the execution of the king, the excitement of the battle,
and tension of the siege. He devotes most of the biography to Blake's
adventures at sea, especially his pursuit of Prince Rupert, which took
him on an odyssey from the coast of Ireland into the Mediterranean, and
to the English and Dutch War of the early 1650s, in which Blake played
so large a part. Regarding this war, Johnson comments on a conflict "in
which nothing less was contested than the dominance of the sea, and
which was carried on with vigour, animosity, and resolution, proportioned to the importance of the dispute." He writes of the naval power of
Holland, whose strength grew during the "inactive" reign of James I and
the internal "commotions" that preoccupied England after his death.
The historian in Johnson emerges even more conspicuously in passages
such as the following:

> [The Dutch] had arrived to that height of naval power, and that
> affluence of wealth, that, with the arrogance which a long-continued

prosperity naturally produces, they began to invent new claims, and to treat other nations with insolence, which nothing can defend, but superiority of force. They had for some time made uncommon preparations, at a vast expense, and had equipped a large fleet, without any apparent danger threatening them, or any avowed design of attacking their neighbours. This unusual armament was not beheld by the English without some jealousy, and care was taken to fit out such a fleet as might secure the trade from interruption, and the coast from insults. (*Works*, XIV, 190)

Blake's heroism is certainly not ignored: "Blake, for some time, stood alone against their whole force" (p. 191); however, Johnson often blends it into the historical portrait, with the result that the reader is more interested in the outcome of the naval engagements than in the courage and resolve of Robert Blake. At times, Blake seems to disappear from the account altogether. For instance, Johnson mentions the admiral's confrontation with the Dutch fleet in July and September of 1652 (Johnson says only "he," not "Blake") and then shifts the focus to the ships themselves and the battle that ensued. For the remainder of the paragraph and the two that follow, Blake becomes no more than a blur in the historical account, as Johnson treats the particulars of the engagement, the number of ships lost, the vexation of the Dutch admirals, and the maturity of the English that allowed them to make the most of their victory. Again the historian speaks: "Such is the general revolution of affairs in every state; danger and distress produce unanimity and bravery, virtues which are seldom unattended with success; but success is the parent of pride, and pride of jealousy and faction; faction makes way for calamity, and happy is that nation whose calamities renew their unanimity. Such is the rotation of interests, that equally tend to hinder the total destruction of a people, and to obstruct an exorbitant increase of power" (pp. 193–194). Johnson's observation and application of historical events to contemporary life befit the articulate and eloquent mind of the best kind of historian.

Blake, as we would expect, resumes his rightful place in the narrative, but for many sections he is not the subject of the piece. Johnson's depiction of the historical events is simply too successful to make the *Life of Blake* a good study of the man. Even when he analyzes Blake's refusal to retire in the face of innumerable odds, Johnson approaches the matter as a historian as well as a biographer: "To mention the impetuosity of his own courage, is to make the blame of his temerity equal to the praise of

97

his valour; which seems, indeed, to be the most gentle censure that the truth of history will allow" (p. 196). Apparently inspired by the sound of exploding guns, Johnson properly emphasizes the historical drama in the action he describes. Although the final passages are devoted entirely to the admiral's character, the *Life of Blake* smells too much of cannon smoke and burning ships to deny Johnson the role of historian.

Francis Drake offered Johnson another opportunity to display his historical talents. In many respects the pattern and nature of the observations in the *Life of Blake* apply equally to the biography of Elizabeth's great admiral. For example, early in the life, Johnson mentions Drake's voyage to the West Indies and comments on "the mercantile or adventurous part of mankind" during the sixteenth century:

> Fresh discoveries were frequently made, new countries and nations never heard of before, were daily described, and it may easily be concluded, that the relaters did not diminish the merit of their attempts, by suppressing or diminishing any circumstance that might produce wonder, or excite curiosity. Nor was their vanity only engaged in raising admirers, but their interest, likewise, in procuring adventurers, who were, indeed, easily gained by the hopes which naturally arise from new prospects, though, through ignorance of the American seas, and by the malice of the Spaniards, who, from the first discovery of those countries, considered every other nation that attempted to follow them, as invaders of their rights, the best concerted designs often miscarried. (*Works*, XIV, 209)

Later in the biography, Johnson subordinates Drake to an examination of the march of the Symoren Indians across Panama, a section that might have easily been condensed with no loss to the biographical account (pp. 226–231).[14] In two other places he becomes the social historian and anthropologist as he discusses Indian customs, dress, and bodily appearance. Unable to suppress his interest in these aspects of the past, Johnson writes in the first instance of Indian body paint: "Such was the practice of the first inhabitants of our own country. From this custom did our earliest enemies, the Picts, owe their denomination. As it is not probable that caprice or fancy should be uniform, there must be, doubtless, some reason for a practice so general, and prevailing in distant parts of the world, which have no communication with each other" (p. 257). He then offers some practical explanations for Indian body painting. Surely, these paragraphs allow us to see through Drake's eyes as he explored the alien culture, but one could not fault the biographer for leaving them out or shortening them considerably. Johnson, however, believed his readers would broaden their perspectives with such glimpses at the history of mankind.

Johnson enjoyed not only mentioning or illuminating historical events but also offering causes and motives for them. And in doing so he provided more than dry particulars; rather he took an interest in presenting short, though readable and entertaining, analyses of early colonization. Although Drake is more prominently and consistently displayed as the center piece of the life than was Blake, readers cannot help drawing as much wisdom and pleasure from Johnson's historical account of Drake's adventures on sea and land as they can from an understanding of the admiral's character and heroism. And many biographers, although seeing the importance of historical knowledge to an understanding of their subject, might not allow themselves the kinds of historical digressions in which Johnson delighted.

In the biography of Francis Cheynel, published in *The Student* for 1751, Johnson depicts some of the turbulence characteristic of the mid seventeenth century. Throughout this short life, he maintains a proper balance between the subject and his times but assumes the historian's stance when he writes of Cheynel's visit to Oxford in 1646 to reform the pulpits.[15] As noted in chapter two, we learn that the delegation from Parliament, of which Cheynel was a member, "offended" the Oxford establishment with their empty, noisy, and unusual discourses and their radical demeanor and neglect of the Lord's Prayer. One draws from Johnson's account much of the tension that gripped the secular and spiritual levels of society during the period. Although Cheynel is conspicuous in this section of the life, his part does not dominate the piece; he becomes rather the major player in the historical drama unfolding at the time. Johnson provides as well some insight into the zealous philosophy and activity of the "Independents," mentioning, for example, the influence of William Earbury, a charismatic preacher who at times led a group of his spirited followers and disputed "with great vehemence" against the Presbyterians. The religious debate between the groups clearly paints in the needed background for Cheynel's role in the controversy, but it moreover stresses the kind of "confusion" reflective of the age. Again, this is no mere accident or by-product of biography, for Johnson considered the religious controversies far more interesting than the personality of Cheynel.

Johnson's *Life of Roger Ascham* (1763), his last biographical work before the *Lives of the Poets*, exhibits in addition to the comments on Elizabeth identified in chapter two the author's attraction toward the Renaissance period and fascination with intellectual history or the history of ideas. We have already witnessed in the lives of Sarpi and Drake, the review of Tytler's *Enquiry,* the edition of Shakespeare, his poetry, and allusions in the periodical papers Johnson's enthusiasm for the era that produced a profound change in England's role in world affairs and her position among the intellectual community of Europe. Although he could characterize the taste of the time in unflattering terms, he perceived sixteenth-century events and personalities as breathing the spirit of dignity and grace into an already courageous and proud nation. To Johnson the Renaissance years saw England move from a wild, vibrant, though at times awkward and confused, adolescence to a more sophisticated and powerful, though hardly an ideal and polished, young adulthood. He knew, however, that as it grew more refined and intelligent as a nation, drawing on its long experience to influence its destiny, England might still look back to those years as one of the most exciting times of its life.

Early in the biography, Johnson writes of Ascham's entering Cambridge University "at a time when the last great revolution of the intellectual world was filling every academical mind with ardour or anxiety" (*Works,* XV, 92). He next mentions the sweeping changes overtaking the land: "Learning was, at that time, prosecuted with that eagerness and perseverance, which, in this age of indifference and dissipation, it is not easy to conceive. To teach or to learn, was, at once, the business and the pleasure of the academical life; and an emulation of study was raised by Cheke and Smith, to which even the present age, perhaps, owes many advantages, without remembering, or knowing, its benefactors" (p. 93). Ascham on occasion fades in and out as the major focus of the work as Johnson discusses or alludes to further evidence of Renaissance learning, university studies and politics, and patronage. In addition he establishes the period as one of high tension and drama as Mary assumes the throne after the death of her brother Edward in 1553 and attempts to pull her country back into the mainstream of Roman Catholicism: "morality was never suffered, in the days of persecution, to protect heresy" (p. 107).

Mention of Ascham's *Toxophilus,* his work on the art of shooting, prompts from Johnson a digression of several paragraphs on the transition from longbow to firearms: "in the long peace of king James, the bow was wholly forgotten. Guns have from that time been the weapons of the English, as of other nations, and, as they are now improved, are certainly more efficacious" (pp. 100–101). Reference to Ascham's pension from Henry VIII merits commentary on the value of money in early sixteenth-century England—all of which is relevant to Ascham's life but suggestive nevertheless of Johnson's interest in nearly all aspects of history, from military to monetary. He enjoyed illuminating the subtler topics of the historical periods he treated; never do we sense that he was performing the perfunctory function of filling in background.

That Ascham received a pension serves almost as a pretext for a more general observation: "Men are rich and poor, not only in proportion to what they have, but to what they want. In some ages, not only necessaries are cheaper, but fewer things are necessary. In the age of Ascham, most of the elegancies and expenses of our present fashions were unknown: commerce had not yet distributed superfluity through the lower classes of the people, and the character of a student implied frugality, and required no splendour to support it" (p. 102). The *Life of Ascham,* then, gives the reader a sense of the intellectual and social climate of the mid sixteenth century. One comes away from the life wishing Johnson had written more, not on Ascham himself, but on the society and times in which he lived.

Johnson's association with the *Literary Magazine* in 1756 resulted in several pieces relating to the current Seven Years' War (see chapter five), one of which was a life of Frederick the Great (1712 to 1786), then the king of Prussia and leading member of the European political and military order. But Johnson's account is primarily concerned with Frederick's role in the War of the Austrian Succession in the 1740s (he does not bring his biography up to 1756). Other than a few general remarks on the habits and motives of kings, he provides some of the flavor of Prussian life in the early eighteenth century by treating the reign and military passion of Frederick's father and the young king's early years on the throne. But soon Johnson raises the curtain on the few years that dominate the life: "On the 9th of October, 1740, half Europe was thrown into confusion by the death of Charles the sixth, emperour of Germany" (*Works,* XV, 13). The reader learns of the "pragmatic sanction," the dissension it caused, and the many claimants who emerged to fill the political vacuum opened by the emperor's death. The complexity of the period prompts Johnson to write that "the narrow plan of this essay will not suffer" him to relate as many aspects of the times as he might wish: "Let them be told by some other writer of more leisure and wider intelligence" (p. 14).

Modesty aside, Johnson plunges into the historical account, keeping in mind the necessity of accurate yet lively narration: "Upon the emperour's death, many of the German princes fell upon the Austrian territories, as upon as dead carcass, to be dismembered among them without resistance" (p. 14). Johnson, we shall discover in another chapter, placed much importance on the historian's style, and with the vivid metaphor chosen above, he is able to depict the disintegration of order at Charles's death far more intelligibly than a more ponderous account. Frederick's declaration that he had an "ancient" claim to Silesia prompts further historical analysis: "Such a declaration was, I believe, in the opinion of all Europe, nothing less than the aggravation of hostility by insult, and was received by the Austrians with suitable indignation" (p. 15). The reader follows Frederick as he advances on coveted territory, guided by Johnson's competent and at times exciting narration. As in the *Life of Blake*, he does not permit his subject to dominate the piece. Owing to Johnson's choice and arrangement of materials, the great Prussian shares the stage with the historical event itself and in some places with Maria Theresa of Hungary and Charles of Bavaria.

Johnson notes that one "of the most remarkable events of the Silesia war, was the conquest of great Glogau, which was taken by an assault in the dark, headed by Prince Leopold of Anhalt Dessau" (p. 18). He then adds details, clearly unnecessary to a purely biographical account, about combat after nightfall. In other places he examines the plan and goal of battles and the political complexities that dictated events. Maria Theresa and the Austrian court and military establishment also command his attention. Cognizant of his frequent historical emphasis, he attempts at one point to check himself: "To settle property, to suppress false claims, and to regulate the administration of civil and criminal justice, are attempts so difficult and so useful, that I shall willingly suspend or contract the history of battles and sieges, to give a larger account of this pacifick enterprise" (p. 19). But like a connoisseur of fine foods who will admit to anyone nearby that he needs to watch his weight and then several minutes later will succumb once more to the delicious smells emanating from the table, we find Johnson shortly afterward giving in to his insatiable appetite for interesting history: "We now return to the war" (p. 26).

The confrontation at Czaslau between the Austrians and the Prussians sparks the following description:

> On the 6th of May, about seven in the morning, the Austrians began the attack: their impetuosity was matched by the firmness of the Prussians. The animosity of the two armies was much inflamed: the Austrians were fighting for their country, and the Prussians were in a place, where defeat must inevitably end in death or captivity. The

fury of the battle continued four hours: the Prussian horse were, at length, broken, and the way to the camp, where the wild troops, who had fought with so much vigour and constancy, at the sight of plunder forgot their obedience, nor had any man the least thought but how to load himself with the richest spoils.

While the right wing of the Austrians was thus employed, the main body was left naked: the Prussians recovered from their confusion, and regained the day. . . . (p. 30)

Johnson's interest in the military side of history is clearly evident here, as it is throughout the life, and he includes in this succinct account a touch of drama along with a panoramic sweep to the narrative, which here and elsewhere looks upon all of Europe—the monarchs of major powers, their generals, and their clashing troops.

Sprinkled among the narration are several general remarks of a historical nature: "To enlarge dominions has been the boast of many princes; to diffuse happiness and security through wide regions has been granted to few" and "Princes have this remaining of humanity, that they think themselves obliged not to make war without a reason. Their reasons are, indeed, not always very satisfactory" (pp. 19, 38). (Johnson illustrates the latter with the examples of Louis XIV, Peter the Great, and Charles XII of Sweden.) Wherever one turns in this work one finds Johnson charting enthusiastically the historical terrain in which Frederick passed his most exciting years. Although Johnson does well in informing his reader of and breathing new life into his subject's background, social programs, personal weaknesses, and military heroism, the *Life of Frederick of Prussia* is, as Donald Greene has written, more an "exercise in historiography than in biography."[16] Johnson must have taken much pleasure in composing this work because it allowed him to indulge his love of history and to explain for his readers in easily comprehensible form the shifts of fortune and power in Europe during the 1740s, which in turn helped put the present hostilities—the Seven Years' War—in better focus.

In his last great work, the *Lives of the Poets,* Johnson puts to use the historical skills developed over the past forty years and is excellent in providing a revealing glimpse of the social and political milieus of the mid to late seventeenth and early eighteenth centuries, especially in the lives of Cowley, Denham, Milton, Rochester, Roscommon, Sprat, Halifax, Addison, Prior, Swift, and, as Maximillian Novak argued, Dryden. Whereas we expect the commentator in such a large undertaking to provide relevant background material, Johnson on occasion offers historical information or analysis beyond what is required of a good literary critic or biographer. For example, a number of his observations on the individual English monarchs and the English Civil War come, as discussed in chapter two, from the *Lives of the Poets*. In the "Life of Milton" he could have merely mentioned the poet's sympathy and work for Cromwell's government and then gone on to comment on the prose writings, but Johnson's knowledge of and interest in history encouraged a more detailed assessment of the protector's legal claim to authority: "Cromwell had now dismissed the parliament by the authority of which he had destroyed monarchy, and commenced monarch himself under the title of protector, but with kingly and more than kingly power. That his authority was lawful, never was pretended; he himself founded his right only in necessity" (*Poets*, I, 115–116).

A careful reading of the *Lives* discovers Johnson's use of historical, rather than biographical, transitional devices such as "Oliver was now dead; Richard was constrained to resign" and "The state of both England and Ireland was at this time such, that he who was absent from either country had very little temptation to return." The lives of Waller, Prior, and Swift may be the most historical, for in each Johnson offers commentary that frequently reaches beyond the bounds of the purely biographical to embrace the historical events and personalities of each man's period. In his remarks on Waller (Clarendon being the major source of the life) Johnson devotes considerable attention to the poet's parliamentary career and the so-called Waller's plot concerning the reluctance of some to continue the war against Royalist forces. Johnson is also excellent in supplying the reader with a sense of the tension and high drama of the time, and although Waller is the central player Johnson has him share the stage with the parliamentary debates and intrigues that typified the era of Pym, Hampden, and Cromwell. Johnson used the occasion of Waller's *Panegyrick* on Cromwell to assess the lord protector and the methods he employed to gain power: Waller's "choice of encomiastick topicks is very judicious, for he considers Cromwell in his exaltation, without enquiring how he attained it. . . . The act of violence by which he obtained the supreme power is lightly treated, and decently justified." Comfortable in his slight digression from Waller and his work, Johnson mentions what he had read in Bulstrode Whitlock's *Memorials of the English Affairs*, that Cromwell "was very desirous . . . of adding the title to the power of monarchy, and is supposed to have been with-held from it, partly by fear of the army and partly by fear of the laws, which, when he should govern by the name of King, would have restrained his authority." Adding a vivid scene to this recollection, Johnson writes of those who came forth with an invitation to accept the crown: after much thought, Cromwell refused it, "but is said to have fainted in his coach when he parted from them" (I, 269–270). Perhaps Johnson could have trimmed a few of these remarks without lessening the reader's knowledge of Waller and his verse, but the biography is far more memorable for Johnson's having allowed his historical interests to guide him in the inclusion of these details and observations: the reader can more easily recall these indelible historical moments and then connect them with the literary work or character of a writer such as Waller.

The "Life of Prior" is set amid the political and military climate of the early eighteenth century, and the following comment sets the tone for most of the biographical account: "A great part of Queen Anne's reign was a time of war, in which there was little employment for negotiators" (*Poets*, II, 186). The first major historical event of Johnson's life, the War of the Spanish Succession, no doubt intrigued him, but as "Prior" demonstrates he took a hard look at the event and reflected accurately on its effect on the populace: "The nation in time grew weary of the war, and the queen grew weary of her ministers. The war was burdensome, and the ministers were insolent. Harley and his friends began to hope that they might, by driving the Whigs from court and from power, gratify at once the queen and the people" (II, 187). Instead of writing something similar to "During the war of Queen Anne's time, Prior was engaged in efforts to resolve the conflict through what would be called the Treaty of Utrecht," Johnson chose a more historically worded comment because he was fond of assuming the role of historian, even if only for two sentences or a paragraph. The politics of Anne's reign and the maneuvering leading up to the Treaty of Utrecht, Johnson believed, were worthy of attention and commentary, even in a critical and biographical preface. Because they were at least related to Prior's life, Johnson felt justified writing these brief historical digressions, but at one point, probably realizing that his remarks might indeed be seen as digressive, he admonishes himself as follows: "My business is not the history of the peace, but the life of Prior" (II, 189). Regardless of this attempt to rein in his enthusiasm for history, Johnson provides further historical details, certainly helpful though not crucial to an understanding of Prior, throughout the remainder of the life.

The "Life of Swift" afforded Johnson yet another opportunity for historical commentary, especially considering Swift's relationships with the powerful Tories in Anne's regime. In addition to these relationships and their literary by-products, the reader is privy to Johnson's assessment of Anne and the "October Club": "They thought, with great reason, that the ministers were losing opportunities; that sufficient use was not made of the ardour of the nation; they called loudly for more changes and stronger efforts, and demanded the punishment of part, and the dismission of the rest, of those whom they considered as publick robbers" (III, 17). Johnson moreover devotes an entire paragraph to Robert Harley and Anne, which again is primarily influenced by his interest in early eighteenth-century history more than by his desire to shed light on Swift and his writings. And when efforts like those of Swift began to move the populace toward accepting an end to the War of the Spanish Succession, Johnson writes, the "people, who had been amused with bonfires and triumphal processions, and looked with idolatry on the General [Marlborough] and his friends who, as they thought, had made England the arbitress of nations, were confounded between shame and rage when they found that 'mines had been exhausted and millions destroyed,' to secure the Dutch or aggrandize the emperor, without any advantage to ourselves; that we had been bribing our neighbours to fight their own quarrel, and that amongst our enemies we might number allies" (III, 18). Here, as elsewhere in the *Lives,* Johnson adds in a sentence or clause an observation merely for the historical record: "the death of the Queen broke down at once the whole system of Tory politicks" (p. 26). One senses in these and other like comments and emphases in the *Lives* Johnson's irrepressible desire to write in the historic vein. There is more historical flavor in the above remark, after all, than there would be in writing "after the death of Anne, which put an end to Tory influence, Swift was left with no choice but to return to Ireland," because the former is allowed to stand as a historical statement without being subordinated to a main clause concerned with Swift. As many have argued, in the last of his great literary achievements, the *Lives of the Poets,* one finds the essence of Johnson's critical beliefs. But more than this, the *Lives* displays Johnson's strong historical sense at work, shaping, embellishing, and complementing the impressive biographical and critical observations.

Johnson's biographical writings are infused with his knowledge of and enthusiasm for history. Although he was like all good biographers, who appreciate the importance of comprehending the events, personalities, and social milieu of their subject's age and include those details that significantly relate to their subject's life, Johnson often went beyond the biographical/historical realm into the province of history alone. He took pleasure in commenting on historical matters only in part because he believed the reader would thereby gain a better perspective through which to view one man's life; moreover, he wished to indulge his historical fancy, to apply his command and analysis of the facts to topics of much interest and importance to him. Several modern biographers have similarly engaged in considerable historical examination, often leaving their biographical subject pages behind, but here too the author is in fact a historian as well as and in places even more than a biographer. One cannot relegate the history in Johnson's biographies to being merely the natural result of writing lives of persons who lived during memorable times.

An examination of Johnson's historical sense cannot ignore the Vinerian law lectures of Robert Chambers, more specifically those sections that show evidence of Johnson's hand or influence. Until recently, Johnsonians have assumed with some confidence that the passages identified by E. L. McAdam, Jr., in *Dr. Johnson and the English Law* (1951) were indeed composed by Johnson. But Thomas Curley has now warned us not to accept without qualification and reservation the sections McAdam claimed as Johnson's alone.[17] Regardless of whether he wrote all or parts of these passages, Curley argues, we can safely assume Johnson at least supervised, possibly inspired, but certainly collaborated with Chambers on the law lectures that contain some of the most memorable and eloquent historical commentary. We find treated in their historical contexts such topics as the law,[18] government, customs, warfare, religion, feudal tenures, monarchal power, Parliament, antiquities, currency, elections, feudal organization, church government, exploration, migration, and learning. Although the scope is large in the passages McAdam attributed to Johnson, the author handles each topic with Johnson's characteristic facility, making these aspects of medieval and early English life comprehensible to those unfamiliar with these periods.

The author writes, for example, of the inability of law and learning to stem the power of the sword: "But by what laws soever the Britons were governed before the arrival of those German tribes whom we generally call by the name of Saxons, the subsequent expulsion of the Britons themselves by those northern invaders must undoubtedly have been attended with the expulsion of their laws. Hardly any conquest was ever followed by such fatal consequences to the conquered, or any change so total ever produced as those which were effected by that ferocious people."[19] These lectures, if we can assume he authored or coauthored at least some parts of them, were an excellent showcase for Johnson's historical talents, and he must have relished the chance to play the role of historian without having to focus on his literary or biographical topic. The following is only part of the excellent commentary on migration McAdam has attributed to Johnson:

> When such bodies of men transplanted themselves from Sarmatia or Scythia into Germany and Scandinavia, they must, to make room for themselves, have driven out the former inhabitants of those countries, who would of necessity therefore endeavour to obtain new territories by the expulsion of their more polite and more effeminate neighbors, or at least by conquering them and intermixing with them. And this perhaps was the cause of that extraordinary change which happened in the state of Europe in the fifth, sixth, and seventh centuries, when many various flights of northern barbarians invaded those countries which had been first conquered, then civilized, and at last deserted by the Romans. . . . When men were once persuaded that to slaughter was the highest honor, and that to be slaughtered at last the highest happiness, we need no longer inquire why they engaged themselves in unnecessary wars. (McAdam, pp. 86–87)

The author seems especially interested in the relationship of war and the evolution of learning; he sees the military conflicts as having had an ebbing and flowing effect, for when they receded they left a residue of progress and law. Societies did not for the most part emerge in all their radiant splendor; rather they inched along, suffering various setbacks and only occasionally sprinting far ahead. With his audience in mind, many of whom lacked a knowledge or feel for medieval history, the author explains the past in easily comprehensible prose: "The king was maintained in times of peace, not by taxes or imposts, but by the profits of his own lands, which in reigns of luxury and negligence were diminished by wanton grants, or profuse alienations, and in times of contest or tyranny, were increased by seizures and forfeitures. As he subsisted upon his own revenues, he had very little dependence upon his people. But in a time of war, whether incited by ambition or enforced by necessity, he was compelled to summon his feudatory lords, whose greatness was such that when they combined against him he had scarcely power to compel their attendance" (p. 90). He takes the reader into the shadows of England's fascinating past, leading and illuminating the way with his effective historical narration and analysis. To this historical analyst it is important his readers learn that "Nations as well as individuals have their childhood," and like a modern psychologist he realizes a true understanding of adults can never be achieved without an investigation into their youth, into the many experiences that molded them as they moved to maturity. The commentator forces his readers to look carefully at England's childhood, marked by "prejudice and ignorance," as a way to understand not only their country's history but themselves as well.

The author takes the opportunity throughout these sections of the lectures to dispel popular though erroneous notions about government and law and to challenge the assumptions of those who have little knowledge of life in the past: "We now live at a time when by diffusion of civility and circulation of intelligence the manners of the whole nation are uniform, when by determinations of acknowledged authority the limits of all jurisdictions are fixed; when a long course of records and precedents has furnished models for almost every civil transaction, and experience has supplied what reason wanted in the art of government. To us, therefore, it is natural to think that former ages glided on with the same regular and uniform tranquility. But when we search into early times this idea must be carefully driven from our minds" (pp. 97–98). Whether or not Johnson himself composed the above passages, he would have agreed that this searching "into early times" could be a taxing and humbling experience, often leaving a bitter taste in the mouths of many readers disinclined to disturb the security of their misinformed views. Yet he realized that those without a feel for history should make the effort because all individuals have the obligation to know the truth about their nation's past and the evolution of institutions, laws, and customs.

The judiciousness of the author's remarks may best be illustrated by his observations on Alfred the Great, a monarch whose reputation was enhanced by a romanticized view of the past. Should the following indeed be by Johnson, we discover how easily he put aside a boyish fascination with history's great leaders and commented as a disinterested historian should.

Of the laws which have given so much renown to the name of Alfred, it will naturally be expected that something should be said. So far as we can judge of his Code by the fragments which time has left us, it seems to be the effort of benevolent power endeavoring to rescue a people yet unformed from the insecurity and unhappiness of savage license. He seems to have it more in his thought to avert evil than to procure good. His institutions are such as the sense of present inconvenience would naturally dictate; but the nation had not then experience or knowledge sufficient to open prospects into remote futurity, to fix the exact bounds of civil rights, or regulate with nice adjustment the distributions of property and evolutions of succession. (pp. 88–89)

We also find in the lecture passages attributed to Johnson a sense of historical humility, which checks one's confidence in discerning the truth merely from a reading of histories. Implied throughout these sections is the belief that a considerable amount of knowledge about England's past has escaped the scrutiny of historical writing and that historians have not always done an adequate job treating the subjects they have examined in detail. The author writes at one point, "To deduce the history of the courts of justice and fix the time of their institution is very difficult, for most things at their beginning are small and what is small is necessarily obscure" (p. 118). But the search must be made regardless of the difficulty, or else one wrongly assumes that government and legal systems emerged like a comet from the sky, intact and developed in their present states. He therefore warns the reader of (or listener to) the lectures: "The methods of government and processes of jurisdiction have not been devised at once, or described and established by any positive law, but have grown up by slow and imperceptible degrees, as experience improved and necessity enforced them; and what is known of them in early times has been gathered not from any distinct and positive narrations of history but deduced by inference and conjecture from rolls and registers, from obscure hints and incidental circumstances" (pp. 118–119), a point reflecting the view of no less a historian than David Hume.

In regard to the shortcomings of historical writers, the commentator asks younger scholars to be suspicious of those "modern historians" who mislead their readers when they "search for profound policy and subtle refinements in temporary expedients, capricious propositions, and stipulations offered with violence and admitted by compulsion and therefore broken and disregarded when that violence ceased by which they were enforced." Almost incredulous at the apparent naiveté of some historical writers, the author goes on to point out that our "political historians too often forget the state of the age they are endeavoring to describe—an age of tyranny, darkness, and violence, in which perhaps few of the barons, to whom the contrivance of this wonderful system of government is ascribed, were able to sign their names to their own treaties, and in which therefore there could be little foresight of the future because there was little knowledge of the past" (p. 92). One might from this assessment detect and object to an insensitivity regarding the learning and sophistication of the Middle Ages, but the author's point is that students must understand the nature of life, government, and law of earlier times to comprehend adequately the unique nature of contemporary life. And he did not consider the earlier periods of English history as a convenient object of ridicule to which modern society could be favorably compared; rather he saw a historical perspective as a means to provide for the future growth of society. No society could learn from its mistakes or benefit from its successes if it had no knowledge of what those errors and achievements actually were.

Regardless of the extent to which Johnson contributed to the Vinerian law lectures—whether he wrote or dictated every word McAdam claimed, shaped these passages, or merely approved and encouraged them—the evidence strongly suggests that had he so chosen Johnson would have written effective history of whatever length. And although, as Curley reminds us, to accept without question McAdam's attributions dismisses too lightly Chambers's talent for prose and his historical vision, so much of what McAdam prints echoes or coincides with what Johnson had previously written or would later write that it seems almost impossible for him not to have had a hand in the composition of at least some of the passages examined here.[20] As Curley remarks further, "Perhaps the debatable issue of Johnson's specific contributions to the Vinerian course is less important than the question of the general impact of the collaboration on his mind."[21] The lectures refined further Johnson's historical knowledge and perceptions of how society and government developed, modified, and progressed over the centuries. In its entirety, Curley summarizes, *A Course of Lectures on the English Law* must "stand as a notable work of rare historical insight, whose value is enhanced by the fact that Johnson helped inspire it."[22]

Chapter Five

Johnson as Historian:
Looking at the Modern World
in the Light of History

Johnson firmly believed that when men and women considered the world around them a knowledge of history could help to clarify many of the questions, dispel much of the confusion, and provide the proper context in which to characterize and evaluate contemporary events and significant political and social issues. As a man deeply interested in his world and anxious to comment on it, Johnson had frequent opportunity to sharpen his perspective with the aid of history. He took much gratification in assuming the mantle of historian as he discussed and analyzed carefully those contemporary events and issues affecting the course his country was taking in the period 1756 to 1775, when it emerged as a world power and faced the serious political and military problems such a status created.

Although Johnson had already "documented" contemporary history when he composed the *Parliamentary Debates,* it was his experience with the *Literary Magazine* in 1756 that first gave him ample occasion to act as historian of his times.[1] The *Literary Magazine* announced its interest in contemporary history: Johnson himself writes in the introduction to the periodical, "Our design is to give the history political and literary of every month" (Hazen, p. 129). And in 1756 he wrote several works treating aspects of the ongoing Seven Years' War, and even though they rightly belong to his political or journalistic writings, they nevertheless reveal him drafting a chapter of contemporary history. The contradictory emotions of excitement and distress many felt over Britain's course at the time suggested to Johnson that these years would rank as important ones in the eventual history of the eighteenth century. He most likely sensed the urgency of the moment and may have realized that whatever he wrote on the war might serve future generations as an account of and commentary on the important issues that either guided or retarded Britain's and Europe's destiny. But he would not allow himself to be swept up in the tide of patriotic fever, which exulted in the exploits of battles with the French and the policy of colonization in the New World.

Remarks on the Militia Bill, for example, establishes the context of the debate over Britain's desire to arm a home-trained militia as a supplement to the unpopular standing army and foreign mercenaries. In his printing of the bill's wording and in his evaluation of specific passages, Johnson, though probably not intending to do so, in effect provided a historical service for subsequent readers as well as a polemic for his contemporaries.[2] Accordingly, modern historians of the period would be severely amiss if they did not consult remarks such as Johnson's, for these separate publications indicate popular and dissenting sentiment. And the same may be said of *Observations on a Letter From a French Refugee in America,*[3] which discusses the state of the American colonies; *On the Russian and Hessian Treaties,* which speaks primarily of alliances resulting in a dependence on foreign troops to fight Britain's battles on the continent, in the colonies, and on the seas; and *Observations on the Present State of Affairs.* The latter is of special interest, for besides being masterfully written,[4] it succinctly looks to the past for the causes of the current conflict: "It is allowed on both sides, that hostilities began in America, and that the French and English quarrelled about the boundaries of their settlements, about grounds and rivers to which, I am afraid, neither can shew any other right than that of power" (*Political Writings,* p. 186). Johnson suggests that a fait accompli is hardly justification for defending colonial holdings; one must consider the history of the colonization. If it be argued that the Indians have already granted to the British and French the land now under contention, "these grants can little add to the validity of our titles, till it be experienced how they were obtained." Johnson argues furthermore that if research shows the grants to have been extorted or induced by fraud, threats, or broken promises they are "but new modes of usurpation" and "new instances of cruelty and treachery" (pp. 186–187). He strongly advises his readers to consider these issues in a historical context: "It cannot be said, that the Indians originally invited us to their coasts; we went uncalled and unexpected to nations who had no imagination that the earth contained any inhabitants so distant and so different from themselves" (p. 187). One must recall, Johnson adds, the methods employed by the British over the past two hundred years to establish a claim to Indian lands. One finds much wisdom in the following terse summary remark, which contains the author's historical lesson:

"The American dispute between the French and us is therefore only the quarrel of two robbers for the spoils of a passenger" (p. 188).[5] Outside the context of history, however, this assessment suggests only a man in opposition to administration policies, rather than a man with a keen grasp of past events and the ability to interpret them correctly. We have applauded Johnson's views on Indian rights as an example of his modernity, but we need to keep in mind that his perspective was shaped not only by his humanity but also by his historical sense.

Johnson moreover emphasizes in the *Present State* the unfortunate result of ignoring history: "When a quarrel has been long carried on between individuals, it is often very hard to tell by whom it was begun. Every fact is darkened by distance, by interest, and by multitudes. Information is not easily procured from far . . ." (p. 188). In other words, each country's inability or lack of desire to discover true facts pertaining to a dispute—"those whom the truth will not favour, will not step voluntarily forth to tell it"—allows it to interpret or make its own history to support its individual self-interest. Johnson seeks next to answer the larger historical question, "by whom were the hostilities in America commenced?" He generalizes that there must have always been antagonism and conflict between the two parties: "Two powerful colonies enflamed with immemorial rivalry, and placed out of the superintendence of the mother nations, were not likely to be long at rest" (p. 188). He considers the historical as well as the natural causes of the boundary disputes and then recalls the hostilities between England and France during the present century, from the squabble over the English settlement on the Island of St. Lucia in 1723 to the War of the Austrian Succession: "The events of the war are well known, we pleased ourselves with a victory at Dettingen, where we left our wounded men to the care of our enemies, but our army was broken at Fontenoy and Val; and though after the disgrace which we suffered in the Mediterranean we had some naval success, and an accidental dearth made peace necessary for the French, yet they prescribed the conditions, obliged us to give hostages, and acted as conquerors, though as conquerors of moderation" (p. 193). One finds no hint of a patriotic historian who takes liberties with the truth or his analysis of events in order to favor his own country. Johnson's assessment, except for the use of first-person plural, may leave the patriot cold or belligerent, but it offers a far more objective historical account than others had been willing to give. He is interested in determining the causes of the Seven Years' War as a way to understand both the reasons for the conflict and the nature of disruptions and war in general. Suggested throughout the *Present State* is his wish that the nations knew better the history of their claims, territories, and antagonism. Here Johnson forwards a grasp of history as an antidote to the horror of war.

We furthermore find Johnson documenting major contemporary historical events in his 1756 reviews of the Byng pamphlets[6] and in his contributions to the "Historical Memoirs" section of the *Literary Magazine,*[7] and his essays in the "Foreign History" department of the *Gentleman's Magazine*[8] certainly trained him well for writing on contemporary history in the *Literary Magazine* and for the "Observations" in the *Universal Chronicle* (1758), in which he discussed the British successes at Cherbourg and Louisbourg and the activities of Frederick of Prussia. But of all Johnson wrote for the *Literary Magazine,* nothing is more clearly historical than the *Introduction to the Political State of Great Britain,* published in the magazine's initial number (April/May 1756). Fully embracing the role of historian, Johnson saw as his task the documentation of the causes leading up to the Seven Years' War, then at its beginning. Again, we must pay careful attention to his choice of focus and boundaries for the narration: as Greene points out, "It is not every historian, let alone journalist, who feels it incumbent on him to begin his study of the origins of a war at a point two hundred years before the actual commencement of hostilities" (*Political Writings,* p. 127). But such was the influence of his historical sense, which broadened his perspective on matters many years into the past in quest of answers for modern questions. Accordingly, he opens the *Introduction* with words almost every historian would applaud: to understand the present state of affairs one must first become familiar with the historical background, in this case the history of England's relationship with the continent. "Without this previous knowledge," he adds, "either recollected or acquired, it is not easy to understand the various opinions which every change in our affairs produces" (pp. 129–130).

This "succinct account of British affairs," as he terms his work, begins at the reign of Elizabeth, which to Johnson is most appropriate, for in the second half of the sixteenth century England's general satisfaction with Protestantism allied it with the reformed states and placed it in opposition to the Catholic powers, Spain and France, thereby opening a new chapter in his nation's long history. Whereas he thoroughly enjoyed reflecting on all aspects of the Renaissance period—the powerful personalities, the culture, the intellectual and literary accomplishments—in the *Introduction* he is most concerned with England's diplomatic relationship with the continent and its activities in trade and exploration, the latter being one of his favorite historical subjects. The competition for the overseas riches and trade routes, he argues, had a profound effect on England's recent history: "We began in the same reign to extend our trade, by which we made it necessary to ourselves to watch the commercial progress of our neighbours; and, if not to incommode and obstruct their traffick, to hinder them from impairing ours" (p. 130). One learns early in the *Introduction* that the personalities and prowess of monarchs or the inevitable result of long-standing political differences are not the primary causes of all historical events, in this case the Seven Years' War. Reflective of his habit as a historical writer, Johnson rejects the noble and exalted rhetoric of such patriotic historical analysis as "It was England's duty to fight the tyranny of France's domination," and instead makes the causes for the current strife rather demeaning to the British as well as to the French and Spanish: "We seem to have snatched [distant dominions] into our hands, upon no very just principles of policy, only because every state, according to a prejudice of long continuance, concludes itself more powerful as its territories become larger" (p. 130).

Johnson next discusses the rise of the Dutch, who understood that power "is the consequence of wealth" (i.e., commerce), and the French, whose emergence on the international scene at a time "which seems to be the period destined for the change of the face of Europe" led them to assume "an air of superiority" (p. 132). The narrative is unencumbered by digressions or subtleties in its relation of facts or its analysis; in treating the events Johnson above all wishes to make intelligible those complicated changes of power and fortune characteristic of the late sixteenth century: "France was now no longer in dread of insults and invasions from England. She was not only able to maintain her own territories, but prepared, on all occasions, to invade others, and we had now a neighbour whose interest it was to be an enemy, and who has disturbed us, from that time to this, with open hostility or secret machinations" (p. 132).

Having done considerable reading on Renaissance and seventeenth-century history (not so much in preparation for the *Introduction* but rather in the years before 1756), Johnson feels comfortable pointing out other historians' shortcomings. Remarking on the accession of James I in 1603, he notes, "It has not, I think, been frequently observed by historians at how critical a time the union of the two kingdoms happened." Sound deduction and speculation on events and scenarios that did not transpire are allowed in good historical writing if they illustrate a point of importance; therefore, Johnson considers the probable effects on England had

James of Scotland remained in the north: "Had England and Scotland continued separate kingdoms, when France was established in the full possession of her natural power, the Scots, in continuance of the league [with France], which it would now have been more than ever in their interest to observe, would, upon every instigation of the French court, have raised an army with French money, and harrassed us with an invasion, in which they would have thought themselves successful, whatever numbers they might have left behind them" (p. 133). This passage displays effectively Johnson's historical perspective, because he goes far beyond simple narration of events to an analysis of what might have occurred had another decision been taken 150 years earlier. It was important to him that readers view the history of any country as the result of decisions made or opportunities lost, rather than the force of destiny or the will of a dynamic leader. Perhaps only the slightest deviation from the course actually taken might well have changed drastically the history of England.

Emphasizing his theme that the desire for wealth has had a profound effect on recent history, Johnson points to the issue of ship money as giving "occasion to the civil war" (p. 134). He does not, of course, discount the personality and decisions of Charles and the growing tension between the king and Parliament, but he implies once more that events are precipitated by seemingly mundane matters, many times more so than by grand gestures. His ability to suppress the romantic side of his historical sense made him a good historical thinker because he knew that to understand the past one had to dirty one's hands with unglamorous, though highly important, causes, decisions, and events. He goes on to mention the ground England lost while it ravaged itself with a civil war: "the power of France and Holland was every day increasing. . . . The French, who wanted nothing to make them powerful, but a prudent regulation of their revenues, and a proper use of their natural advantages, by the successive care of skilful ministers became every day stronger, and more conscious of their strength" (pp. 134–135). Taking up colonial expansion, Johnson writes of the early French colony in Canada and the plight of the native Indians. Even though this section of the *Introduction* offers him an opportunity to vent his anger at those who afflicted other human beings in the name of God and country, he moreover reminds his readers that the history of any nation contains much to be deplored, much that the historian would be remiss in ignoring. Knowing that many have the talent for *simple* narration, Johnson thought the best kind of historical writing should force readers to think and to struggle with their own perception of the past. English people reading his historical writings could not sit back and revel in the glories of their history; Johnson undoubtedly made many angry because he painted the harsher as well as the brighter tones onto his historical canvas.

In his discussion of the English and Dutch wars of the 1650s, Johnson once more demonstrates his ability to portray an accurate picture of history: "In this contest was exerted the utmost power of the two nations, and the Dutch were finally defeated, yet not with such evidence of superiority as left us much reason to boast our victory" (p. 137). Cromwell's subsequent quarrel with Spain, he also notes, was prompted by covetousness for territory in America, so that he could "exalt his own reputation, and inrich the country." Even here, readers see not only the prevalent theme that a desire for money dictated events but also Johnson's fairness in historical analysis. Rather than explaining simplistically Cromwell's colonial ambitions as the result of his lust for grandeur and power, he argues that practical and even altruistic considerations were also weighed. Readers never sense the author is writing polemically or malevolently (or at least they *should not* feel this way); instead they feel confident that the historian is knowledgeable of his facts and objective in his determinations. Although the enthusiastic eighteenth-century patriot was no doubt offended and rankled by some of Johnson's assessments such as "Our own troubles had left us very little desire to look out upon the continent, and inveterate prejudice hindered us from perceiving, that for more than half a century the power of France had been increasing, and that of Spain had been growing less" (p. 138) or the many negative observations regarding the English monarchs identified in chapter two, the modern reader trusts Johnson's judgment and admires his independence as a historian. Furthermore, his objective and cautious historical persona and willingness to consider multiple explanations for events are evident in the following remarks: "In every change there will be many that suffer real or imaginary grievances, and therefore many will be dissatisfied. This was, perhaps, the reason why several colonies had their beginning in the reign of Charles the Second. . . . The Dutch still continuing to increase in wealth and power, either kindled the resentment of their neighbors by their insolence, or raised their envy by their prosperity" (p. 139).

Keeping in mind his purpose of explaining the causes of the Seven Years' War, Johnson stresses that with the ministry of Jean-Baptiste Colbert (1661 to 1683) the power of France "became formidable to England," for combined with Charles II's shortsightedness and lack of resolve the French began reaping the rewards of shrewd economic and commercial policy: "The king of France was soon enabled to bribe those whom he could not conquer, and to terrify with his fleets those whom his armies could not have approached" (p. 140). The reader comprehends through Johnson's narration and emphasis on commerce why the "influence of France was suddenly diffused over all the globe." France could thunder on the coasts of Africa and receive ambassadors from Siam because its rulers understood and capitalized on the power of "selling much and buying little." Johnson's mercantilist theory that colonies "are always the effects and causes of navigation" was hardly as glamorous as a pamphlet praising the martial ardour of Louis XIV, William III, and the Duke of Marlborough, but he did not set out to write an exciting history or to provide standard assessments of historical periods so dear to many of his day. Rather, he wanted his readers to learn the truth about their past by looking at history in a new way, one that contradicted their impressions of England's glorious achievements. Those who came to grips with their unsettling feelings, however, would have greatly broadened their perspectives and thus learned the lesson about historical thinking Johnson had been trying to teach throughout this and his other historical works. He furnished his readers then with a highly readable overview of the events leading up to the Seven Years' War, even if they extracted nothing else from his efforts. With impressive historical evaluation and analysis, considering the limitations of a work of this kind, Johnson provided a further example of his strong historical sense. The *Introduction* was an important contribution because Johnson's historical sketch would have been a handy document for those less inclined to peruse the larger and poorly written histories available to them.

The remarks on colonial expansion in the *Introduction to the Political State of Great Britain* and the *Observations on the Present State of Affairs* indicate the kind of attention Johnson paid to the movements of people and societies throughout history. He was a historian concerned with far more than the growth of his own nation; the scope of his historical interests embraced not only Europe but also ranged beyond the seas to America. He knew that journeys of exploration and the migrations of people by land and sea had a profound effect on the course of Western history. He was both fascinated by the spirit compelling travelers and settlers to sacrifice the security of a life in their native countries and horrified by the suffering inflicted and the avarice displayed by those who explored and conquered new shores. And as an example of the attention Johnson paid to this aspect of history, we can point to his little-read introduction to *The World Displayed,* a monthly periodical that ran from December 1759 to July 1761.[9]

Drawing from the historians Manuel de Faria y Sousa and J. F. Lafitau,[10] Johnson provides in the introduction a condensed history of fifteenth-century navigation and discoveries up to the time of Columbus in 1492. He mentions initially the ancient voyages, about which "little certain is known," and then moves on to emphasize the significance of the compass to the improvement and spread of navigation, demonstrating once more his belief that history is comprised of and dictated by small inventions and refinements as well as monumental decisions and victories. He depicts the early sailors as a tentative lot, lacking either "knowledge or courage," unwilling to sail too far from the familiar coastline. But with the advent of Prince Henry the Navigator, sea exploration grew from its infancy into its rugged and dauntless youth. Johnson infuses his account with bits of drama and attempts to make his reader understand the fear and excitement experienced by the early seamen. We learn as well that Henry's motives went beyond mere curiosity and sense of personal destiny; he also desired to convert the heathens who inhabited the new lands. Always searching for multiple causes for historical decisions and individual accomplishments, Johnson believed too many of his contemporaries retreated to the sanctuary of the simplistic cause without perceiving history as often a complex study that seldom reveals all its meaning on the surface level.

Unwilling to portray unthinkingly the early period of European exploration as representative of the grandeur of Renaissance man, Johnson adds to his account that human greed both tainted and encouraged further discovery: "The desire of riches and of dominion, which is yet more pleasing to the fancy, filled the courts of the *Portuguese* Prince with innumerable adventures from very distant parts of *Europe*" (Hazen, p. 224). Following a brief sketch of the early discoveries of and settlements on the Canary Islands, Johnson writes of the explorers' domestic practices such as leaving cattle behind and planting crops and plants they felt would thrive in the new environment. Once again we find him interested in the less resplendent aspects of history, in this case the agricultural, because he realized that each had its part to play in the total evolution of a new society. And he was also different from many historical thinkers in his sensitivity for those displaced and conquered by the European discoverers. Johnson's historical vision was never myopic, for he scanned the breadth and depth of the historical canvas and viewed its subtle as well as its impressive hues.

In the introduction he allows the reader to imagine the discovery of new lands from the natives' perspective as well as from that of the Europeans. At one point he disagrees with his source Lafitau, who wrote that the natives on shore thought the approaching ships were either large birds or large fishes, depending on whether the sails were spread or lowered: "Such is the account given by the historian, perhaps with too much prejudice against a negroe's understanding; who though he might well wonder at the bulk and swiftness of the first ship, would scarcely conceive it to be either a bird or a fish; but having seen many bodies floating in this water, would think it what it really is, a large boat; and if he had no knowledge of any means by which separate pieces of timber may be joined together, would form very wild notions concerning its construction, or perhaps suppose it to be a hollow trunk of a tree, from some country where trees grow to a much greater height and thickness than in his own" (pp. 226–227). As this passage indicates, Johnson did more than simply translate into English the words of the Spanish and French historians, and he refused to subscribe to the popular notion existing among those with a distorted historical vision that the natives who lived in the newly discovered lands were ignorant and often loathsome savages, unable to comprehend the very notion of progress and undeserving of their home in territory now rescued from oblivion by the superior race of Europeans. As we have seen in the *Life of Drake,* Johnson found the culture of the Indians unique and worthy of examination. Surely he bristled at the imperialists' mentality, which patronized the uncivilized natives on the one hand and condemned their existence on the other. Accordingly, he took a special interest in considering the new relationship between the "civilized" Portuguese and their "savage" hosts: "They did not understand each other, and signs are a very imperfect mode of communication even to men of more knowledge than the negroes, so that they could not easily negociate or traffick; at last the *Portugueze* laid hands on some of them to carry them home for a sample; . . . On what occasion, or for what purpose cannons and muskets were discharged among a people harmless and secure, by strangers who without any right visited their coast; it is not thought necessary to inform us" (p. 227).

Because he saw history as a tool of morality, Johnson, in the introduction's most interesting passage, assails the "wanton merriment" of the Europeans as they murdered a large number of the natives: "We are openly told, that they had the less scruple concerning their treatment of the savage people, because they scarcely considered them as distinct from beasts; and indeed the practice of all the *European* nations, and among others of the *English* barbarians that cultivate the southern islands of *America* proves, that this opinion, however absurd and foolish, however wicked and injurious, still continues to prevail. Interest and pride harden the heart, and it is vain to dispute against avarice and power" (p. 227). Not even his own country escapes Johnson's moral censure, which has the justification and sanction of the historical record.

Whereas he believed a historical account should go far beyond the exploits of a major figure, Johnson appreciated the power of the individual to affect the course of history. Of Prince Henry he writes, he was "the first encourager of remote navigation, by whose incitement, patronage, and example, distant nations have been made acquainted with each other, unknown countries have been brought into general view, and the power of *Europe* has been extended to the remotest parts of the world. What mankind has lost and gained by the genius and designs of this Prince, it would be long to compare, and very difficult to estimate" (p. 228). But Johnson insists, as was his custom, in presenting the other side of the historical coin; although navigation and exploration have propelled civilization to the outer reaches of the globe and have added vast knowledge and immeasurable benefits to European life, they have also spawned despicable cruelty and a subversion of basic religious principles and moral laws, which have been "outrageously and enormously violated." Johnson's critical attitude toward indiscriminate colonial expansion, well publicized by Donald Greene, no doubt colors the following observation, but it nevertheless depicts him as an interpretive and moral historian: "The *Europeans* have scarcely visited any coast, but to gratify avarice, and extend corruption; to arrogate dominion without right, and practise cruelty without incentive. Happy had it then been for the oppressed, if the designs of *Henry* had slept in his bosom, and surely more happy for the oppressors" (p. 228). As he continues his narration, Johnson never fails to stress the hypocrisy of the "Christian" discoverers, those far removed from their apostolic ancestors, who did not enter defenseless territories armed with swords: "they built no forts upon ground to which they had no right, nor polluted the purity of religion with the avarice of trade or insolence of power" (p. 230).

Johnson's introduction to *The World Displayed* contains a good mixture in fact, analysis, character study, and moral commentary. Even though he basically follows Sousa and Lafitau in the ordering of particulars, his own hand shapes the most interesting parts of the account; he could never simply retell or translate the work of others without putting his stamp upon the finished product. The introduction performs a valuable service to the reader by providing a competent historical narrative, parts of which, as Allen Hazen remarked in 1937, "are still of more than passing interest to the social historian and to the general reader" (p. 216), and, more important, by forcing his readers to question some long-standing assumptions about exploration and colonization and their nation's moral justification for its actions. And this is what a good historian should do: encourage deeper thought as well as disseminate the facts.

The movements of mankind across the seas and the subsequent attempts at exploration and settlement are again prominently featured in Johnson's *Thoughts on the Late Transactions Respecting Falkland's Islands* (1771).[11] True to his belief that complicated issues require a knowledge of historical events, parallels, and precedents, he makes clear his intentions early in the *Thoughts* when he writes, "The Rubicon was ennobled by the passage of Caesar, and the time is now come when Falkland's Islands demand their historian" (*Political Writings,* p. 350). One should note the purpose and enthusiasm in Johnson's words; he no doubt felt totally confident in his ability to assume the mantle of historian. He points out early, however, that the subject of his account is not the conquering heroes or political intrigues of and in the Falkland Islands, because few grand events have occurred on the islands to merit recording. Even so, the reader will gain valuable insight into the present crisis through the history of the islands' discovery and settlement.

Following the preamble, Johnson does not begin his history with the presumed first sighting of the Falkland Islands by John Davis in the 1590s; rather he takes up where he left off twelve years earlier in the introduction to *The World Displayed* with a discussion of exploration and colonization in the late fifteenth and throughout the sixteenth centuries. Once more his disdain for colonial expansion permeates the historical account: the Spaniards, he writes, "were made at once insupportably insolent, and might perhaps have become irresistibly powerful, had not their mountainous treasures been scattered in the air with the ignorant profusion of unaccustomed opulence" (p. 350). Unable for several reasons to "dip their own hands in the golden fountain," the other major European nations left the ocean lanes free for English ships to emulate the Spanish routes and discoveries. Johnson does far more than provide mere facts pertaining to this period of history: he analyzes motives and causes for and effects of the events about which he writes. He furthermore comments on the logic that motivated action: "By the war between Elizabeth and Philip, the wealth of America became lawful prize, and those who were less afraid of danger than of poverty, supposed that riches might easily be obtained by plundering the Spaniards. Nothing is difficult when gain and honour unite their influence; the spirit and vigour of these expeditions enlarged our views of the new world, and made us first acquainted with its remoter coasts" (p. 351). Johnson's independence from blatantly patriotic assumptions about England's motives for exploration is one of his finest qualities as a historian. A good many readers of this work had to be disturbed by the aspersions the author cast at his own country, but Johnson allowed no individual monarch or nation, including his own, to escape the responsibilities of their actions. Because he believed passionately in discovering the truth in history, he boldly pushed his way into the corridors of the past, stepping on any toes that were in his way. That he offended some of his contemporaries would not have troubled him, because he believed the historian should be equipped with a thick enough skin to ward off the barbs of romanticism and patriotism, those powerful weapons that deter one from viewing history objectively and analytically.

Johnson moves rapidly from the early discoverers of the Falkland Islands and their seeming insignificance throughout the seventeenth century, for he knew readers would best understand the current conflict with a knowledge of mid eighteenth-century events. One central question is whether the islands are of strategic importance. Granting their use in times of war, Johnson nonetheless adds, "But war is not the whole business of life; it happens but seldom, and every man, either good or wise, wishes that its frequency were still less" (p. 353). Other than being universal in its application, the comment reflects his general view of historical study, not universally shared by his contemporaries, that the history of a nation must concentrate on the "business of life" as well as the great leaders and conflicts dominating the history books. He moves on to conclude that the islands have no clear use in peacetime, for "what use can it have but of a station for contraband traders, a nursery of fraud, and a receptacle of theft?" (p. 354).

Following some general commentary of a political nature, Johnson takes the reader to 1748, the date of George Anson's influential account,[12] recalling an English voyage to the islands that infuriated the Spanish, who claimed dominion over the area. Johnson presents both the English and Spanish positions regarding the motives of their voyages to the Falkland Islands, which is a further illustration that he was no prejudiced political or national historian. After some seventeen years of generally ignoring the islands, he writes, Britain in 1765 sent "Foul-weather Jack" Byron to claim them for the mother country. Now entering the crucial period in his narrative, Johnson next discusses the subsequent settlements, the geographical properties of the islands, and the animals, vegetation, and minerals discovered by the British seamen. The colony, he notes, seemed doomed from the outset because it was unable to maintain itself sufficiently; therefore, the government, at great expense, sent provisions for the new Falklanders' survival. At this point Johnson turns his attention to the motives for historical decisions: although logic and monetary wisdom could not support the distant colony, the "shame of deserting a project, and unwillingness to contend with a projector that meant well, continued the garrison, and supplied it with regular remittances of stores and provisions" (p. 358). As he knew, one would find it impossible to count the number of historical actions motivated primarily by national pride and an unwillingness to begin or end a commitment because of fear or shame. Citizens would naturally balk at accepting the view that their government's inability to admit its error or weakness, not bad luck or destiny, was most responsible for a disastrous battle or a barren settlement. But history is often unpleasing to the eye and sour to the taste, and yet if one is to benefit from it one must force oneself to look at and then digest the kinds of historical truth about which Johnson writes. It is too tempting not to consider how his words on the Falkland Islands garrison might be applied to America's Vietnam withdrawal policy in the late 1960s and early 1970s.

The peaceful yet expensive sovereignty over the islands, Johnson goes on to point out, was challenged in the fall of 1769 when the Spanish once again protested British presence in the area. Of Captain Anthony Hunt's assertion that by right of first discovery and first settlement the British had claim to the islands, Johnson remarks, "This was an assertion of more confidence than certainty. The right of discovery indeed has already appeared to be probable, but the right which priority of settlement confers I know not whether we yet can establish" (p. 359). Johnson never hesitates to sweep away the mists of patriotic rhetoric or misapplied logic to see the past as it really was. He performs very effectively the function of the good historian by citing the rationale of the historical figures involved and then challenging it. Although poor historical writers can as a result descend into mere polemics, successful historians are able to mix harmoniously their narrative and their analysis of character and events. Without a sense of timing and proportion in these matters, the history becomes a source of irritation to the reader. An examination of Johnson's historical writing, however, shows that he combines the elements always satisfactorily and often brilliantly.

Continuing his narrative, Johnson reminds the reader of the diplomatic and naval salvos of the recent months (leading up to March 1771). One senses the tension of the period as both Britain and Spain crept closer to a violent confrontation: "Having while he was writing received the letters of warning written the day before by the English captains, [a Spanish officer] told them, that he thought himself able to prove the King of Spain's title to all those countries, but that this was no time for verbal altercations. He persisted in his determination, and allowed only fifteen minutes for an answer. . . . Finding the Spaniards disposed to make no other acknowledgements, the English ministry considered a war as not likely to be long avoided. In the latter end of November private notice was given of their danger to the merchants at Cadiz, and the officers absent from Gibraltar were remanded to their posts. Our naval force was every day encreased, and we made no abatement of our original demand" (pp. 361, 365). Even though the Spanish landed and easily "conquered" the English force, Johnson strongly advises that one not make too much of the "petty revolution": "The conquest, if such it may be called, cost but three days" (p. 362). Johnson likely wished to set the record straight for future generations contemplating the event: he understood that many students of history often exaggerated the significance and effect of some military confrontations and that this misunderstanding of history could be tragically used as a pretext to further and larger aggression.

Johnson's depiction of the subsequent haggling and animosity is reflective of the *Thoughts* as a whole: he writes with clarity and succinctness when he relates the facts, determined in his own mind that all readers have a clear understanding of the events leading up to the present tension over those small islands off the coast of South America. But strategically placed within his narrative are bits of summary and analysis that steer the reader away from drawing hasty conclusions from the facts about the islands' history. In addition to the example given above regarding the Spanish "conquest" of the Falkland Islands in June 1770, Johnson writes of the impressive and speedy preparation of the British fleet, which he praises, but then adds that it was "obstructed by the utmost power of that noisy faction which has too long filled the kingdom, sometimes with the roar of empty menace, and sometimes with the yell of hypocritical lamentation. Every man saw, and every honest man saw with detestation, that they who desired to force their sovereign into war, endeavoured at the same time to disable him from action" (p. 363). With an eye to posterity, Johnson did not wish to leave the impression that all of England burned with the same patriotic fervor and commitment. He knew how easily historians or historical thinkers give in to the temptation of a handy generalization when considering the actions and moods of the past. Finally, as Donald Greene informs us, Johnson's account was so lucid that in 1948, after Argentina had reopened the dispute, the *Thoughts* was reprinted as "the clearest exposition available" of the islands' complicated history (p. 346).[13] Reading Johnson's history, one feels secure not only in the facts revealed but also in the historian's judgments and analyses and in his independence from the pressures of party or state.

Johnson viewed himself at least partly as a historian in the *False Alarm* (1770), another of his major political tracts of the 1770s. In his attack on the growing cant surrounding the Wilkes affair and the misunderstanding of parliamentary law, Johnson employed his knowledge of history in an attempt to refute radical arguments as well as popular sentiment. Early in the piece he informs his readers that there is historical basis for the Commons' decision to oust one of its own members regardless of the will of the people. The exemption of the House from other legal bodies, he writes, was "first established in favour of the five members [Pym, Hampden, Hollis, Strode, and Haselrig] in the Long Parliament" of 1642. (Charles I, it may be recalled, attempted to arrest the five inside the Commons.) Adding a precedent from the time of Elizabeth (1580) and others from the reigns of James I, Charles II, and Anne, Johnson argues that the power of Commons to punish its own has been "so long exercised" it cannot successfully be challenged (*Political Writings*, p. 322). It is "uncontrovertibly certain," he contends further, that "the Commons never intended to leave electors the liberty of returning them an expelled member" (p. 328), and he therefore emphasizes once more the weight of historical example: "I must forever remind these puny controvertists, that those acts are laws of permanent obligation" (p. 331). The decision to expel Wilkes, Johnson summarizes, is therefore "agreeable to custom and reason" and "consistent with the practice of former times" (p. 333).

Near the conclusion of his pamphlet, Johnson again invokes history to draw a comparison to the uproar over Wilkes's situation: he mentions the Wat Tyler revolt in 1381 (or perhaps the Robert Kett uprising in 1549) and the peasant riots of the Jacquerie in 1358 as fit historical parallels of contemporary "low-born railers" (pp. 341–342). George III, he adds, has been insulted far more rudely than William III, James II, and Charles I in their times of trouble (p. 342), an exaggerated, though historically oriented, observation. Johnson warns his readers that history has much to teach an intemperate populace: "Had Rome fallen by the Catilinarian conspiracy, she might have consoled her fate by the greatness of her destroyers; but what would have alleviated the disgrace of England, had her government been changed by Tiler or by Ket?" (p. 343). Should these references be too far removed from some of his readers, Johnson punctuates his view by adding, "The civil war was fought for what each army called and believed the best religion, and the best government. The struggle in the reign of Anne, was to exclude or restore an exiled king. We are now disputing, with almost equal animosity, whether Middlesex shall be represented or not by a criminal from a jail" (p. 343). Johnson's intent is to refresh the reader's historical knowledge and then equate the emotional fervor of those violent times with contemporary reaction to Wilkes, the result of which might lead to further internal disorder or even the deaths of English citizens at the hands of their own. Certainly, Johnson exploits history for a polemical purpose here, but his point nevertheless has far more than a semblance of truth behind it. Although his views in the *False Alarm* have not been universally seconded, we should not fail to recognize that his fine sense of historical perspective as well as his desire to engage in political argument affected the composition of the pamphlet.

Even in the shorter piece *The Patriot* (1774), Johnson employs history to refute widely accepted though illogical assumptions such as that Protestantism is in danger because "Popery is established in the extensive province of Quebec." Johnson answers such as "shameless falsehood" with the following: "the inhabitants, being French, were always Papists"; "persecution is not more virtuous in a Protestant than a Papist; and that while we blame Lewis the Fourteenth, for his dragoons and his gallies, we ought, when power comes into our hands, to use it with greater equity"; and "when Canada with its inhabitants was yielded, the free enjoyment of their religion was stipulated; a condition of which King William, who was no propagator of Popery, gave an example nearer home, at the surrender of Limerick" (*Political Writings,* p. 393). While writing in the political vein, Johnson had at his disposal to supplement his powerful, analytical, and independent mind not only his command of logic and understanding of human nature, its nobility and pettiness, but also his quick recall of historical events. Believing that no society exists apart from its past, he encouraged his readers to heed the lessons of history before they decide on political questions of importance. Knowing one's history meant being free from the debilitating effects of political propaganda, cant, and fashionable, though purely fictitious, assessments of rulers and their descendants.

But no other political work so instilled in him the sense of being a contemporary historian than *Taxation No Tyranny* (1775). Keenly aware that the debate over colonial independence would probably lead to a critical moment in England's long history, Johnson desired to answer his opposition by providing what he considered a more temperate view of a highly emotional issue. At this time much of Europe sat nervously awaiting word from Philadelphia, Boston, New York, and Baltimore as to which direction the Continental Congress would take. Regardless of one's support or disdain for the American cause, all realized they were on the threshold of a major historical event. As Donald Greene points out, Johnson appears to have known by the time he sat down to write *Taxation No Tyranny* that the congress had already resolved for American autonomy (*Political Writings,* p. 402). He was thus, like many others, awaiting the inevitable clash of arms.

Underlying his introduction of the colonies' position in the first several paragraphs of the pamphlet is Johnson's anger at the Americans' desire to sever themselves from their British heritage and their history: "it never has been my fortune to find, either in ancient or modern writers, any honourable mention of those, who have with equal blindness hated their country" (p. 412). As he vigorously counters each point raised against taxation by the Americans and their British supporters, Johnson again finds the need to establish a historical context. At one point he seeks to explain the impetus for migration and colonization: "the history of mankind informs us," he notes, of only two kinds of migration. The first is comprised of those who left their native land for whatever reason and never looked back or expected aid from their former homeland: "Of this kind seem to have been all the migrations of the early world, whether historical or fabulous, and of this kind were the eruptions of those nations which from the North invaded the Roman Empire, and filled Europe with new sovereignties" (p. 420). The second mode, those who depended on each other and their homeland for support, developed when "wiser laws and gentler manners" evolved.

Beginning to assume more fully the mantle of historian, Johnson forwards his own analysis of the history of migration: "Had the western

129

continent been discovered between the fourth and tenth century, when all the northern world was in motion; and had navigation been at that time sufficiently advanced to make so long a passage easily practicable, there is little reason for doubting but the intumescence of nations would have found its vent, like all other expansive violence, where there was least resistance; and that Huns and Vandals, instead of fighting their way to the south of Europe, would have gone by thousands and by myriads under their several chiefs to take possession of regions smiling with pleasure and waving with fertility, from which the naked inhabitants were unable to repel them." Johnson contends that in those days several states would have been produced from each expedition: "The Scandinavian heroes might have divided the country among them, and have spread the feudal subdivision of regality from Hudson's Bay to the Pacifick Ocean" (p. 420).

Johnson next writes of the changes in society by the time Columbus sailed to the New World: no longer could a single man lead his people and establish separate colonies by the sword, for by the fifteenth century he "that committed any act of hostility by land or sea, without the commission of some acknowledged sovereign, was considered by all mankind as a robber or a pirate" (p. 421). Johnson speculates on the responses to Columbus's venture had he lived in a remoter time. Instead of standing alongside a mighty family of warriors, he was forced to wander "from court to court, scorned and repulsed as a wild projector, an idle promiser of kingdoms in the clouds" (p. 421). In his role as historian Johnson demonstrates an unwillingness to agree that the brilliance of individuals or the idea of individual destiny could always rise above the historical setting in which one was placed. The "great man" theory of historical causation, he thought, too often exaggerated the significance of the person, no matter how charismatic or powerful he or she was. Johnson was too sophisticated a historian to believe a Caesar, Alexander, or Cromwell would have accomplished what they did had each been placed in another period of history.

Johnson next mentions the Portuguese discovery of a passage to the Indies and the Spanish exploration of the American coast. As he indicates, Europe soon became fired with boundless expectations of new wealth with each new territory explored; but his historical perspective did not overlook the darker aspects of the "glorious" discoveries: "the adventurers were contented with plunder; though they took gold and silver to themselves, they seized islands and kingdoms in the name of their sovereigns" (p. 422). He then considers the evolution of colonial government and the unalterable fact that "territories thus occupied and settled were rightly considered as mere extensions or processes of empire." They were kept "flourishing and spreading," he adds, "by the radical vigour of the mother-country" (p. 422). Although he was always opposed to colonization because it exploited usually helpless natives and encouraged greed and violence, Johnson saw the need in *Taxation No Tyranny* to present a general assessment of colonial expansion so that his arguments against American autonomy might carry the weight of authenticity and history rather than simply reflect the ideas of an energetic debater. And the inclusion of this historical preface is a masterful stroke of polemics as well; after a highly charged start to the pamphlet he allows the reader to agree with the facts of history and to see him as a sensible historian, which will then pave the way to a fuller acceptance of him as a credible spokesman.

Even in the midst of his argument, Johnson continues to emphasize history's importance to the debate: "To him that considers the nature, the original, the progress, and the constitution of the colonies, who remembers that the first discoverers had commissions from the crown, that the first settlers owe to a charter their civil forms and regular magistracy, and that all personal immunities and legal securities, by which the condition of the subject has been from time to time improved, have been extended to the Colonists, it will not be doubted but the Parliament of England has a right to bind them by statutes . . ." (pp. 425–426). As for the colonists' contention that their ancestors were entitled to all the "rights, liberties, and immunities" of free and natural-born English subjects, Johnson again challenges the assertion in the context of history: "If their ancestors were subjects, they acknowledged a sovereign; if they had a right to English privileges, they were accountable to English laws, and what must grieve the lover of liberty to discover, had ceded to the King and Parliament, whether the right or not, at least the power, of disposing, 'without their consent, of their lives, liberties, and properties,' " (p. 429). If the colonists wish to invoke history, Johnson is all the better equipped to counter their move: "Their ancestors left a country where the representatives of the people were elected by men particularly qualified, and where those who wanted qualifications, or who did not use them, were bound by the decisions of men whom they had not deputed." Although one may charge Johnson with rhetorical overkill in this and the following remark—"they have therefore exactly what their ancestors left them, not a vote in making laws, or in constituting legislators, but the happiness of being protected by law, and the duty of obeying it" (p. 431)—he cleverly uses to his own advantage the Americans' allusions to the past by countering them with harder historical evidence for his arguments.

Johnson's employment of history in *Taxation No Tyranny* does not support the assumption that he was indulging in a bit of party propaganda, for his knowledge of the history of colonization compelled him to draw several derogatory conclusions about the English as well as the French settlers and their governments' motives for encouraging further exploration and eventual conflict, conclusions that could not have amused many who supported Johnson's general attack on the American position. Few in the government would have applauded his refusal to endorse the patriotic cant extolling the colonization of foreign lands by a superior English people, as if such settlements were the nation's manifest destiny or global noblesse oblige. Johnson's unclouded historical vision, which allowed him to see the true history of migrations and colonization, helped to keep him independent from party loyalists.

The commentary in chapters one and three on Johnson's responses to Scotland during his journey in 1773 indicate that for him a full picture of Scotland could not be drawn without substantial coloring from the past. We have seen him ponder seriously the local customs and the historical ruins scattered across the Scottish landscape: "Edifices," he noted, "either standing or ruined, are the chief records of an illiterate nation" (*Journey*, p. 73). And we know that he was highly sensitive to the effects of the political and religious upheaval in the sixteenth and seventeenth centuries; for example, the "tumult and violence of Knox's reformation." More than this, Johnson reflected on the economic conditions of Scotland before the Union of 1707, the state of learning in earlier times, Cromwell's effect on the Scottish spirit, and the nature of Highland warfare—all in the hope of understanding more clearly the nature of modern life in Scotland's largest cities and smaller villages in the Highlands and Western Islands. His sense of history made him responsive toward and especially qualified to assess the effects of the terrain, social and political isolation, and large-scale emigration on the land and on its people. And, as Edward Tomarken has recently written, the *Journey to the Western Islands* "concludes by considering how the past influences the future."[14]

That Johnson's discussion of the Highlanders is rich in historical insight is clearly evident in his depiction of the landmarks, battles, warriors, and feuds of these virile and curious men and women. Consistent with his view that geography was one of history's "necessary preparatives and attendants,"[15] he stresses the influence of the land on the history and development of a people: "Mountainous regions are sometimes so remote from the seat of government, and so difficult of access, that they are very little under the influence of the sovereign, or within the reach of national justice. Law is nothing without power; and the sentence of a distant court could not be easily executed, nor perhaps very safely promulgated, among men ignorantly proud and habitually violent, unconnected with the general system, and accustomed to reverence only their own lords" (p. 46).[16] Taking seriously his occasional role of historian, Johnson wishes to point out that a nation's past has its nooks and crannies not easily discernible at first glance. As a historical thinker, Johnson was knowledgeable of and sensitive to the details of history, the lesser names, the smaller events, and the more particular aspects of the past, whether social, political, military, or traditional. And yet he was aware that the history of such small pockets of the globe, such as the Highlands and Western Islands of Scotland, share much with the events and psychology of larger countries: "A claim of lands between two powerful lairds was decided like a contest for dominion between sovereign powers" (p. 47). To punctuate this remark, he writes of the last open war of the clans—that between Mackintosh and Macdonald—fought near the end of William III's reign.

Johnson was particularly interested in life near and on the Western Islands, because "Every thing in those countries has its history" (p. 49). Although generally suspicious of oral tradition, he argued that the stories of feuds and warfare at least "deserve the notice of a traveller, because they are the only records of a nation that has no historians, and afford the most genuine representation of the life and character of the ancient Highlanders" (p. 50). Accordingly, he took much pleasure in passing on information he gleaned regarding the clans of the Macleods and the Macdonalds (pp. 68–74). He strongly implies that an account of contemporary Hebridean and Highland life would be incomplete and less impressive without an understanding of its history. His near meticulous concern with reviewing the past goes beyond recounting the battles between clans; he seeks to portray a once-thriving spirit among these people as as contrast to the current state of malaise and mass emigration: "This was, in the beginning of the present century, the state of the Highlands. Every man was a soldier, who partook of national confidence, and interested himself in national honour. To lose this spirit, is to lose what no small advantage will compensate" (p. 91). Johnson portrays in his historical account a people worthy of interest and admiration and a decline in the quality of their life and in their communal and national temperament. These are therefore no mere snippets of fact thrown in gratuitously by a historically minded commentator; they are rather significant observations of an unusual culture deduced and embellished by an artistic, philosophical, and moral genius.

While discussing the island of Skye, Johnson considers the thinning population of the northern regions and again stresses the importance of historical precedents: "Migration, while the state of life was unsettled, and there was little communication of intelligence between distant places, was among the wilder nations of Europe, capricious and casual" (p. 97). And then, after an allusion to Caesar and the wandering Helvetians, he writes of the military ardor of the Highlanders, which led them on journeys of adventure in other lands, and of England's use of Highland troops in America (p. 98). As a competent historian should, Johnson considers multiple reasons for the depletion of the population (for example, agricultural deficiencies that resulted in famine), but concludes that the "northern regions were not, when their irruptions subdued the Romans, overpeopled with regard to their real extent of territory, and power of fertility" (p. 99). For all the praise due the *Journey to the Western Islands* for its examination of "men and manners," Johnson's historical writing in the book added a brilliant luster to it and made more intelligible an understanding of those people and their manners. And, as Edward Tomarken furthermore argues, the *Journey* "demonstrates that the author's process of coming to terms with the Hebrides affords an insight into the historical dilemma of the islands."[17] The *Journey*, written at a time when his grasp of history had reached its mature stage, is a significant illustration of Johnson's encompassing historical sense: it demonstrates the connection he made between a place and its past, the symbolism and lessons drawn from historical landmarks, an appreciation for the importance of customs, the enjoyment in recalling historical battles and feuds, and, most important, a perception and interpretation of contemporary life gained only through a keen awareness of history.

Johnson's writings on contemporary events and societies in the light of history, his historical reviews, his sense of historical perspective in his literary criticism, his historical commentary in his biographies, and his involvement with the Vinerian law lectures of Robert Chambers amply illustrate his talent for historical writing. We must therefore regret that he did not attempt more writing in the purely historical vein, because as this and the previous chapters have shown, his compositions were marked by the sensitivity for dramatic moments, the energy, and the excitement characteristic of William Robertson, the power of narration and humanistic sentiments we associate with Edward Gibbon, and the clarity of style, critical independence, and moral judgments we find in David Hume.

As an epilogue to this discussion of Johnson the historian we should look to some of the historical projects he contemplated over the years. Other than the "Historical Design" he mentioned to Edward Cave in 1743, Johnson wrote Thomas Warton on 27 October 1757, although apparently the letter was not sent, about several projects on which a scholar in the university could work—projects, we may trust, of interest to Johnson himself. These included an "Ecclesiastical History of England," a "history of the Reformation, (not of England only, but of Europe;)," the "Life of Richard the First," and the "Life of Edward the Confessor." These projects show again that he was not insensitive to the Middle Ages. An investigation into the life of Richard would probably have fascinated Johnson, because one could easily find uplifting the exploits of the warrior king and find challenging and rewarding at the same time an attempt to dispel that romantic view by judging Richard as an administrator in absentia and his conduct during the third Crusade. Johnson's birthday resolution for 1760 contains a reminder to "Send for books for Hist. of war" (*DPA*, p. 71). Boswell believed the reference was to a history of the Seven Years' War, then in progress; perhaps Johnson wished to enlarge upon or complete what he had begun in the *Introduction to the Political State of Great Britain*. One must wonder, however, what books he would be referring to concerning a war that still had over two years remaining before the Peace of 1763. A more likely candidate would be the War of the Austrian Succession during the 1740s. Johnson had already composed part of that history in his life of Frederick of Prussia in 1756. Other possibilities would be a history of the English Civil War, or an aspect of that struggle, or even a history of war in general, as G. B. Hill suggested.

Johnson also "seriously entertained the thought" of translating De Thou's (Thuanus) *Historia sui temporis* (*Life*, IV, 410). Boswell felt he would have written an excellent account of the Seven Years' War: "He would have been under no temptation to deviate in any degree from truth, which he held very sacred, or to take a license" and, taking Boswell's own biases into account, a good "*Tory History* of his country"

(*Life*, I, 355: IV, 39). Boswell also tells us that he regretfully lost an opportunity to have his family's history "recorded and illustrated by Johnson's pen." Johnson told him, "Let me have all the materials you can collect, and I will do it both in Latin and English"; he believed that there "should be a chronicle kept in every family" (*Life*, IV, 198; *Tour*, p. 181). Other projects he had at one time considered were (1) translations of Herodian's *History*, Benzo's *New History of the New World*, and Machiavelli's *History of Florence;* (2) a history of the State of Venice, "in a compendious manner"; (3) a body of chronology in verse, with "historical notes"; (4) a dictionary of ancient history and mythology; (5) a history of the British constitution; and (6) a history of the revival of learning in Europe (*Life*, IV, 381–382; Hawkins, pp. 285–286). Johnson, like other fecund minds, formulated topics that would remain only plans or outlines on discarded pieces of paper, but one rarely considers devoting time to subject matter in which one is not sincerely interested. It is quite possible, before the pension in 1762 at any rate, that he lamented not having the leisure to take up some of these projects in earnest, or he might have lamented his inability, after 1762, to sit down and discipline himself to desk and pen. Regarding a history of the British constitution, he may have tried his hand at part of this topic in the sections of the Vinerian law lectures attributed to him. But for all these planned accounts he would have undoubtedly preferred to work on and complete the "History of the Revival of Learning in Europe." His friends Joseph and Thomas Warton, along with others, had hoped to accomplish this formidable task, Thomas Warton's *History of English Poetry* being conceived at one point as a part of a larger whole. We cannot forget what he wrote in *Rasselas:* "There is no part of history so generally useful as that which relates the progress of the human mind, the gradual improvement of reason, the successive advances of science, the vicissitudes of learning and ignorance, which are the light and darkness of thinking beings, the extinction and resuscitation of arts, and the revolutions of the intellectual world. If accounts of battles and invasions are peculiarly the business of princes, the useful or elegant arts are not to be neglected; those who have kingdoms to govern have understandings to cultivate" (p. 118).

Relative to Johnson's own desire to compose in the historical vein was his encouragement of others to write history. Boswell relates that when he bemoaned the lack of an authentic history of the 1745 Jacobite uprising, Johnson chided, "If you were not an idle dog you might write it, by collecting from every body what they can tell, and putting down your authorities" (*Life*, III, 162; *Tour*, p. 384). And in 1772 when Boswell, then intending to write a history of Sweden, asked if one might write the book without "going thither," Johnson replied, "Yes . . . one for common use" (*Life,* II, 156). Johnson also suggested to William Maxwell that he attempt a history of Ireland and he implored Charles O'Connor to write on early Irish history: "If you could give a history, though imperfect, of the Irish nation from its conversion to Christianity, to the invasion from England, you would amplify knowledge with new views and new objects. Set about it, therefore if you can, do what you can easily do, without anxious exactness. Lay the foundation, and leave the superstructure to posterity" (*Letters,* II, 172–173). In addition, Johnson offered his assistance to William Strahan in getting Robert Watson's *History of Philip II* ready for the press (*Letters,* II, 151), and Lord Hailes found him helpful in more than mere vocal support: Johnson took a good deal of his time in the mid 1770s to read, comment on, and revise portions of Hailes's *Annals of Scotland.*

The considerable number of historical allusions and perceptive historical commentary, those works in which Johnson is chiefly the historian, and the many historical projects he considered and encouraged make clear the importance of history to Johnson's career as a writer. When he came to compose the important political pamphlets of the 1770s, the *Journey to the Western Islands,* and the *Lives of the Poets,* he had both a vast amount of historical knowledge and much experience incorporating that knowledge and an acute historical perspective into almost everything of importance he ever wrote.

Chapter Six

Thinking about the Philosophy and Presentation of History: Johnson on Historiography and the Historians

An examination of Johnson's historical writings has uncovered ample evidence that he had definite ideas on what constituted effective history. This chapter will explore more fully his requirements for successful historical composition and his impressions of history as an art and as a science. By placing Johnson into the intellectual context of his times, we will find him far more aware of and responsive to eighteenth-century historical theory and the recent efforts of historians than we have ever imagined. A comparison of Johnson's views with those of Bolingbroke, Hume, Robertson, Gibbon, and others leaves us with the inescapable conclusion that Johnson deserves a place among the more advanced historical thinkers of his age.

A good place to begin an investigation of Johnson's perception of historical writing would be with a discussion of the most notorious incriminating documents that Macaulay and others since have used to prove Johnson's ignorance and rejection of history and historical fact in particular. Hester Thrale relates that her friend was never less pleased with a conversation "than when the subject was historical fact or general polity." "What shall we learn from *that* stuff," she quotes him as saying. Johnson, she continues, never "desired to hear of the *Punic war* while he lived": he believed such conversation was "lost time" and that it "carried one away from common life, leaving no ideas behind which could serve *living wight* as warning or direction" (*Misc,* I, 201–202).[1] Regarding the Catiline Conspiracy, Thrale writes of the time she asked her friend about the conversational power of Charles James Fox. Johnson said, "He talked to me at club one day . . . concerning Catiline's conspiracy—so I withdrew my attention, and thought about Tom Thumb" (*Misc,* I, 202–203).

Hester Thrale's anecdotes, while probably not fabricated or exaggerated, are nevertheless highly misleading. One should not assume from these comments that Johnson despised history or even historical fact; rather he disdained the pedantic or fashionable repetition of these facts—common fare, it seems, in his day. David Hume's remark to Hugh Blair in 1769 that history had become the "Favourite Reading"[2] suggests that frequently during this period men and women read history not seriously, but too fashionably for their own good. One can envisage a modish gathering of leisurely people addressing the subject of classical history and the inevitable "learned" commentary on the Punic War and Catiline Conspiracy. References to these events were assuredly part of the cant Johnson warned his friends to avoid (e.g., *Life*, IV, 221). We have noted in the 1756 review of Blackwell's *Memoirs of the Court of Augustus* Johnson's intolerance for the romantic view of Rome as a model for contemporary society, and surely this attitude affected the manner in which he responded to these classical historical allusions.

Besides, Johnson himself was not at all averse to mentioning or using both the Punic War and Catiline Conspiracy. For instance, he employs Hannibal, a major figure in the second Punic War, as an object lesson about passivity in *Rambler* 127: "It was said of Hannibal that he wanted nothing to the completion of his martial virtues, but that when he had gained a victory he should know how to use it" (IV, 314). Johnson mentions Catiline several times in his writings (*Rambler* 60 and *Adventurer* 99) and refers to the conspiracy in *The False Alarm*: "Had Rome fallen by the Catilinarian conspiracy, she might have consoled her fate by the greatness of her destroyers" (*Political Writings*, p. 343). And among Johnson's papers was found a "translation" of a book he possessed in his library—Sallust's *De bello Catilinario*.[3] These events did not raise Johnson's anger because they were historical; they were able to evoke a spirited retort only because he had heard them mentioned in an atmosphere of illegitimacy. Instead of being included in conversation to make an intelligent historical point or parallel, they were used too often as cheap window dressing for fashionable talk. History was too important to Johnson to allow such liberties freedom from censure.

In addition, far too many readers of the nineteenth and twentieth centuries have taken memorable anecdotes like those of Hester Thrale at face value, without considering the tone of Johnson's voice, of whom or to whom he spoke, or his habit of talking for victory, considerations particularly relevant to many of his observations in Boswell's *Life of Johnson*. Although we can trust that he preferred a broad application of history to contemporary life,[4] that he was annoyed at the mindless repetition of historical details merely to sustain a conversation, that he was well aware of historians' penchant (especially pre-Hume) for cramming into their works unnecessary amounts of information, that he agreed with Hume's contention that the historian must abridge and retain in most cases only "the more material events" (*History*, II, 143), and that he believed there was far more to historical writing than providing accurate data, Johnson actually respected and enjoyed the factual side of history, especially when it served a useful purpose. First of all, one need only recall the many facts included in his historical writings that did not lead to philosophical or moral reflection. In places he freely added particulars to his narrative and analysis, understanding that historical works are all the more interesting when they include information the reader would merely like to *know*, not necessarily *use*. In this light it is noteworthy to remember what he said of Lord Hailes's *Annals of Scotland* (1776, 1779). When he characterized the work as a "Dictionary" containing "mere dry particulars," which seems to support Hester Thrale's assessment above, Johnson was being matter-of-fact: annals are inferior to histories because specifics are by design their focus. But more significant is what he wrote and said to Boswell regarding Hailes's work: "The exactness of his dates raises my wonder. He seems to have the closeness of Henault without his constraint[;] . . . it has such a stability of dates, such a certainty of facts, and such a punctuality of citation. I never before read Scotch history with certainty" (*Letters*, II, 83; *Life*, III, 58, 404). These comments hardly suggest a man who dislikes the factual aspects of history. Painfully aware that many historians and self-professed historical thinkers were widely and at times comically off the mark regarding dates and other particulars, his wonder and enthusiasm were all the more raised by the achievement of Hailes's *Annals*.

To refute further the impression left by Thrale's anecdotes, we should examine Johnson's observations on a major component of historical fact: chronology, which he considered one of the "necessary preparatives and attendants" of history.[5] He once told Hester Thrale, "Do not remit the practice of writing down occurrences as they arise, of whatever kind, and be very punctual in annexing the dates. Chronology you know is the eye of history" (*Letters*, II, 201–202). In his preface to Du Fresnoy's *Chronological Tables* (1762), he wrote that the "necessity of Chronology to a distinct and exact knowledge of history, is too evident to require proof. History is little more than romance to him who has no knowledge of the succession of events, the periods of dominion, and the distance between one great action and another" (Hazen, p. 88). Johnson's appreciation of chronology reflects the belief reaching maturity in England in the seventeenth and eighteenth centuries that an adherence to this factual part of history helped check the urge to distort the truth in order to enhance the author's literary product. During the Renaissance, as Peter Burke points out, history was in many circles thought of "as a branch of rhetoric. Form was sometimes thought of as more important than content; a good style more important than an interest in what had actually happened, or why."[6]

Although, as we shall shortly see, Johnson put significant weight on the historian's style as one key to the success of a historical work, he held that the structure of history—chronology, geography, and the facts—must be strongly and carefully laid before the architect can allow his or her imagination to express itself in the design. Certainly, to place the heavy blocks in their proper position can be an arduous task, and frequently the success of the structure is judged only by the appearance and ingenuity of the exterior design; but Johnson knew the back-breaking work had to be done and done correctly if the entire edifice were to have strength and true value. These thoughts are most eloquently reflected in his preface to *The Preceptor* (1748): "*History* can only be made intelligible by some Knowledge of *Chronology,* the Science by which Events are ranged in their Order, and the Periods of Computation are settled; and which therefore assist the Memory by Method, and enlighten the Judgment, by shewing the Dependence of one Transaction on another. Accordingly it should be diligently inculcated to the Scholar, that unless he fixes in his Mind some Idea of the Time in which each Man of Eminence lived, and each Action was performed, with some Part of the contemporary History of the rest of the World, he will consume his Life in useless reading" (Hazen, pp. 182–183). We must reject forcefully the notion that he despised the factual side of history; Hester Thrale's anecdotes, as memorable and entertaining as they are, have no authority unless they are compared with and conformed to Johnson's own writings.

Johnson's wide reading in history afforded him the opportunity to think seriously about the art and intent of historical writing. Classical writers such as Polybius, Cicero, Dionysius of Halicarnassus, Livy, Tacitus, Lucian of Samosata, Thucydides, and Herodotus raised questions about the utility, truth, literary quality, and educative value of history—topics of continued interest and heated debate in Johnson's century. In the medieval and Renaissance chroniclers and the Renaissance and seventeenth-century historians (for example, Eusebius, Bede, Robert of Gloucester, Scaliger, Polydore Vergil, Machiavelli, Holinshed, Bacon, Paolo Sarpi, Camden, Burnet, Clarendon, and De Thou) Johnson saw what was effective historically, what was tedious or enlightening, what was stylistically pedestrian or daring, what was worthy of analysis or mention, and what theory or philosophy of history and causation was best suited to the student and to the truth of the past. And in the important work of his own century—that of Bolingbroke, Du Fresnoy, Rapin, Charles Rollin, Vico, Montesquieu, Voltaire, Hume, Henault, Robertson, and Gibbon—Johnson had the opportunity, though not always taken, to further his understanding of historiography and to determine his own view of how history should be written.

Regardless of the materials and historical minds available in the eighteenth century, we must not fall prey to the common fallacy that assumes writers merely echo what they have read or what is "common" knowledge. What we know of Johnson's intellectual capacities and independence discredits any notion that he nodded unthinkingly in assent to contemporary theories. If we find him agreeing with many other historical thinkers and the historical authorities of earlier times or his own day, his positions were *his own,* not accepted because they came from an authority but approved of because they met *his* criteria for historical writing. Having made this observation, I wish to stress Johnson's awareness of recent developments in and debates on historiography and his willingness to write and speak on the subject. Apparently flippant, narrow-minded, or negative remarks in Boswell's *Life of Johnson,* Thrale's anecdotes, and even in his own *Rambler* essays largely distort the amount of attention he gave to the art of historical writing. Because history was one of his major intellectual priorities, he would naturally ponder the very issues that concerned the most perceptive historians and historical thinkers of the eighteenth century. And like many of these first-rate scholars and writers, he was able to perceive the importance of and difficulty in composing good history.

Although the study of history advanced at times rapidly toward the day when the *érudit* would eventually triumph over the *philosophe*[7]— when historians would concentrate on showing the times as they really were rather than applying historical lessons to modern society—it did not easily shake free from the traditions of the "exemplary history," as George Nadel deftly terms it. And the tradition had its roots deep in antiquity, for Polybius had long before emphasized the utility of history:

"the surest and indeed the only method of learning how to bear the vicissitudes of fortune is to recall the calamities of others."[8] Dionysius of Halicarnassus, Tacitus, Lucian of Samosata, and Livy also believed that history should teach by example, that it remains immortal only because it is applicable to contemporary times, and, in the case of Tacitus, that one could better learn proper behavior from the examples and experiences of others than from any inner understanding of goodness or morality. Many medieval writers obscured history for "exemplary" reasons, to which hagiography attests, and in the fifteenth and sixteenth centuries the view remained an integral part of historical theory (e.g., that of Machiavelli). Therefore, those holding the same position in the eighteenth century had the staunch support of nearly two thousand years of authority. And they furthermore had the endorsement of some first-rate historical thinkers nearer their own time. In the late seventeenth century, Père Le Moyne, Rapin, and Degory Wheare upheld the arguments of the classical exemplary historians. In the eighteenth century Lenglet du Fresnoy argued that history should teach the reader prudential rules and virtues; Charles Rollin held that history should be studied before other subjects because it offers many lessons of moral conduct; Bolingbroke, in his influential historical essays, reinforced the view that history provides morality and wisdom to mankind; David Hume further noted that history's chief use "is only to discover the constant and universal principles of human nature"; Robertson, in his histories, sought to emphasize the universal and permanent aspects of history; and in his pamphlet on historical composition Peter Whalley wrote that improvement and instruction are the chief ends of history.[9] And, finally, a young Edward Gibbon remarked that to the philosopher events and facts "are the least interesting part of history. It is the knowledge of man, morality and politics he finds there that elevates it in his mind."[10]

These views are reflective of the "humanist" school of historical theory, one to which Johnson subscribed enthusiastically; like other eighteenth-century historical thinkers he was unable or at least unwilling to break the grip of the humanist tradition, even though he saw that it held back the rapid development of a scientific approach to history. As Paul Fussell has written, the eighteenth-century humanist "is pleased to experience a veneration . . . for the past, a feeling accompanied by a deep instinct for the tested and the proven in the history of human experience. This reverence for the past is inseparable from the humanist belief in the historical uniformity of human nature."[11] One does not have to read too far in Johnson to discover an agreement with the humanist credo: "We are all prompted by the same motives, all deceived by the same fallacies, all animated by hope, obstructed by danger, entangled by desire, and seduced by pleasure" (*Rambler* 60, III, 320). Like the eighteenth-century historians in the humanist camp, Johnson believed history should discover the constant and universal in human nature and that it should be used as an educative tool. An examination of the periodical essays and the *Vanity of Human Wishes* reveals him employing history as a teaching device; again, as he wrote in *Adventurer* 95, the moralist may enforce his doctrine and deliver and illustrate his sentiments "by historical examples" (p. 426). His frequent use of such wording as "history will inform us" and "Every page of history . . . will furnish us"[12] testifies to his position that history is not only significant as an intellectual study but also important to human beings in the shaping of their own lives and conduct: "Let us be warned," he writes in Sermon 23, by the "calamities of past ages."[13] And in his pamphlet on the Falkland Islands he asserts that "the history of mankind does not want examples that may teach caution to the daring, and moderation to the proud" (*Political Writings,* p. 372). Once more we find Johnson and Hume in general agreement, for as Hume pointed out in his early effort, "Of the Study of History" (1741), historians and histories have been "the true friends of virtue."

Because he tied history closely to morality, Johnson charged historians with the responsibility of censuring the disreputable and destructive acts of historical figures (*Rambler* 79, IV, 54). He was much less concerned with moral transgressions in the private lives of historical figures. Gibbon would argue similarly over twenty years later in the *Decline and Fall* that history, "which undertakes to record the transactions of the past, for the instruction of future ages," cannot "plead the cause of tyrants" or "justify the maxims of persecution."[14] We should therefore not misconstrue such statements as the "general and rapid narratives of history . . . afford few lessons applicable to private life" and historical examples are too often "employed for shew than use, and rather diversify conversation than regulate life"[15] as evidence of Johnson's disregard for history. He is actually saying that many of the histories he had read and examined by and during the 1750s (those "general and rapid narratives" of which there were far too many) simply provided details of battles and reigns and therefore glossed over their subjects in a manner that precluded the kind of analysis and moral stress he found so appealing and necessary to good history. (His second comment is moreover an obvious reflection on the use of historical references to decorate fashionable talk.) True historians must select carefully from the mass of information available those details necessary to an accurate account, but they must also emphasize the significance of that account to the reader. As a test of a good historical work Johnson as humanist historian would ask, "Is all of this information necessary?"; "How effectively does this information apply to contemporary life?"; and "What might a reader learn from this account other than names, places, and dates?" As William Keast observes, Johnson's "repeated expressions of impatience with history as usually written reflect his deep conviction of its potential value."[16] Johnson disdained the wasted efforts of those historians who, because of their infatuation with detail or their political prejudice, could not see to the very heart of moral and educative history.

The exemplary theory of history, so roundly assailed in the nineteenth century for obstructing an appreciation of the uniqueness of any given historical period, stood squarely in the way of the emerging scientific approach to history, which held that historians should tell things as they were rather than concern themselves with philosophical and moral emphasis (i.e., Ranke's "Wie es eigentlich gewesen"). As R. N. Stromberg pointed out, most of the humanist historians saw rational man in a static society, not historic man in a moving society.[17] But in Johnson's day there could be no doubt that historiography was in a period of transition, in which the historians were pulled in two directions: by tradition and by an increasing acceptance of a more scientific emphasis. Evidence of the slow but steady transition would be the rise in the eighteenth century of the "Rationalist" or "Enlightenment" school of historiography.[18]

Even though Voltaire, Hume, Robertson, and Gibbon held differing views on historical theory, there was enough uniformity in their methods and interests to enable us to generalize about the school of Rationalist historiography[19] and compare its conception of history to that of Johnson. The Rationalists encouraged the idea that the scope of history should be broadened widely beyond the bounds of the military, political, and religious realms to encompass social history, the history of trade, law, institutions, literature, families, music, taste, travel, customs, exploration, colonization, ideas, and the histories of lands far removed from Britain. Important historical minds of the later eighteenth century, most notably Scots such as Adam Smith, Lord Kames, Adam Fergusson, Lord Monboddo, James Barry, John Brown, and Gilbert Stuart, examined and illuminated less-publicized areas of history, especially law, manners, trade, institutions, and language. They began to see more clearly the often complex interdependence of the individual and society. Robertson's *History of America* expanded considerably his readers' historical scope, as did Gibbon with his commentary on migration and geography in the *Decline and Fall*. And through his discussion of manners and commerce in the *History of England* (*Great Britain*) and his essays "Of Commerce," "Of the Balance of Trade," "Of the Balance of Power," and "Of the Populousness of Antient Nations" (1752), Hume served notice that the days of the insular historian were surely numbered.

Giving Voltaire credit for influencing the broader application of historical inquiry, Hugh Blair noted that the historian should examine "laws, customs, commerce, religion, literature, and every other thing that tends to show the spirit and genius of nations. It is now [ca. 1783] understood to be the business of an able Historian to exhibit manners, as well as facts and events; and assuredly, whatever displays the state and life of mankind, in different periods, and illustrates the progress of the human mind, is more useful and interesting than the detail of sieges and battles."[20] With all of this Johnson was in enthusiastic agreement many years before 1783.[21] As we have seen throughout chapters four and five Johnson was fascinated by the various shades of history: the structures and societies of an earlier Scotland, the history of exploration, migration, and colonization in the New World, and the history of the law. The portion of the law lectures that McAdam believes Johnson wrote for Chambers suggests a growing appreciation for the development of laws in environments of violence and social instability, and, as Hawkins informs us, Johnson expressed a "profound reverence" for the English constitution: "He understood it well, and had noted in his mind the changes it had at various periods undergone" (p. 224). Johnson therefore shared the belief of Bolingbroke, Hume, and Robertson that enlightened historians had a responsibility to examine the development of political systems and the laws that affected them.

The *Introduction to the Political State of Great Britain* is in large part an investigation of how trade affected foreign and domestic policy, and the *Life of Ascham,* the preface to *Shakespeare,* and his plan to write a history of the revival of learning in Europe demonstrate his belief in the significance of what people thought—their wisdom, superstitions, and perceptions of morality and legality. In this area Johnson was in accord with the most advanced historical theorists of his day, including Giambattista Vico (1668 to 1744), who stressed cohesion of thought, language, and economics as the crucial areas of historical exploration.[22] Once more we should recall Johnson's words in *Rasselas* that "no part of history" is "so generally useful as that which relates the progress of the human mind" (p. 118). He furthermore seconded Lord Monboddo's position that the "history of manners is the most valuable," lightly passing off Boswell's argument that one found manners "in the course of general history": "Yes; but then you must take all the facts to get this, and it is but a little you get" (*Tour*, p. 55). And while considering in 1778 Robert Henry's *History of Great Britain*, he remarked, "I am told it is carried on in separate divisions, as the civil, the military, the religious history; I wish much to have one branch well done, and that is the history of manners" (*Life*, III, 333). As much as he was interested in the military, political, and religious branches of history, Johnson was too advanced in his historical thinking to believe that the total picture could be gleaned from investigating only those parts of the whole. And his trip to Scotland vividly informs us of the importance he placed on all aspects of a people's culture as a way to understand a nation's rich heritage. Not restricted by his humanistic-historical assumptions, Johnson would take the magnifying glass of the scientist and search diligently for the particles of history—the unglamorous and often ignored data of "common life"—that, when pieced together, gave him a far more accurate depiction of the past than the more impressive accounts of famous battles and reigns. In this area, Johnson's own work pointed in the direction toward which the best historical minds wanted the study of history to go.

From classical times, historians have made a special plea for accuracy in historical narration. Thucydides, Polybius, and Cicero advocated an adherence to truth, and in the second century A.D. Lucian of Samosata, in his "How to Write History," stated that the "historian's sole task is to tell the tale as it happened."[23] Even though the modern student may assume that this basic tenet was quickly and universally inculcated, the most influential eighteenth-century historical thinkers knew it had not been and therefore reminded historians of this classical precept, much like a parent giving seemingly common-sense advice that the child, for some reason, rarely follows or completely understands. In the introduction to his *Histoire d'Angleterre* (2nd edition, 1727), Paul de Rapin Thoyras stressed that historians should have no biases; they must above all else speak the truth. In 1746 Peter Whalley wrote in his *Essay on the Manner of Writing History* that the historian must have a "religious Regard to Truth": "To be *exact, honest,* and *impartial,*" he emphasized, "is what we have a Right to demand in an *Historian*."[24] Likewise, David Hume argued that the "first Quality of an Historian is to be true and impartial."[25] And as emphatic on this point as any of the historians, classical or modern, was Samuel Johnson: the "first law of History," he wrote in 1758, is the "Obligation to tell Truth."[26]

Johnson's passion about the pursuit of truth is conspicuous throughout Boswell's *Life*,[27] but is perhaps best summarized by Thomas Percy's statement that no man had a "more scrupulous regard for truth; from which . . . he would not have deviated to save his life" (*Misc*, II, 218). Accordingly, Johnson was quick to criticize those historians who distorted the truth, either knowingly or unconsciously, for whatever reason. For example, in his *Life of Frederick of Prussia* (1756), he takes Voltaire to task for the seemingly venial sin of asserting that voluntary subscriptions from English ladies, rather than Parliament, were solicited for the benefit of Maria Theresa's war efforts: "It is the great failing of a strong imagination to catch greedily at wonders. He was misinformed, and was, perhaps, unwilling to learn, by a second inquiry, a truth less splendid and amusing" (*Works*, XV, 27). Because he knew that even the slightest untruth in a historical account may perpetuate the error into posterity and that even a minor deviation from the facts might affect greatly the manner in which a nation, society, or individual is viewed, Johnson felt a strong obligation to point out and correct if possible whatever falsehood he found. Regarding the Renaissance Scot historian Hector Boece (Boethius), Johnson could applaud his place in literary history and the style of the *Scotorum historia* (1527), but he nevertheless had to place blame on the work's "fabulousness and credulity" (*Journey*, pp. 14–15, 30–31). And in 1773 he severely questioned Gilbert Burnet's historical veracity as it appeared in the *History of His Own Times* (1724–1734): "I do not believe that Burnet intentionally lyed; but he was so much prejudiced, that he took no pains to find out the truth. He was like a man who resolves to regulate his time by a certain watch; but will not inquire whether the watch is right or not" (*Life*, II, 213).[28] He laments, therefore, that there are no adequate punishments for those who deceive, because "no crime" is "more infamous than the violation of truth" (*Idler* 20, p. 62).

In his desire to prevent others from accepting unsupported assertions from disreputable or careless historians, Johnson advocated active skepticism in historical inquiry. In the review of the *Account of the Conduct of the Duchess of Marlborough* (1742), and thus early in his career, he argues energetically for historical verity by encouraging distrust as a "necessary qualification" of the student of history: "Distrust quickens his discernment of different degrees of probability, animates his search after evidence, and, perhaps, heightens his pleasure at the discovery of truth; for truth, though not always obvious, is generally discoverable, nor is it any where more likely to be found than in private memoirs, which are generally published at a time when any gross falsehood may be detected by living witnesses" (*Works*, XIII, 165). Part of the problem in Johnson's mind was that too many historians, from classical days to the present, willingly colored the facts with their own prejudices, analyses, and laudatory intentions.

For many eighteenth-century historians, the search for historical truth was severely hampered by the unreliability of existing histories and other accounts. At times the historian was faced with two assessments of an event or personality so extreme and diametrically opposed that he could only hope to ascertain the truth by taking a middle position, as Gibbon was often forced to do. Hume too applied a "common-sense" approach to contradictory or sketchy evidence by distrusting most generalized narratives and then filling in the blanks or foggy spaces with assumptions about what might have actually happened based on the principles and workings, as he saw them, of human nature. But more than this, Hume was the heir of seventeenth-century historical skepticism and its radical branch of Pyrrhonism, and it is important to understand the effect of this intellectual tradition, which Isaac Kramnick considers "at the heart of the Enlightenment's attitude to history," on historians such as Bolingbroke and Hume to understand better Johnson's call for skepticism as the "necessary qualification" of the student of history.[29]

Doubt about the validity and value of historical data, theory, and interpretation has loomed like an ominous cloud from classical times, but with the heated debate over the historical accuracy of the Bible the climate turned hostile to many who sought the truth in historical accounts. In France, the home of seventeenth-century skepticism and Pyrrhonism, Le Vayer and Saint-Evremond dismissed written history as untrustworthy and reflective merely of distorted interpretations by partisan advocates. Studying and writing about history, then, resulted in the furthering of myth, falsehood, and propaganda. The climax of seventeenth-century Pyrrhonism was reached in the work of Pierre Bayle, who in his *Historical and Critical Dictionary* (a favorite reading of the *philosophes*) refused to accept not only the accuracy of all kinds of history but also the remotest possibility that man, with his limited vision, could ever hope to discover the truth about the past. All historical writing, past, present, or future, Bayle argued, was an elaborate exercise in futility. Those unwilling to accept Bayle's intemperate negativism, however, sought in the late seventeenth and early eighteenth centuries a form of compromise that would allow for rules of evidence and at least for some truth in earlier sources. But undoubtedly the effects of the French skeptics and especially Bayle were not easily shaken by the more advanced historical thinkers of the eighteenth century. Bolingbroke, most notably before Hume, brought from his historical studies in France a vigorous skepticism as evidenced in sections of his *Letters on the Study and Use of History*.

In David Hume's skepticism, though, there is a brilliant radiance bursting through the dark clouds of doubt. Although he believed that complete certainty was far beyond the grasp of any historian and that so much of written history deserved censure if not neglect, he did not throw up his hands in disgust or despair (or with glee, it appears, as did some of the French exponents of Pyrrhonism), but rather he rolled up his sleeves and set to work at applying his skepticism to a historical method. Hume believed that historians must put written evidence and oral testimony through a rigorous examination regarding their authenticity and reliability and the bias, self-interest, and reputation of the author or eyewitness. In short, historians must look harshly with the skeptic's eye at all historical records. Even so, as Hume, Gibbon, and others knew, conclusions about evidence and the nature of historical truth ultimately depended on the experience, fairness, and common sense of the historians themselves. Hume's skepticism was therefore a healthy expression because it led him closer to the truth and toward a more scientific approach to the study of history.

Johnson's skepticism was also of the healthy, not the debilitating, variety. For instance, he could write that "it is impossible to read the different accounts of any great event, without a wish that truth had more power over partiality" and still have confidence that a historian like Clarendon could write a work "agreeable to the admirers of elegance and the lovers of truth": "many doubtful facts may now be ascertained, and many questions, after long debate, may be determined by decisive authority" (*Idler* 20, p. 62; 65, p. 201). On the one hand, Johnson believed some degree of historical truth was attainable, while on the other he was convinced that earlier and some contemporary histories were filled with errors of fact and, more seriously, errors of judgment and deliberate distortion. This conviction may have compelled him to warn young students against relying too heavily on "modern historians" who he suspects "often deceive themselves and their readers."[30] Johnson's strict regard for the truth and his historical skepticism must be recalled when reading such statements as "We must consider how very little history there is; I mean real authentick history. That certain Kings reigned, and certain battles were fought, we can depend upon as true; but all the colouring, all the philosophy, of history is conjecture" (*Life,* II, 365–366). Even granting that he might have been trying to upset Edward Gibbon, who was present in his company, Johnson was not slighting history as a subject of study in this remark, as one might assume; rather he was asserting an unfortunate fact: it is difficult to distinguish the truth in many histories because there seem to have been very few reliable eyewitness accounts to corroborate or deny what the authors wrote, and because this is so, all but demonstrable facts about historical figures and events must be read with suspicion, if not discounted entirely.

Johnson's desire to have "gross" historical falsehoods detected and amended lies at the heart of his perception of good history. Therefore, like Polybius, Johnson looked with more favor on those historians who were contemporaries of the events they described: "We may know historical facts to be true, as we may know facts in common life to be true. Motives are generally unknown. We cannot trust to the characters we find in history, unless when they are drawn by those who knew the persons; as those, for instance, by Sallust and Lord Clarendon" (*Life,* II, 79). Even though he questioned the veracity of Gilbert Burnet, he found the first part of his history "quite dramatic," for in this section the author seemed to be "actually engaged in what he narrated" (*Tour,* p. 253). The penetrating and dauntless skepticism that marked his own character would, Johnson presumed, serve the student of history better than a scholar's knowledge of the facts or a gifted writer's talents for prose style. Without a distrust of earlier historical writers, justifiable or not, the modern historian serves little purpose other than that of a sleeping sentry by which falsehood creeps stealthily forward into posterity. Again, Johnson would have found as an elegant spokesman Lucian of Samosata, who wrote that the historian should be "fearless, incorruptible, free, a friend of free expression and the truth."[31]

As I have noted, Johnson did not go as far as some of the French skeptics of the seventeenth and eighteenth centuries, who characterized history as a litany of misinformation or a mere fabrication by interested parties, because he believed that the truth *could* be found; but he nevertheless shared with Bolingbroke, most notably among others, a tension in his view of history. Whereas he articulated on occasion one of the skeptics' main positions, that the interpretive aspects of history are generally useless because one could not know for sure what the true motives and personalities were, as we have seen in his own writings he never balked at attempting just that—to analyze, conclude, and then inform.

Johnson was therefore much like Bolingbroke, who in his attempt to reconcile the humanist and Enlightenment traditions wrote in the *Letters* that students must reject the negativism of Bayle and make the best of the situation by choosing from among the historical sources those they believed best approached the truth—as Johnson so chose Clarendon. Histories cannot be rejected outright; they must rather be carefully selected. And Gibbon, who had himself come to abandon the Pyrrhonism of Bayle, could not have agreed more.[32] Certainly one entered dangerous territory in historical inquiry, best approached with a guide who lived and wrote at the time studied, but in his search for historical truth Johnson never feared making the journey reinforced at times with the authority of eyewitnesses, equipped at others with only his own knowledge and historical perspective nourished by his healthy skepticism. His advocacy of truth as the "first law of History," a position he began articulating in the early 1740s, united him philosophically with the best historical writers and theorists—Bolingbroke, Gibbon, and Hume.

The reader will recall how encountering some of Johnson's comments on history outside their philosophical contexts has contributed significantly to the view that he thought little of history. Few observations, for instance, seem to speak less of history's value than the following: "If we view past ages in the reflection of history, what do they offer to our meditation but crimes and calamities?"; "What are all the records of history, but narratives of successive villanies, of treasons and usurpations, massacres and wars?"; and "The history of mankind is little else than a narrative of designs which have failed, and hopes that have been disappointed" (*Adventurer* 120, p. 467; *Rambler* 175, V, 160; Sermon 12, *Sermons*, p. 130). Lest one believe these are the reflections of a hostile or simple-minded approach to history, we should recall that much later Gibbon made the same claim: history, he noted in the third chapter of the *Decline and Fall,* is "little more than the register of the crimes, follies, and misfortunes of mankind." And both Johnson and Gibbon lagged behind Pierre Bayle, who in his *Historical and Critical Dictionary* also characterized history as a catalog of the misfortunes and sufferings of mankind.

That Johnson and Gibbon could echo the sentiments of Bayle suggests the kind of effect seventeenth-century skepticism had on the best historical minds of the eighteenth century. But in Johnson's case, these periodic expressions of frustration at the apparent futility of history—and the above remark in the company of Gibbon is but another example—did not dominate his historical perspective to the point that he relegated history, as did the Pyrrhonists, to the realms of myth, fiction, or deliberate fraud. As another example, we may take Johnson's statement, discussed earlier, to the effect that the "general and rapid narratives of history . . . afford few lessons applicable to private life" and compare it with Gibbon's admission that the "experience of past faults, which may sometimes correct the mature age of an individual, is seldom profitable to the successive generations of mankind" (*Decline and Fall*, chapter 41). In both instances the observation seems to run contrary to the humanistic historian's basic philosophy, but while each reflects the legacy of seventeenth-century skepticism both Johnson and Gibbon shook off such pessimistic pronouncements and went ahead to speak enthusiastically and eloquently of the moral and educative values of history. Johnson was able to keep his strong skepticism in check, and, instead of succumbing to the beast, he tamed it and used its power to his own advantage in his search for the truth about the past.

Even though history was evolving from a branch of belles lettres into a form of science, many eighteenth-century historians had what we would now consider unhistorical outlooks and approaches to their tasks. A good number were never really comfortable about performing detailed research. Even Hume and Gibbon have been criticized for a lack of rigid scholarship.[33] Conjecture and primary reliance on earlier histories were acceptable substitutes, but as the century progressed, more and more historians came to accept research as the sine qua non of the historical process. Several voices, however, spoke out early and strongly for thorough research, at least so far as they understood the term. Peter Whalley, for one, argued that the first "Requisite" for the writer of history is a "perfect *Knowledge* of his *Subject*" (p. 12). And Samuel Johnson was in strong agreement. During his 1773 tour through Scotland he observed "it was but of late that historians bestowed pains and attention in consulting records, to attain accuracy." He mentioned that in writing his *History of Henry VII* Francis Bacon seemed not to have consulted any records but rather took "what he found in other histories, with what he learnt by tradition" (*Tour,* p. 181), an assessment upheld by modern historians.[34]

Whereas he felt as many eighteenth-century historians who had "a horror of pedantry,"[35] Johnson nevertheless saw the need of consulting manuscripts, records, memoirs, and diaries in order to ascertain historical truth. Examining published histories was simply not enough, especially because they were often filled with erroneous facts and conclusions. That is, although he could note in the *Life of Frederick of Prussia* that "Nothing is more tedious than publick records, when they relate to affairs which, by distance of time or place, lose their power to interest the reader" (*Works,* XV, 42), Johnson could also stress that a knowledge of pamphlets and small tracts is of much significance to the study of history, "because many Advantages may be expected from the Perusal of these small Productions, which are scarcely to be found in that of larger Works" (*Introduction to the Harleian Miscellany,* Hazen, p. 55). He was clearly able to distinguish between important historical evidence and historical memorabilia that bear little or no significance to larger historical questions. His appreciation and advocacy of the smaller though more crucial tools at the historian's disposal suggest that in this matter his eyes were turned away from the humanist tradition of historiography and toward the emerging scientific response to history.

Considering the nature of historical evidence, Johnson, evincing a healthy skepticism, reminds historians of his and future days that "He who describes what he never saw, draws from fancy." Historians, he says elsewhere, should not give characters unless they knew their subjects personally *or* "cop[y] from those who knew them" (*Life,* II, 237; III, 404). And in Scotland he observed that Sir John Dalrymple's unsubstantiated assertions as to what people "thought and talked a hundred years ago" are not to be trusted. "All history," he added, "so far as it is not supported by contemporary evidence, is romance" (*Tour,* p. 392). Johnson certainly did not believe that eighteenth-century authors writing about Elizabeth's reign were merely composing romance but rather that these historians must consult and then evaluate vigorously contemporary records of all kinds and the accounts of those who lived during the period, or else their work, no matter how effectively narrated or informed with analysis, may likely be on the whole or in part imaginative fiction. Voltaire would thus serve as Johnson's model to those historians writing of events nearer their own time, for the Frenchman interviewed and corresponded with actual participants in the events described in the *History of Charles XII.* Johnson's advice on these matters is indeed basic and sound and again reflective of his century's advances in historiography, but we tend to lose sight of its wisdom while searching in the above comments for evidence that he disliked history.

We should recall that he said basically the same thing about biography: "nobody can write the life of a man, but those who have eat and drunk and lived in social intercourse with him" (*Life,* II, 166, 446). Few would assume from this observation that Johnson felt his own biographies valueless; on the contrary he believed quite correctly that his *Life of Savage* was superior to his other lives because he had "eat and drunk and lived in social intercourse" with the subject. In the other biographies he made up for a lack of personal knowledge by seeking the contemporary evidence available to him. We now can see more easily the wisdom of Arthur Murphy's assertion that "no man better understood the nature of historical evidence than Dr. Johnson" (*Misc*, I, 479). Considering the imperfect research methods of most eighteenth-century historians, many of whom relied exclusively on earlier and larger accounts or drew only from sources that supported their own partisan view of the past, we should place considerable value on Murphy's assessment and give Johnson high marks, even by modern standards, for his appreciation and support of historical scholarship.

Eighteenth-century Rationalist historians were not the first to show a genuine interest in causation: Polybius, for instance, considered part of the pragmatic function of history to be an understanding of the causes of an event as the first step toward applying a lesson to modern times. This point was refined by Hume, who saw a knowledge of causation not only as the most "satisfactory" but also as the "most instructive" of all historical knowledge because by it one may "control events, and govern futurity." More advanced historical thinkers of the eighteenth century dismissed the time-honored explanations ("God's will" or "divine punishment") as insufficient responses to important historical questions, although many others still held to this "providential" notion. Historians advanced both popular and novel explanations for historical events and the actions of individuals. These would include the influence of catastrophic rather than evolutionary forces; the temper or "spirit" of the times (as Robertson frequently noted); climate and geographical locale; religious, governmental, or military successes and failures; and the calculated decisions and personalities of leaders, or the "great man" theory of causation of which Gibbon at times seemed so fond and which Adam Smith thought so insignificant. Even so, theories of causation were in general contradictory and complex.[36] The philosophical historians were compelled to avoid concentrating on the specific causes for an event and to emphasize instead the general explanations more useful for their purposes. Other historians, such as Gibbon, emphasized one or two major causes as a way of reinforcing the general theme that ran throughout their works. In light of these attitudes, Johnson's comments on the matter are noteworthy, for he certainly was aware of his century's concern with historical causation.

Johnson assumed that almost all the explanations provided above could apply to historical occurrences and that historians should set a priority to a list of relevant causes. But he refused to believe that only one or two determining factors could unlock the secrets of history. He was too historically sophisticated to ignore the less glamorous forces influencing the course of events. Regarding the "great man" theory, for example, Johnson knew that important individuals, whereas they may have had considerable effect on the course of history, were products of their times, shaped and encouraged by the unique social and political dynamics of the day. He would have agreed with Gibbon, then, who noted that "the times must be suited to extraordinary characters" (*Decline and Fall,* chapter 70). Although, as he wrote in the preface to *The Preceptor,* "It is not easy to live without enquiring by what Means every thing was brought into the State in which we now behold it," Johnson, for all his interest in causation, believed as did Lord Kames that historians often wasted their time and misled the reader in their quest for a neatly packaged cause for every historical event.

His most effective statement on the matter of causation is found in his pamphlet on the Falkland Islands:

> It seems to be almost the universal error of historians to suppose it politically, as it is physically true, that every effect has a proportionate cause. In the inanimate action of matter upon matter, the motion produced can be but equal to the force of the moving power; but the operations of life, whether private or publick, admit no such laws. The caprices of voluntary agents laugh at calculation. It is not always that there is a strong reason for a great event. Obstinacy and flexibility, malignity and kindness, give place alternately to each other, and the reason of these vicissitudes, however important may be the consequences, often escapes the mind in which the change is made. (*Political Writings,* pp. 365–366)

Thirteen years earlier he poked fun at Tom Tempest, the Stuart loyalist, for believing "that nothing ill has ever happened for these forty years by chance or error," and wrote more seriously the next week that "Forms of government are seldom the result of much deliberation, they are framed by chance in popular assemblies, or in conquered countries by despotick authority" (*Idler* 10, p. 34; 11, p. 37).

These observations indicate that, like Voltaire, Johnson thought chance never received the attention it deserved when historical causation was debated. By "chance" he meant more than the capricious winds that have blown gentle breezes and violent gales throughout time; he also defined it as the complex interaction among multiple causes, which blend so agreeably that their individual parts are impossible to discern. Like Hume, Johnson saw history in general as the result of a slow and painful growth, not the deliberate creation of one or two superior minds or military leaders. He certainly shared with Hume and Robertson an appreciation of those great moments in time, when profound change was set in motion, and those memorable figures who were significant in effecting such change, but to Johnson history was too complicated a subject to be explained by a facile reference to some popularly held system of analysis; he saw, as did Gibbon, that it was far too complex and monumental a study, which at times laughs in the face of those trying to understand it. Johnson emphasized that even the most perceptive minds could not provide capsulized explanations for historical occurrences to be easily digested by the student and reader. He knew that these capsules could at best act as temporary palliatives but at worst fool the patient into believing in misconceptions and falsehoods about the nature of the past. The healthy historical mind had to reject any notion of simplified cause—which as a result must leave one disillusioned as to the proclivity of one's historical understanding—and accept the prognosis that history will always be a humbling study not always lending itself to easy analysis. Young students should therefore be wary of having too much confidence in those historians who "deceive themselves and their readers when they attempt to explain by reason that which happened by chance."[37]

The development of history as a science naturally cast doubt about its status as an art. Reflective of the transitional period of British historiography and the historian's dilemma is Hayden White's contention that the eighteenth century saw the *study* of history as scientific, the *writing* of history as rhetorical.[38] Regardless, the debate over the nature of historical composition was well under way by mid century, with men like Hume, Adam Smith, Hugh Blair, Lord Kames, and James Moor forging a strong link between history and poetry.[39] Whereas the Rationalists sought to bring literary artistry to historical composition, they refused to employ the affected Latin rhetoric characteristic of many Renaissance historians; nor were they willing to sacrifice content or veracity for a more elaborate style, again as many of their forerunners had done. But they most assuredly thought historians should show clarity and some excitement and avoid tedious digressions and dry formality in their work.

Johnson's views on the issue once more demonstrate his awareness of recent developments in historical debate. From at least his mid twenties on he held that one of the first requirements of good historical writing was effective style. In a 1737 letter to Edward Cave he mentioned that the style of Nathaniel Brent's 1620 English translation of Sarpi's *History of the Council of Trent* was "capable of great Improvements" (*Letters,* I, 8). Five years later, when he reviewed the memoirs of Sarah Churchill, he remarked that the historian "may trace the progress of great transactions, and discover the secret causes of important events. And, to mention one use more, the polite writer may learn an unaffected dignity of style, and an artful simplicity of narration" (*Works, XIII,* 165). In the review of Blackwell's *Memoirs of the Court of Augustus* (1756), Johnson levelled his heaviest blows against the author's style, not his veracity or selection of facts: "His great delight is to show his universal acquaintance with terms of art, with words that every other polite writer has avoided and de-spised" (*Works, XIII,* 175). Later he criticized Gilbert Burnet's style as "mere chit-chat" and found Clarendon, whom he highly respected, guilty of employing a manner of writing he characterized as "the effusion of a mind crouded with ideas, and desirous of imparting them" (*Life,* II, 213; *Rambler* 122, IV, 289).

The significance Johnson placed on *how* a history was written explains best his unqualified praise of Richard Knolles, author of the *General History of the Turks* (1603). Knolles, he concluded, wrote in a clear style and avoided tedious minuteness in his descriptions and over-elaboration in his digressions (*Rambler* 122, IV, 290). And we should not forget his sincere tribute to Lord Hailes's *Annals of Scotland:* "The narrative is clear, lively, and short. . . . It is in our language, I think, a new mode of history, which tells . . . all that is known, without laboured splendour of language, or affected subtilty of conjecture" (*Letters,* I, 409; II, 83). John-son thus agreed with some of the best historical thinkers of his day, who argued profusely and eloquently that it is the historian's duty to write effectively, concisely, but at times dramatically and imaginatively.

But did he agree with James Moor's position that the "proper Art, and method, of Composition, in which a good Historian must excel, re-quires, perhaps, not much less genius and skill, to execute in perfection, than that of any other kind of writing; without excepting Poetry itself"?[40] In *Rambler* 122, his essay on the state of English historiography, Johnson observes that of "the various kinds of speaking or writing, which serve necessity, or promote pleasure, none appears so artless or easy as simple narration. . . . It is natural to believe, upon the same principle, that no writer has a more easy task than the historian" (IV, 287–288). And "Great abilities," he said in July 1763, "are not requisite for an Historian; for in historical composition, all the greatest powers of the human mind are quiescent. He has the facts ready to his hand; so there is no exercise of invention. Imagination is not required in any high degree" (*Life*, I, 424).

Based on these comments, one could easily assume Johnson discredited history as a dull, unimaginative form of writing. But we need to keep in mind that in *Rambler* 122 he was referring to *simple* narration of the kind he had read prior to 1751, and *compared* to the labors of the philosopher and poet the historian *appears* to have the easiest task, for "his materials are provided and put into his hands, and he is at leisure to employ all his powers in arranging and displaying them" (p. 288). And yet, he continues, few have performed this seemingly simple labor with any distinction. Many, like Raleigh, have chosen to "select facts, rather than adorn them" and have "produced an historical dissertation, but seldom risen to the majesty of history" (p. 289). Johnson's choice of words—the "majesty of history"—is testimony to the fact that he did not see the writing of *good* history as artless or easy; to him, the goal of every historian was to elevate his materials, through an effective style, beyond the mere compilation of facts or pedestrian narration. His own historical efforts reveal his theory in practice, for he never allowed his recounting of facts to inhibit his style, which was in various instances vigorous, judicious, interesting, and dramatic.

As for the 1763 assertion that the historian needs comparatively little invention or imagination, Johnson's view may not square with James Moor's or the modern historian's, but it was probably shaped not only by his belief that the historian was to adorn rather than create but also by his strict regard for accuracy and truth in history: too much concentration on the "literary" or rhetorical aspects, he realized, might turn history into "romance." Although the mid and late eighteenth-century historians despised pedantic cataloging of facts, they also disdained idle story telling or dramatic leeway with these facts. Johnson was quite clear in his assessment that poor historical writing is marked by a "mediocrity of stile" and an inability to "confine" the mind "to that even tenour of imagination, which narrative requires" (*Rambler* 122, IV, 289). Even so, he knew the historian's duty was to "decorate known facts by new beauties of method or of style" (*Idler* 94, p. 291). As he noted in his review of Blackwell, the historian should not be censured for writing on a familiar subject, even if the work adds factually little or nothing new to its predecessors, because "the same ideas may be delivered more intelligibly or more delightfully by one than by another, or with attractions that may lure minds of a different form" (*Works*, XIII, 170–171).

Although he could not subscribe without qualification to Gibbon's view that, given the impossibility of discovering absolute truths, historians in effect only create and interpret history,[41] as the following remark from the "Life of Milton" indicates, Johnson eventually came to the conclusion that historians might allow themselves a little more imagination in the presentation of their materials than he might have thought in the 1750s and early 1760s: historians are to "improve and exalt" their material by a "nobler art," animate it by "dramatick energy," diversify it "by retrospection and anticipation" (*Poets*, I, 170). As long as historians did not distort the truth, they were free to use their literary artistry and "dramatick energy" to make a readable and memorable history. Johnson may not have agreed totally with James Moor's position, for he held that the profound genius required to write *Hamlet* was inappropriate for history, but he did embrace the view that the scientific and literary aspects of history could and should blend harmoniously.

Samuel Johnson was well aware of contemporary developments in historical theory and he by and large agreed with the basic tenets espoused by the leading historical thinkers of his day, especially Hume. We see, then, that the anecdotes and selected quotations in Hester Thrale's anecdotes and Boswell's *Life of Johnson* greatly distort his appreciation of history as an emerging science and the art of historical composition. The observations on historical inquiry and composition in the Churchill and Blackwell reviews, published in the widely read *Gentleman's Magazine* and *Literary Magazine,* and those in his periodical papers (the *Rambler, Adventurer,* and *Idler*) and in other miscellaneous prose works (e.g., the preface to *The Preceptor*) reached a significant number of readers, some certainly historians, who would either have seen in Johnson's remarks an important endorsement of their own views on historical truth, causation, and method of composition or have taken from them new and important food for thought. And one of his most influential pieces may have been *Rambler* 122, which appeared on 18 May 1751, at a time when British history had not yet burst forth in all its magnificent colors—the first volume of Hume's *History of Great Britain* was still three years away. In 1751 the potential existed for excellent historical writing, but no one could have then predicted the success of Hume, Robertson, Gibbon, and other mid and late eighteenth-century historians. Johnson's words thus served as a challenge to his contemporaries to fill an embarrassing void: "It is observed, that our nation, which has produced so many authors eminent for almost every other species of literary excellence, has been hitherto remarkably barren of historical genius" (IV, 288–289).

Although perceptive observers like Peter Whalley in 1746 had also noted that few in England had done "Honour to themselves and their Country" with an impressive history, Johnson's reputation as the author of the *Rambler* and the work's respected position in the minds of learned readers gave him the opportunity to reach a far larger audience than others who shared his view. And it is possible Johnson's words triggered Hume's observation to John Clephane on 5 January 1753 that "there is no post of honour in the English Parnassus more vacant than that of History. Style, judgement, impartiality, care—everything is wanting to our historians."[42] (In any event, the remark again shows how similar were Johnson's and Hume's historical minds.) In *Rambler* 122 he encourages a new commitment to historical composition by shaming his countrymen: "if we have failed in history, we can have failed only because history has not hitherto been diligently cultivated." In short, he calls for historical works that will rise to "the majesty of history." Whereas we cannot accurately measure his influence on mid-century historical writing, neither can we assume he had no impact on the growing interest in historiography. We must keep in mind that the large majority of Johnson's historical writings and observations on historical theory were published in the 1740s and 1750s, therefore before Gibbon's and Robertson's histories and at the same time as the first volumes of Hume's *History of Great Britain* and his essays and Bolingbroke's *Letters,* the latter being written between 1735 and 1738 but not published until 1752. At the very least, Johnson marched alongside the eighteenth-century historians as new paths were trod; he cannot be said to have merely followed in their well-worn trail.

We are therefore left to wonder how Johnson's understanding and advocacy of good historical composition have been lost on so many of his readers from the nineteenth century to the present day. One might point first of all, as did Macaulay, to Johnson's impressions of his century's gifted historians. After all, if he so respected historical composition, why did he disparage the best historical writers of the age? Macaulay has no doubt spoken for hundreds over the years when he remarked, although quite erroneously, "historians could, as he conceived, claim no higher dignity than that of almanack-makers; and his favourite historians were those who, like Lord Hailes, aspired to no higher dignity. He always spoke with contempt of Robertson. Hume he would not even read."[43]

Without question, one can collect impressive evidence that seems to support Macaulay's assessment: as we have seen, Johnson had uncomplimentary things to say about the seventeenth-century historians Raleigh, Bacon, and Burnet, and moving to his own period he charged Lord Lyttelton with "the most vulgar Whiggism" in his *History of Henry II,* which he also noted was "elaborated by the searches and deliberations of twenty years, and published with such anxiety as only vanity can dictate" (*Life,* II, 221; *Poets,* III, 453). And one cannot help pitying poor Catharine Macaulay when Johnson "stripped" her to "the very skin": "She is better employed at her toilet," he supposedly bellowed in 1776, "than using her pen. It is better she should be reddening her own cheeks, than blackening other people's characters." When Boswell pointed out that his friend had made Kate Macaulay look foolish, Johnson responded, "That was already done, Sir. To endeavour to make *her* ridiculous, is like blacking the chimney" (*Life,* III, 46; II, 336). When asked if he had read the second volume of her *History of England* (1763–1765), Johnson answered, "No, Sir, . . . nor her first neither" (*Misc,* II, 11–12). Surely, one might argue, he was amiss in his apparent disregard for one of the century's most important historians: her acclaim as a national historian, writes Victor Wexler, "was second only to Hume's in the eighteenth century."[44]

But these comments pale in comparison with his apparent neglect of Gibbon's and Hume's historical work and his frequent criticism of Robertson's. Even though he lived to see three of the six volumes brought out (the first in 1776, the second and third in 1781), Johnson said very little about the monumental *Decline and Fall of the Roman Empire.* Some have wanted to blame Boswell, who appears to have greatly disliked Gibbon, for poisoning Johnson against the historian, as if literary history was somehow cheated because the men were not close friends. There is even speculation that Johnson could never forgive Gibbon for rudely treating his cousin, Phoebe Ford, when she was housekeeper to the historian's step-mother.[45] At best the men only tolerated each other; there appears to have been no warmth or lightheartedness between them.[46] According to John Bailey, the "historian who could not talk was not likely to appreciate the great talker who cared nothing for history"![47] As Boswell informs us, in April 1775 Johnson argued in the company of

Gibbon that there was really very little authentic history being written: "all the colouring," he said, "all the philosophy, of history is conjecture." Gibbon, as Johnson of course knew, was engaged in his historical work, but he did not, as Boswell notes with glee, "step forth in defence of that species of writing. He probably did not like to *trust* himself with JOHNSON!" (*Life*, II, 364–366).

But a simple clash of personalities does not explain Johnson's indifference toward or aversion to the *Decline and Fall*. In March 1776, when Johnson and Boswell were visiting Thomas Warton at Trinity College, Oxford, Gibbon's history was introduced into the conversation. Johnson commented, "However, now that he has published his infidelity, he will probably persist in it" (*Life*, II, 448).[48] In this, the only major reference he made to the great work, which suggests that he was acquainted with at least some of the first volume, Johnson refers more specifically to Gibbon's controversial and skeptical treatment of Christianity. Johnson could not, for example, accept the doctrine that fear lies at the base of religion. Because he sensed the author's hostility toward Christianity, he was unable to appraise objectively one of the masterpieces of the age: as he said a month later, and his words may have been spoken with Gibbon's history in mind, "Every man who attacks my belief, diminishes in some degree my confidence in it, and therefore makes me uneasy" (*Life*, III, 10–11).[49] His insensitivity to the power of the *Decline and Fall,* then, stemmed primarily from his rejection of Gibbon's perceptions of Christianity in the work and secondarily from his dislike of Gibbon the man and thinker; in no fair way can we attribute his attitude to any *antihistorical* prejudice.

In essence, the same can be said of his impression of David Hume. Although he offered his opinion of Hume the man and philosopher whenever it was solicited, Johnson said very little about Hume the historian, which is both unfortunate and ironic considering their general agreement on so many aspects of history and historiography. He mentioned in 1773 that he had not read Hume's *History of England* (*Great Britain*) but noted earlier that the Scot "would never have written History, had not Voltaire written it before him." "He is," Johnson contended, "an echo of Voltaire" (*Life*, II, 53, 236). But as Thomas Campbell related in 1775, Johnson may have indeed read Hume's *History:* "Robertson, he said, used pretty words, but he liked Hume better" (*Misc*, II, 48). In addition, the 1760 review of Tytler's *Historical and Critical Enquiry* includes a section mentioning Hume's argument for the authenticity of the "casket letters" of Mary Queen of Scots, which leads us to believe Johnson knew or read at least one section of Hume's *History*. And as G. B. Hill suggested, Johnson might be borrowing from Hume's *History* in the "Life of Milton" (*Poets*, I, 127).

But if Johnson never read much of Hume's *History* or only skimmed through it, why, then, did he not read it more carefully and praise its historical vision? Certainly, Hume's brief criterion for historical writers has a distinct Johnsonian ring to it: "The first Quality of an Historian is to be true and impartial; the next is to be interesting."[50] The political emphasis of Hume's *History* was undoubtedly more akin to Johnson's own; in fact, Catharine Macaulay's *History of England* was largely undertaken as an answer to Hume's supposed "Tory" history of England. Hume even told Boswell in 1776 that Johnson "should be pleased with my History."[51] But Johnson did not admit to being pleased, and the reason may be attributed to his antipathy toward Hume the man and philosopher. Johnson considered him a "modern infidel," a vain man, a "rogue" and "blockhead," a Tory "by chance," a Hobbist, and a man devoid of all principle.[52] Because of Hume's religious skepticism, which he was adept at publishing, Johnson probably viewed him as a dangerous man and thus refused to quote him as an authority: as Hester Thrale pointed out, Johnson was fearful a quotation might "send People to look in an Author that might taint their Virtue."[53] He might have supposed that to comment on Hume's *History* to any great length or to compliment enthusiastically its style or content would be giving too much credence to Hume as a writer and thinker—something he could not bring himself to do. Johnson was simply unable to separate the work from the man and, in the case of Catharine Macaulay, the work from the woman. He could not stomach, for instance, her insistence on the natural equality of man and the radical sentiments that permeated her works. And who can ever forget her reaction to his suggestion that her footman be invited to sit and dine with them? He "stripped poor Mrs. Macaulay to the very skin" because of her political and social views, not because she was a poor historian. That he placed a copy of her history, perhaps given to him as a present in January 1765 (*DPA*, pp. 84–86), in his library at least offers the possibility that he thought more highly of her historical talents than the famous responses recorded by Boswell suggest.

While Johnson was at work in 1759 on the *Idler* and his edition of Shakespeare, William Robertson brought out his two-volume *History of Scotland*. Enthusiastically received, the work, which takes the reader to 1603, established Robertson's reputation as a historian of the first rank in the minds of Gibbon, Hume, and Horace Walpole, among others. Robertson followed this publication with his three-volume *History of Charles V* in 1769 and his two-volume *History of America* (mainly Spanish America) in 1777. Robertson's efforts did much to elevate historiography as a serious pursuit in the eighteenth century, and even in recent times one commentator has labeled him "an historian's historian."[54] But readers of Boswell's *Life,* especially casual readers, may recall Johnson's ostensible disapproval of Robertson's historical work: "Sir, I love Robertson, and I won't talk of his book" (*Life,* II, 53). In a famous exchange with Boswell on the relative merits of Hume, Goldsmith, and Robertson, Johnson said that he had not read Hume, but Goldsmith's history of Rome was doubtless "better than the *verbiage* of Robertson." When Boswell pressed his friend to admit the superiority of the Scot's "penetration" and "painting," Johnson accused Robertson of writing imaginative romance rather than history and boring the reader with his "cumbrous detail" (*Life,* II, 236–237).[55]

Johnson's remarks necessitate a more careful analysis than most have given them. Initially, his criticism of Robertson's verbosity is consistent with his belief that historical writing suffered from faulty style and "cumbrous detail." And we have seen his dismay at those historians who have taken too much latitude with the facts. Even so, one wonders how much of his criticism was exaggerated for argument's sake. In regard to Giuseppe Baretti's assertion that Robertson's style reminded him of Johnson's, Johnson said, "If Robertson's style be faulty, he owes it to me; that is, having too many words, and those too big ones" (*Life,* III, 173). Concerning the 1773 exchange quoted above, Boswell believed Johnson was merely "talking for victory" rather than expressing "his real and decided opinion" of Robertson (*Life,* II, 238). Boswell is correct in his assessment, for we should remember that he had precipitated the comments by dismissing Johnson's praise of Goldsmith's historical efforts and claiming the superiority of the Scots, Hume and Robertson. Johnson's statement in 1768 that he would not talk of Robertson's book was preceded by Boswell's enthusiastic praise of Scottish literature. Realizing that his friend was assuming his anti-Scots pose, Boswell added that "though he indulged himself in this sally of wit, he had too good taste not to be fully sensible of the merits of that admirable work" (i.e., the *History of Scotland; Life,* II, 53).[56] An evaluation of Johnson's remarks about Robertson in Boswell's *Life* must therefore be tempered by an understanding of the contexts in which they were spoken and supplemented by other evidence within and outside the confines of the biography.

Johnson knew of Robertson's *History of Scotland* at least by 1760, for he mentions in the review of Tytler the historian's arguments for the authenticity of the "casket letters." As the holdings in his library reveal, he came to own a copy of the *History of Scotland* and the *History of America*, parts of which he read to Boswell in April 1778 (*Life*, III, 270). And although there is no record of his having possessed the *History of Charles V* it seems that he helped William Strahan correct Robertson's phraseology when the book was being prepared for press (*Letters*, II, 151). We might also recall what Johnson said in a 1767 letter to William Drummond, in which he advised his correspondent to consult Robertson, "to whom I am a little known. I shall be satisfied about the propriety of whatever he shall direct" (*Letters*, I, 195). Boswell argued that the Drummond letter shows Johnson's true estimation "of the character and abilities of the celebrated Scottish Historian, however lightly, in a moment of caprice, he may have spoken of his works" (*Life*, II, 30). Johnson and Robertson probably met in the summer of 1763, when the historian was in London. (Robertson and Boswell also dined together at this time.) By 1768 there was affection between them, for in that year Johnson asked if "the dog" Robertson talked of him, to which Boswell answered, "Indeed, Sir; he does, and loves you" (*Life*, II, 53). Johnson was moreover greatly pleased to hear that Robertson had "fairly" perused the *Dictionary* "twice over" (Hawkins, p. 142).

In 1773 Robertson wrote Boswell expressing his delight that Johnson would soon be among them in Scotland: "He sometimes cracks his jokes upon us. . . . assure him that I shall be happy to have the satisfaction of seeing him under my roof" (*Tour*, p. 5). His comment suggests again that at least some of Johnson's unflattering opinions of his history might have been in good fun. On 15 August, Robertson arrived at Boswell's lodgings and warmly greeted Johnson; the following day he showed his guest the city of Edinburgh. After Johnson returned from the Western Islands in November, once more warmly greeted by Robertson, the two men discussed a possible history of the 1745 rebellion. Robertson agreed with Johnson's observation that a successful account depended on interviews with those actually involved in the conflict, and he declared it "was now full time to make such a collection" as Johnson suggested (*Tour*, p. 384). The scene titillates the imagination: here was the great Scottish historian acknowledging and embracing Johnson's approach to historical research. Before leaving Scotland, Johnson dined at Robertson's, and Boswell quotes his friend as calling the Scot a "good" and "wise" man (*Tour*, p. 388). And during their conversation in London on

29 April 1778, Robertson seconded Johnson's view that Robert Henry's *History of Great Britain* (1771) should have concentrated more on the "history of manners" (*Life*, III, 333).

On the basis of this evidence one can only wonder at Macaulay's pronouncement that Johnson "always spoke with contempt of Robertson." Even if Johnson actually found the Scot's histories too verbose or imaginative at times, we should not assume that he disapproved of them entirely, especially considering the contexts of the remarks in Boswell's *Life*, for he was a critic who, as his work on Shakespeare demonstrates, could appreciate the overall effect of a work and yet point out its faults. Finally, why has no one presented as evidence Arthur Murphy's recollection that Robertson's *History of Scotland* was the subject of Johnson's "constant praise" (*Misc*, I, 429–430)?

To complete the picture of Johnson and the historians one must recall the compliments as well as the censures. As we have seen, Johnson commended Richard Knolles's "pure, nervous, elevated, and clear" style, but he also regretted that the historian did not employ his talents on English history, for had he done so he would have "secured perpetuity to his name" (*Rambler*, 122, IV, 290). Without doubt, however, Johnson thought more highly of Clarendon than any other seventeenth-century historian. He thoroughly knew the *History of the Rebellion* (posthumously published in three volumes, 1702–1704) and generally agreed with its analysis of the English Civil War. The work was in addition a major source for the lives of Blake, Cowley, Milton, Butler, and especially Waller. Johnson better appreciated Clarendon's historical talents because he knew and understood the period and therefore the viewpoint from which Clarendon approached the events of his time. Johnson would see that, of all the historians he respected, Clarendon was truly a product of history himself.

Although in *Rambler* 122 Johnson criticizes Clarendon's style, he also lauds the historian's "knowledge of nature and of policy; the wisdom of his maxims, the justness of his reasonings, and the variety, distinctness, and strength of his characters" (IV, 289–290). Clarendon, he argued in 1778, is "objected to for his parentheses, his involved clauses, and his want of harmony. But he is supported by his matter. It is, indeed, owing to a plethora of matter that his style is so faulty" (*Life*, III, 257–58). Johnson thought highly enough of Clarendon's work to include many quotations from the *History* in his *Dictionary* and to recommend the work to his friend Daniel Astle (*Life*, IV, 311). He defined Clarendon as a "great historian" and was much pleased when the sequel to the *History*, the *Life of Edward, Earl of Clarendon*, was published in 1759 (*Poets*, I, 266; *Idler*, 65, p. 201).

Regarding the historians of his own century, Johnson read Charles Sheridan's *History of the Late Revolution in Sweden* (1778) "ravenously, as if he devoured it" (a scene that rivals a reluctant Gibbon being "dragged" away by the dinner bell from *his* "intellectual feast," the *Continuation of Eachard's Roman History*)[57] and his appreciation of Thomas Carte's *History of England* (1747–1755) is apparent in his recommending it as well to Daniel Astle as a proper study (*Life*, III, 284; IV, 311). Johnson was also impressed with the historical work of Robert Watson, one of the distinguished professors at St. Andrews. In October 1776, he wrote William Strahan to offer the printer assistance in getting Watson's *History of Philip II* ready for press (*Letters*, II, 151). Even though he disagreed with several of the Scot's contentions, he thought the book "much esteemed" in the literary world and took "great delight" in meeting its author when visiting St. Andrews in 1773 (*Letters*, II, 162; *Tour*, pp. 38–40). He moreover praised Oliver Goldsmith's historical efforts, most notably his *Roman History* of 1769 (another book he recommended to Daniel Astle), which he felt surpassed Florus, Eutropius, and even Vertot in certain places. He told Boswell that whether we take Goldsmith "as a poet,—as a comick writer,—or as an historian, he stands in the first class"; his "plain narrative," he added, "will please again and again" (*Life*, II, 236–237). Although posterity has not agreed with his high assessment of Goldsmith's historical work, Johnson's emphasis on style as a criterion of good history elucidates once again his position that a historical work ought to please as well as instruct the reader.

Macaulay ridiculed Johnson's appreciation of Lord Hailes's *Annals of Scotland*, but, as Godfrey Davies noted, the work has "great merit" and is a "valuable guide" to the history of Scotland and an important foundation for later histories of the country.[58] And following his 1773 journey to Scotland, Johnson would have taken special interest in histories of the land to which he had given much thought. For those sensitive to the power of history there is a need to understand better the significance of the place explored; the works of historians are thus able to educate readers to the fine details they were unable to discover or appreciate when they were attempting to absorb the broader context before their eyes. As much as he had read before traveling north in 1773, Johnson, after returning home, would have looked with more interest at works like Hailes's that dealt with the history of Scotland.

Although apparently the men were together only when Johnson was in Scotland, Hailes had become a favorite of Johnson's in July 1763. At that time Boswell read the following passage from a letter he had recently received from Hailes, then Sir David Dalrymple: "I envy you the free and undisguised converse with such a man. May I beg you to present my best respects to him, and to assure him of the veneration which I entertain for the author of the Rambler and of Rasselas" (*Life*, I, 432–433). Johnson was much pleased by the compliment, and a week later drank a bumper to Dalrymple "as a man of worth, a scholar, and a wit"; later he said to Boswell, "Does Lord Hailes love *me*? I love *him*."[59] Johnson finally met Hailes when he traveled to Edinburgh, and on 17 August 1773 he and Boswell dined with the Scot, at which time the men discussed Johnson's own writings. Hailes noted, for instance, that he had long suspected his guest's authorship of the *Life of Cheynel* (1751), to which Johnson replied, "No one else knows it." Johnson had, as Boswell puts it, one of his "best days" that 17 August, and part of the reason was that Hailes "pleased him highly" (*Tour*, pp. 30–31). He again dined with Hailes on his return from the Hebrides in November, and although Boswell regrets not having recorded the conversation at the time, he does remember that the men spent a "most agreeable day" (*Tour*, p. 388).

One of the topics Johnson and Hailes probably discussed in Edinburgh was the Scot's historical project, on which he was then working. Johnson might have offered his assistance to Hailes, perhaps as a matter of courtesy; in any event, the Scot decided to solicit Johnson's aid through his intermediary Boswell. Therefore, on 12 May 1774 Boswell sent along to Johnson not only Hailes's "best respects" but also some specimens of his manuscript. Enclosed as well was Hailes's request of Boswell: "If I could procure Dr. Johnson's criticisms, they would be of great use to me in the prosecution of my work, as they would be judicious and true. I have no right to ask that favour of him. If you could, it would highly oblige me" (*Life*, II, 278). Hailes realized he was risking the displeasure of the Englishman, who might feel obligated to agree, but he obviously felt the risk was worth taking. But Johnson was in fact happy to assist his friend, even though he found it difficult to read and revise the sheets as promptly as Hailes might have wished. The delays were in no way due to the sheets themselves (Johnson basically revised only stylistic problems or edited Scotticisms); rather they were caused by his inability, for various and characteristic reasons, to sit down and plunge into the task. (There would be similar bouts of procrastination when Johnson worked on the second volume of the *Annals* after 1776). As a result, he felt it necessary to apologize to Hailes (through Boswell) for his indolence. Johnson's sincere compliments regarding the accuracy and style of the *Annals* are only in part attributed to his respect and fondness for the Scot, for we know he demanded of the historian some of the very qualities Hailes possessed. Because the *Annals* were not as inherently conducive to effective writing, Johnson saw all the more reason to shower his praise on Hailes's efforts: the *Annals,* he said, "have not that painted form which is the taste of this age; but it is a book which will always sell" (*Life,* III, 58).

In addition to the often misleading commentary on the historians, readers have also misread Johnson's views on history because of several comments appearing prominently in Boswell's *Life of Johnson* and in the *Rambler* and *Idler.* I have already provided an explanation for such observations as great abilities "are not requisite for an Historian," but what of the following point made in May 1772: "Talking of a modern historian [Robertson, no doubt] and a modern moralist, he said, 'There is more thought in the moralist than in the historian. There is but a shallow stream of thought in history' " (*Life,* II, 195). Here again he was having fun at Boswell's expense; this was only one of several occasions on which he poked fun at Robertson to Boswell's face. As I have noted, Boswell reminded his readers shortly afterward that Johnson, "who owned that he often 'talked for victory,' rather urged plausible objections to Dr. Robertson's excellent historical works, in the ardour of contest, than expressed his real and decided opinion" (*Life,* II, 238). As was his habit, Johnson would provide an almost incontrovertible fact—"There is more thought in the moralist than in the historian"—and follow it with an audacious statement intended to annoy or shock the listener, therefore keeping one foot firmly entrenched in truth and logic and with the other kicking wildly at anything that moved. That is, Johnson could easily defend the position that moralists, by nature of their task, must put more hard effort into their work, which ideally should reach all readers for the betterment of their lives, than historians who simply relate the facts—the kind of historian Johnson probably means in this instance. (We have already seen that he never considered good history divorced from morality.) The second assertion—"There is but a shallow stream of thought in history"—may apply in those cases (and there were more than we should care to imagine) in which historians merely collect and display data for digestion by their readers. His own historical writings and his commentary on the intellectual, moral, and philosophical nature of history easily refute the notion that he could have dismissed history with such a back-handed comment. Boswell knew what Johnson was up to and informed his readers of it, and yet many have chosen to take Johnson's retorts literally, as if they were gospel truth.

In the case of the *Rambler* and *Idler,* where there are no instances of Johnson's "writing for victory," I have explained earlier in this chapter why he argued that the "general and rapid narratives of history" offered "few lessons applicable to private life" (*Rambler* 60), that history is too often "employed for shew than use" (*Idler* 84), that "no writer has a more easy task than the historian" (*Rambler* 122), and that "little is the general condition of human life understood by panegyrists and historians" (*Rambler* 202). One might assume Johnson wishes in *Ramber* 60 and *Idler* 84 to elevate biography at the expense of history by pointing out that only biography can stimulate the interest and morality of the reader by encouraging, as most history does not, empathy with the subject. This view, of course, leads logically to such conclusions as "Johnson's dislike of history is directly antithetical to his great affection for biography."[60] There may be some validity in the argument that he is robbing Peter to pay Paul in these pieces if he has in mind mere factual histories, but I cannot help noting that his enthusiasm for biography is tempered by criticisms of the form reminiscent of several remarks he made on history. In *Idler* 84 he writes, "He that recounts the life of another, commonly dwells most upon conspicuous events, lessens the familiarity of his tale to increase its dignity, shews his favourite at a distance decorated and magnified like the ancient actors in their tragick dress, and endeavours to hide the man that he may produce a hero" (p. 262), and earlier in *Rambler* 60, "biography has often been allotted to writers who seem very little acquainted with the nature of their task, or very negligent about the performance" (III, 322). And in Scotland Johnson remarked that he was unaware of "any literary man's life in England well-written" (*Tour,* p. 204). No one would dare assert that because he finds fault with the manner in which some biography is written Johnson thinks little of the form, for after all it is his view of biography's potential that is important. And yet the same logic has not been generally applied to his evaluation of history.

Isolated from the context of Johnson's total impression of history, these "negative" comments in the *Life of Johnson,* Thrale's anecdotes, and the periodical papers, so effective and memorable in their wording, seem powerful evidence indeed that he had no mind for history as a subject of study or writing. But this evidence wilts rapidly when compared with Johnson's true estimation of historical works and his deep interest in historical theory. The judicious value he placed on historical facts, his support of the humanistic branch of history, his commitment to discovering historical truth, his healthy historical skepticism, his respect for the more scientific aspects of historical inquiry (research and causation), his broad historical scope, and his advocacy of effective historical writing all demonstrate his awareness of current questions and movements in historical thought and his participation in the debate over what constituted good history. His was one of the best historical minds of the age.

Chapter Seven

The Significance of History: Conclusions

Johnson's appreciation of history is wonderfully summarized in the "Life of Milton": "Whether we provide for action or conversation, whether we wish to be useful or pleasing, the first requisite is the religious and moral knowledge of right and wrong; *the next is an acquaintance with the history of mankind,* and with those examples which may be said to embody truth and prove by events the reasonableness of opinions. . . . Those authors, therefore, are to be read at schools that supply most axioms of prudence, most principles of moral truth, and most materials for conversation; and these purposes are best served by poets, orators, *and historians*" (*Poets,* I, 99–100; italics mine). His words more than emphasize the tradition of the humanist historian, for they demonstrate how significant he believed history to be to the continuing welfare of the individual and society. He therefore shared the view of Gibbon that history "undertakes to record the transactions of the past for the benefit of future ages" (*Decline and Fall,* chapter 16). At no time under the spell of any widely held views, Johnson over the years and with much careful thought came to the conclusion that his generation and posterity could gain in dignity, moral strength, self-knowledge, and intellectual stature and vision if they cultivated a knowledge of history. Because he saw human nature as fallible and in constant need of example, he resisted vigorously any assumptions that men and women could ignore the past and concern themselves only with present realities. As his sage Imlac concludes, "To judge rightly of the present, we must oppose it to the past, for all judgment is comparative, and of the future nothing can be known" (*Rasselas,* p. 117).

History was to Johnson both a touchstone and a Rosetta stone of human experience. One could test many theories regarding the relationship between humans and their society, between government and its people, and between nation and nation by comparing contemporary problems with similar ones in history. The English Civil War, as we have seen, served Johnson well in this regard. And history could help to unlock a good many secrets and explain national and individual behavior, which might remain mysteries to those unwilling to look beyond the confines of their own times. Johnson knew that many of his contemporaries, as in any age, unnecessarily lose confidence and hope in mankind because they foolishly believe national and personal crises and troubles to be the province of their age alone. But with a strong sense of history, a society can gain strength and comfort from the fact that identical or worse problems had afflicted earlier generations, who overcame these hardships and in many cases advanced workable solutions.

Johnson's contemporaries could gain considerable wisdom by realizing that divine providence, fate, or bad luck were not responsible for the English Civil War or the Jacobite Rebellions in 1715 and 1745, for an understanding of the real causes that led to these events helps protect each subsequent generation from the kind of error and upheaval that can tear a nation apart. "As man is a being very sparingly furnished with the power of prescience," he wrote in 1754, "he can provide for the future only by considering the past" (*Adventurer* 137, p. 487). In Johnson's mind, avoiding the mistakes of the past was as important to the future progress of society as the initiating of imaginative proposals for growth. Agreeing with Hume, who wrote in his "Of the Study of History" that it is "an unpardonable ignorance in persons of whatever sex or condition" not to be acquainted with history, Johnson went further to stress that a grasp of history was the moral obligation of every intelligent man and woman. Again Imlac speaks eloquently for him: "The present state of things is the consequence of the former, and it is natural to inquire what were the sources of the good that we enjoy or the evil that we suffer. If we act only for ourselves, to neglect the study of history is not prudent; if we are entrusted with the care of others, it is not just. Ignorance, when it is voluntary, is criminal; and he may properly be charged with evil who refused to learn how he might prevent it" (*Rasselas,* pp. 117–118).

Johnson's strong historical sense, as I have noted in chapter three, was in large part responsible for his desire to keep customs alive and to respect, if useful and moral, long-standing institutions. But he rejected the view of many historical thinkers from 1400 to 1800 that "change" was usually change for the worse in political, religious, moral, cultural, and economic terms and that mankind was in a long period of decline.[1] Nor did he believe, as did Bayle and the Pyrrhonists, that over the centuries humanity has made no discernible political or moral progress, even if there has been no measurable decline. To Johnson, innovation for innovation's sake was often dangerous and detrimental to social and political welfare, but in regard to the history of humanity he perceived, given occasional periods of regression, a continuing ascent rather than a decline, not only from the medieval period but from classical times as well. There was no sense of nostalgia in Johnson's historical remarks (except in *London*), as one finds, for example, in Gilbert Stuart's examination of past cultures in his *View of Society in Europe* (1778). It was an "undoubted proof" of Johnson's good sense, Boswell informs us, that he was "never querulous, never prone to inveigh against the present times, as is so common when superficial minds are on the fret. On the contrary, he was willing to speak favourably of his own age; and, indeed, maintained its superiority in every respect, except in its reverence for government" (*Life*, III, 3). In Scotland, Johnson took issue with Lord Monboddo's contention that their ancestors were better men than they: "No, no, my Lord. . . . We are as strong as they, and a great deal wiser" (*Tour*, p. 53).

Johnson's attitude was partly prompted by the cant of so-called historical thinkers who championed Rome and medieval times at the expense of the "corrupt and imitative" eighteenth century, but his view of progress may be likened to Fontenelle's, who in his *Digression on the Ancients and the Moderns* (1688) argued that, although in matters of biology and artistic expression there has been no measurable progress from the ancients, other areas (e.g., science and industry) have clearly demonstrated the superiority of modern times. This position does not ignore the past or relegate it to a dark age of primitivism, but it does portray the world as moving steadily forward, making modifications based on both experience and imagination. Johnson agreed as well with Hume and especially Gibbon, who not only emphasized the barbarism of the past but also stated or implied throughout the *Decline and Fall* a faith in the possibility, if not the necessity, of continuous progress. That Johnson shared such views of progress is perhaps most evident near the end of his life, at a time when he might have been most inclined to take refuge in and champion the past: "Men in the ancient times dared to stand forth with a degree of ignorance with which nobody would dare now to stand forth. *I am always angry when I hear ancient times praised at the expense of modern times.* There is now a great deal more learning in the world than there was formerly" (*Life*, IV, 217; italics mine).

As Johnson knew, comments on the superiority of the past were due in part to an unbridled romantic impression of history. Such romanticism was a part of human nature; there were many like Richard Hardcastle in

Goldsmith's *She Stoops to Conquer* who enjoyed living in their own or the historic past, escaping from the apparently ever-changing present and seeking shelter in the comforts of earlier times, when life was simpler and nobler. Johnson furthermore understood that, artistically at least, a nation could gain or regain strength and a sense of purpose by recalling the exploits of its most famous historical figures, by evoking the memories, as he did in *London,* of Alfred, Edward, and Henry. And even though his general view of history was morally and intellectually serious, he never forgot that history "seems to be one of the most natural Delights of the Human Mind."[2] It could be an enjoyable study, feeding the imagination and allowing one to escape temporarily into the exciting world of the past. Again, Hume may speak for Johnson's position: history, he noted in "Of the Study of History," was an "agreeable entertainment to the mind," which "amuses the fancy" as well as "improves the understanding" and "strengthens virtue." "What spectacle can be imagined, so magnificent, so various, so interesting? What amusement, either of the senses or imagination, can be compared with it?" Johnson's conception of history was not one of conflict in the sense that his romantic and rational sides were at war with each other, pulling in both directions at once. Nor did he have to struggle with a periodically emerging sense of historical romanticism, which he pushed down by the strength of his intellectual powers. Instead, he perceived the romantic side of history as a healthy recreation, dangerous only when it softened and distorted the mind and clouded the truth about the past. As seriously as he viewed history as a moral and teaching device and intellectual study, he found time to put his feet up and relax with visions of the pomp and circumstance of a bygone era.

Bolingbroke wrote in one of his *Letters* about the development of one's historical sense: "The child hearkens with delight to the tales of his nurse: he learns to read, and he devours with eagerness fabulous legends and novels: in riper years he applies himself to history, or to that which he takes for history, to authorised romance: and, even in age, the desire of knowing what has happened to other men, yields to the desire alone of relating what has happened to ourselves. Thus history, true or false, speaks to our passions always."[3] Johnson's romantic impressions of history began during his boyhood. But even then, as he was learning about the glories of the past, he saw, read, and heard about the destructive legacy of the English Civil War. Therefore, at the same time he developed a boy's love of the past, he also came to appreciate the symbolism and lessons of history applicable to contemporary life. His immersion into the alleys of

Grub Street opened his eyes wider to the amount of historical material available to the curious reader, and in the 1740s he began to see the study and writing of history in their complex shades and as serious intellectual pursuits that deserved the attention of England's best writers and thinkers. So much of his work in these years was historically oriented, in part or in whole, and it is not difficult to imagine how different his writings would have been had he lacked a strong historical sense. *Rasselas* would have been diluted of much of its power had he not voiced through Imlac his eloquent defense of history; there would have been no *Introduction to the Political State of Great Britain;* and such pieces as the *Vanity of Human Wishes,* the *Thoughts on the Late Transactions Respecting Falkland's Islands, Taxation No Tyranny,* the *Journey to the Western Islands,* the *Lives of the Poets,* and many of the biographies and some of the important reviews would have been far less successful had it not been for his love of history. As the remarks from the "Life of Milton" indicate, to the end of his life Johnson maintained his deep respect for the study of history. As he grew older he saw better history being written and heard more debate about the nature of historiography, both of which must have pleased and interested him greatly. To the debate he contributed his own views, which show him advancing along with his age toward a more scientific approach to the events of the past. As any scholar who has devoted a lifetime to a particular subject—the years diminishing neither appreciation nor enthusiasm—Johnson refined his historical sense rather than altered the impressions he developed in the 1740s and 1750s. That the age *agreed with him* in many aspects of historical composition only reinforces his position as one of the century's most erudite thinkers.

But there is another aspect of history that appealed to Johnson, one more personal than intellectual in nature. Anyone who has read the *Rambler* essays or Boswell's *Life* knows of Johnson's inordinate sensitivity to the inevitability of death; he could not, as Boswell wrote, "bear to have death presented to him in any shape," and Johnson frequently shared with his readers and friends such advice as "the remembrance of death ought to predominate in our minds" (*Tour,* p. 374; *Rambler* 78, IV, 47). Understandably, then, he took much pleasure and comfort in finding evidence of permanence in a world that offered him far too much documentation of mutability. What could last over the centuries, far beyond the life of the individual, appealed to him immensely, whether it was ancient literature, customs, language, or even the large trees that decorated the landscape.[4] He sought the timeless and the constant in his own life and in the broader context of history; religion, with its prospect of eternal life, rarely comforted him. To discover things that would last, he believed, was the only way men and women could feel reconciled to the inevitability of their own ends. He therefore resolved to keep a journal and encouraged others to do likewise so that their life histories would remain accurate and not a mere wisp of memory. He also advised Boswell to record the "antiquities of the feudal establishment": "The whole system of ancient tenures is gradually passing away; and I wish to have the knowledge of it preserved adequate and complete" (*Letters,* I, 280). He implored Charles O'Connor to study and preserve Irish literature and language because if such learning "be suffered to remain in oblivion for another century" it "may perhaps never be retrieved" (*Letters,* I, 101). He felt furthermore that the inscriptions on Scottish monuments should be in Latin, "as everything intended to be universal and permanent should be," and that to preserve "good actions from oblivion" is both "the interest and the duty of mankind."[5] Finally, he called for the preservation and restoration of important religious and secular structures in Britain.

These bits of evidence suggest a man encouraging permanence as an antidote to the horrors of mutability. And history too conveyed the idea of permanence, for as one well versed in the past Johnson saw himself in the larger spectrum of history rather than in the narrow confines of the present. It must have been reassuring to him, considering his dread of decay, that people have basically been the same throughout the ages, because in this sense they are a permanent fixture not entirely modified by time. Reading about earlier periods and famous historical figures kept them alive in Johnson's mind and relevant to the present. He knew that as long as history was studied, the accomplishments and failures of civilization, of which he was a part, would not fall into the abyss of oblivion. Not only did history help him fight the omnipresent fear of mutability, but it also added a sense of stability to his own existence. As a man who throughout his life struggled against the psychological demons threatening him with mental breakdown, Johnson needed as much evidence of stability and permanence as he could find.[6] He had to take some solace from the fact that the world has witnessed and recovered from far more serious afflictions than those tormenting his mind.

Serving as an excellent illustration of his position is the preface to the *Dictionary.* Near the end of that impressive philological essay, Johnson resigns himself to the inevitability of change in the language: "If the changes, that we fear, be thus irresistible, what remains but to acquiesce with silence, as in the other insurmountable distresses of humanity?" However, he insists that an attempt be made to achieve some degree of permanence: "Life may be lengthened by care, though death cannot be ultimately defeated: tongues, like governments, have a natural tendency to degeneration; we have long preserved our constitution, let us make some struggles for our language" (*Works*, XI, 258–259). In this desire to make "some struggles" we discover Johnson's conviction that one must seek and encourage permanence whenever and wherever possible. The preface protrays a man fully aware of the inevitability of decay but determined as well to slow down the process. It is each generation's responsibility, he implies, to preserve what it can, for by doing so it may gain in dignity and strength, even though its opponent is too powerful ever to defeat. To take part in the struggle, to feel oneself as an extension of the past, was for Johnson one of humanity's noblest pursuits. History helped him make the good fight.

Few misconceptions about Samuel Johnson have been as glaring as his supposed dislike of history. And even those rejecting the pronouncements of Macaulay and others who followed have not fully appreciated the large place history assumed in Johnson's intellectual and philosophical priorities and his writings. Had he only published all his thoughts on history in a pamphlet or small book he would have been hailed as a first-rate historical mind, the rival in many respects of Bolingbroke, Gibbon, and Hume. But the information has been there all along, lying slightly underneath a surface many have passed over while looking for other treasures. Charmed more easily by Boswell's *Life of Johnson* and Hester Thrale's anecdotes, many have ignored the testimony of some of Johnson's other contemporaries, such as Arthur Murphy, who noted that no one understood the nature of historical evidence better than Johnson, and William Cooke, who wrote in 1785 that in history Johnson "possessed an intimate knowledge of the ancient and modern parts. . . . In this useful study he did not merely content himself with exploring the ravages of tyrants, the desolation of kingdoms, the routs of armies, and the fall of empires, but with the different passions, tempers and designs of men—the growth and infancy of political and theological opinions, the gradual increase and declension of human knowledge."[7] Even though history was one of several important channels flowing into the whole of Johnson's intellectual and moral concerns, it was a far wider channel than we have ever assumed.

Notes

Introduction

1. As recently as 1977 Greene wrote that Macaulay's "influence in shaping and perpetuating the Johnson myth of the nineteenth century and later was enormous—and still remains so" (*Political Writings*, p. xxii).

2. Macaulay's review of Croker's edition of Boswell's *Life of Johnson* in *Edinburgh Review*, September 1831, reprinted in James T. Boulton, ed., *Johnson: The Critical Heritage* (New York: Barnes and Noble, Inc., 1971), pp. 428–429.

3. Krutch, *Samuel Johnson* (New York: Holt and Company, Inc., 1944), p. 75; Wimsatt, *The Prose Style of Samuel Johnson* (New Haven: Yale University Press, 1941), p. 96; Low, "Edward Gibbon and the Johnsonian Circle," *New Rambler* (June 1960): 11; Peter Quennell, *Samuel Johnson: His Friends and Enemies* (New York: American Heritage Press, 1972), p. 262. See as well Donald Greene's remarks in his introduction to *Samuel Johnson: A Collection of Critical Essays* (Englewood Cliffs: Prentice-Hall, Inc., 1965), p. 1, note 1.

4. *The Huntington Library Quarterly* 12 (1948): 1–21.

5. In Frederick W. Hilles, ed., *New Light on Dr. Johnson* (New Haven: Yale University Press, 1959), pp. 247–256.

6. Most notably in Greene's *The Politics of Samuel Johnson* (New Haven: Yale University Press, 1960) and Curley's *Samuel Johnson and the Age of Travel* (Athens: University of Georgia Press, 1976).

7. *Samuel Johnson* (New York: The Viking Press, 1974), p. 303.

8. John Butt, *The Mid-Eighteenth Century*, ed. Geoffrey Carnall (Oxford: Clarendon Press, 1979), p. 191.

9. In his impressive biography, Walter Jackson Bate relegates Johnson's attitude toward history to the following parenthetical comment: "Johnson's supposed antipathy to 'history' was only a pose—partly an attempt to remind himself and others that we are 'free agents' and not the passive products of history, and partly a rebuke to historical pedants" (Bate, *Samuel Johnson* [New York: Harcourt Brace Jovanovich, 1977], p. 507).

10. In addition to the books by Greene and Curley, one should consult Robert Folkenflik, *Samuel Johnson, Biographer* (Ithaca: Cornell University Press, 1978) and Richard B. Schwartz, *Samuel Johnson and the New Science* (Madison: University of Wisconsin Press, 1971).

Chapter One

1. The work of Clarendon and Burnet appeared initially in 1702–1704 and 1724, respectively.

2. Greene, *Samuel Johnson's Library: An Annotated Guide* (University of Victoria, 1975) and Fleeman, *The Sale Catalogue of Samuel Johnson's Library* (University of Victoria, 1975).

3. *Account of the Harleian Library* in *Works*, XII, 95.

4. See James L. Clifford, *Young Sam Johnson* (New York: McGraw-Hill Book Company, 1955), pp. 46–58.

5. Ibid., p. 66.

6. Ibid., p. 64.

7. Ibid., pp.81–86; Bate, *Samuel Johnson*, pp. 43–55.

8. Chapin, *The Religious Thought of Samuel Johnson* (Ann Arbor: University of Michigan Press, 1968), p. 50.

9. Aleyn Lyell Reade, *Johnsonian Gleanings* (privately printed 1909–1952), vol. 5, p. 213.

10. See Curley, *Age of Travel*, p. 162.

11. Recent scholarship has discovered much more in this work than Johnson's preface suggests. As Joel Gold has noted, "Virtually every page of the English version, *including* the dissertations, indicates the extent of Johnson's activity: he translated in places, epitomized in others, omitted some sections, expanded others, added asperity to the tone, or softened the wording, rearranged elements for greater clarity, balanced phrases for smoother syntax, inserted translations for easier reading, and interspersed editorial comments to point the moral." See Gold, "Johnson's Translation of Lobo," *PMLA* 80 (March 1965): 51–61.

12. Greene, *Politics*, pp. 66–72. See also Gold, "Translation of Lobo."

13. For an analysis of these years see Edward A. Bloom, *Samuel Johnson in Grub Street* (Providence: Brown University Press, 1957).

14. Clifford, *Young Sam Johnson*, p. 250.

15. It is possible that the pamphlet led to a warrant for Johnson's arrest. See Hawkins, p. 41 and *Political Writings*, p. 20.

16. See Greene's introduction to the abridgment in *Political Writings*, pp. 74–79. Johnson may have furthermore edited a version of *Monarchy Asserted*. See also Hazen, pp. 248–250.

17. See Bloom, *Grub Street*, pp. 51–62; Greene, *Politics*, pp. 112–135; and Benjamin B. Hoover, *Samuel Johnson's Parliamentary Reporting* (Berkeley: University of California Press, 1953).

18. Greene, *Politics*, p. 123.

19. *Gentleman's Magazine* 11 (1741): 339–340, 351.

20. *Gentleman's Magazine* 11 (1741): 411.

21. Hoover, *Parliamentary Reporting*, p. 141.

22. Johnson supposedly warned Smollett against accepting the speeches as

authentic (Hawkins, p. 59; *Misc,* II, 342). He wrote in the introduction to the *Literary Magazine* (1756), "We shall not attempt to give any regular series of debates, or to amuse our Readers with senatorial rhetoric. The speeches inserted in other papers have been long known to be fictitious, and produced sometimes by men who never heard the debate, nor had any authentic information" (Hazen, p. 129).

23. Greene, *Politics,* p. 133.

24. For background and an assessment see Thomas Kaminski, "Johnson and Oldys as Bibliographers: An Introduction to the Harleian Catalogue," *PQ* 60 (1981): 439–453.

25. *Account of the Harleian Library* in *Works,* XII, 95.

26. Clifford, *Young Sam Johnson,* p. 270.

27. See Donald Greene, "Johnson and the 'Harleian Miscellany,'" *Notes and Queries,* N.S. 5 (1958): 304–306 and Clifford, *Young Sam Johnson,* pp. 270–271.

28. *Letters,* III, 122. See also Edmond Malone's notation on *Burton's Books* in the 6th edition of Boswell's *Life of Johnson* (1811); reprinted as the one-volume Modern Library "Giant" edition (New York: Random House, 1931), p. 1080.

29. Curley, *Age of Travel,* p. 79.

30. Clifford, *Young Sam Johnson,* pp. 26–43 and Henry J. Callender, "Johnson and His Lichfield," *Johnson Society Transactions* (1973): 4–18.

31. Clifford, *Young Sam Johnson,* p. 35.

32. See ibid., pp. 35–37 and chapter 2 of this book.

33. Johnson spent a short though miserable period of his life as a tutor at Market Bosworth. As the now famous story goes, George II asked Sir Wolstan Dixie, the combative and boorish patron of Bosworth School, "Bosworth— Bosworth! Big battle at Bosworth, wasn't it?" Dixie, recalling a recent fist fight with a neighbor and displaying his insensitivity toward history, answered, "Yes, Sire. But I thrashed him" (Clifford, *Young Sam Johnson,* p. 137).

34. Johnson would have also appreciated the older colleges he saw at Cambridge University in 1765, most notably Corpus Christi (founded in 1353), Pembroke (1347), Clare (1326), and Peterhouse (1281). The dates for the colleges at Oxford and Cambridge are from Dorothy Eagle and Hilary Carnell, eds., *The Oxford Guide to the British Isles* (Oxford: Clarendon Press, 1977).

35. For more on Johnson's views on customs and landmarks see chapter three of this book.

36. Schwartz writes, "With his knowledge of men and books, Johnson surely was taken by the history which enveloped him there. . . . [For example,] Fleet Street was religious in its associations. The Blackfriars had arrived at their Thames location in 1276. The Carmelite settlement at Whitefriars was there and was laid in ruins by Henry VIII. . . . The Temple Church, which occasioned pilgrimages, numbered among its relics wood from the true cross, some of Christ's blood, and the sword which killed Thomas à Becket" (Schwartz, "Johnson's Day, and Boswell's," in John J. Burke, Jr., and Donald Kay, eds., *The*

Notes to Chapter 1

Unknown Samuel Johnson [Madison: University of Wisconsin Press, 1983], pp. 86, 87–88).

37. Johnson had the opportunity to further his awareness of continental history by viewing the historic sites and structures during his short trip to France in 1775.

38. He wrote to Hester Thrale that in the area many chapels sprang up, but "by the active zeal of Protestant devotion, almost all of them have sunk into ruin" (*Letters*, I, 366).

Chapter Two

1. All quotations from Johnson's poetry will come from E. L. McAdam, Jr., ed., with George Milne, *Poems* (New Haven: Yale University Press, 1964).

2. For an extension of the references to "Edward" see John A. Vance, "Edward III or Edward, the Black Prince? Esoteric Symbolism in Thomson, Pope, and Johnson," *ELN* 17 (1980): 256–259.

3. Modern historians believe Charles was killed by enemy artillery fire, not murdered by an aide-de-camp.

4. Regarding the exploits of the eighteenth-century "successor" to Tamerlane, Nadir Shah (Kuli Khan), Frederick Bernard considers the possibility that Johnson was involved in the publication of a "rare pamphlet, *The History of Tahmas Kuli Khan, Shah, or Sophi of Persia,* anonymously translated from the French and published by [J.] Wilcox in 1740." See Bernard, "The History of Nadir Shah: A New Attribution to Johnson," *British Museum Quarterly* 34 (1969–1970): 92–104.

5. Johnson may be alluding to the prophecy in Daniel 2:36–45, in which four kingdoms will be succeeded by one that "shall never be destroyed" and "shall stand for ever."

6. *DPA*, p. 71; *Letters*, I, 15; and *Life*, IV, 235.

7. For commentary on Johnson's *Life of Frederick* see chapter four.

8. Beauclerk was Charles II's great-grandson, descended from the king's amour with Nell Gwynne.

9. To Hester Thrale he wrote, "Camps are the habitations of those who conquer kingdoms or defend them" (*Letters*, II, 257).

10. For Johnson's distortion of Mary's departure from Scotland see Mary Lascelles, "Johnson's Last Allusion to Mary Queen of Scots," *RES*, N.S. 8 (1957): 32–37.

11. *Thoughts on the Late Transactions Respecting Falkland's Islands*, in *Political Writings*, p. 374, and Johnson's review of William Tytler's *Historical and Critical Enquiry, in Works*, XIII, 261. David Hume noted that the Whigs "have long indulged their prejudice against the succeeding race of princes by bestowing unbounded panegyrics on the virtue and wisdom of Elizabeth" (*History of England*, 8 vols. [London: T. Cadell, 1796], vol. 5, pp. 389–390).

12. *Life,* IV, 13; *Shakespeare,* I, 72; *Political Writings,* pp. 130–131; and Hazen, p. 57.

13. *Introduction to the Political State of Great Britain,* in *Political Writings,* p. 130.

14. In the *Life,* Boswell deviated little from his journal account of that evening's conversation.

15. Johnson's review of Tytler in *Works,* XIII, 261.

16. Greene, *Politics,* p. 182. Greene adds that Johnson's opinion of the institution of monarchy was, "to say the least, unenthusiastic" (p. 3).

17. Historians have agreed on this point but have stressed that James and Charles I were unable to understand the English temperament as had the Tudors and thus erred in undiplomatically confronting Parliament.

18. *Introduction to the Political State of Great Britain,* in *Political Writings,* p. 133.

19. In his notes on Shakespeare's *Henry V,* Johnson writes of James that "with all his faults, and many faults he had," he was "such that Sir Robert Cotton says, 'he would be content that England should never have a better, provided that it should never have a worse' " (*Shakespeare,* II, 529).

20. *Introduction to the Political State of Great Britain,* in *Political Writings,* p. 134; *Poets,* I, 261.

21. *Life of Thomas Browne,* in *Works,* XV, 75. This piece, published in 1756, praises the king's judiciousness and popularity and mentions his ability to "discover excellence, and virtue to reward it with such honorary distinctions, at least, *as cost him nothing*" (italics mine).

22. *Poets,* I, 272, 303; "Drury-Lane Prologue" (line 21); and *Idler* 69, p. 216.

23. *Life,* I, 442; II, 41; and *Poets,* I, 126.

24. Although William *and* Mary were considered by law joint sovereigns until Mary's death in 1694, William was in practice England's sole monarch throughout the period 1689 to 1702. Stuart blood coursed through his veins; his maternal grandfather was Charles I and he was thus the nephew of Charles II and James II as well as James's son-in-law. In 1742 Johnson warned his readers that the traditional picture of Mary as "the popular, the beneficent, the pious, the celestial Queen Mary, from whose presence none ever withdrew without an addition to his happiness" is not supported by Sarah Churchill's correspondence and reminiscences. Instead, Mary appears to have been insolent, resentful, vengeful, "desirous of controlling where she had no authority," and "backward to forgive, even when she had no real injury to complain of" (*Works,* XIII, 167).

25. *Tour,* p. 218; *Political Writings,* p. 342; *Poets,* II, 85, 239; III, 4; and Johnson's *Review of the Account of the Conduct of the Duchess of Marlborough,* in *Works,* XIII, 166–167.

26. *William III* (New York: Collier Books, 1967), p. 115.

27. Johnson's review of Tytler's *Historical and Critical Enquiry* in *Works,* XIII, 261.

28. Greene, *Politics,* p. 183.

29. For the effect of Sarah Churchill's memoirs on the popular tradition of

Anne's passivity and stupidity, which Johnson helped forward, see David Green, *Queen Anne* (New York: Charles Scribner's Sons, 1970).

30. The period may be defined as 1640 (the commencement of the Long Parliament) to 1658 (the death of Oliver Cromwell).

31. "That memorable period of the English history, which begins with the reign of king Charles the First, and ends with the Restoration, will almost furnish a library alone" (*Works*, XII, 95).

32. Burnet, *History of His Own Times* (London: William Smith, 1838), vol. 1, p. 1.

33. Greene, *Politics*, pp. 22–34 and Clifford, *Young Sam Johnson*, pp. 35–37.

34. "Life of Milton," in *Poets*, I, 125.

35. Greene, *Politics*, pp. 29–30.

36. Johnson said the custom might have ended in 1700 had a time limit been imposed initially, but because that was not done it would be appropriate to continue the practice for another century. It was abolished in 1859.

37. *Introduction to the Political State of Great Britain*, in *Political Writings*, p. 139.

38. John Phillips, *The Reformation of Images: Destruction of Art in England, 1535–1660* (Berkeley: University of California Press, 1973), pp. 184–185.

39. Ibid., p. 202.

40. Christopher Hill, *The World Turned Upside Down* (New York: The Viking Press, 1972), pp. 24–25, 88, 144–146, 150–152, 211.

41. "Life of Butler," in *Poets*, I, 214.

42. It was also a time, Johnson might have recalled, when the Ranters considered as acceptable sexual intercourse out of wedlock, when groups argued for female nudity, and when men and women advocated the trading of marriage partners (see Hill, *Upside Down*, pp. 252–254).

43. *God's Englishman: Oliver Cromwell and the English Revolution* (New York: Harper and Row, Publishers, 1970), p. 270.

44. *The History of the Rebellion and Civil Wars* (Oxford: University Press, 1849), vol. 6, p. 110. See Hill, *God's Englishman*, pp. 265–267 for early assessments of Cromwell.

45. According to E. L. McAdam, Johnson made the remark in parts of a law lecture he wrote for Robert Chambers. See E. L. McAdam, Jr., *Dr. Johnson and the English Law* (Syracuse: Syracuse University Press, 1951), p. 97.

46. See George Rudé, *Hanoverian London, 1714–1808* (Berkeley: University of California Press, 1971), pp. 162–227.

47. The Gordon Riots of 1780, for example, had already realized some of Johnson's fears.

Chapter Three

1. In this number Johnson writes of a society into which some members were admitted who were "totally ignorant of all that passes, or has lately passed, in the

world" (*Rambler* 177, V, 171). Hirsutus, the "eldest and most venerable" member, may have been Johnson's characterization of William Stukeley. For more on the society see Joan Evans, *A History of the Society of Antiquaries* (Oxford: University Press, 1956).

2. Johnson's view of the antiquarians has been considered by R. W. Ketton-Cremer in "Johnson and the Antiquarian World," *New Rambler* (January 1968): 5–11.

3. Lort, who lent Johnson books, was proposed in December 1782 for membership in The Club but was rejected (*DPA*, pp. 355–356).

4. Curley, "Johnson's Secret Collaboration," in Burke and Kay, eds., *The Unknown Samuel Johnson*, pp. 103–104. Further commentary on the Vinerian law lectures will appear in chapter four of this book.

5. Hart, ed., *Minor Lives: A Collection of Biographies by John Nichols* (Cambridge: Harvard University Press, 1971), p. xviii.

6. Edward L. Hart, "Some New Sources of Johnson's *Lives*," *PMLA* 65 (1950): 1088–1111.

7. Davis, "A Matter of Dispute: Thomas Percy and Samuel Johnson," *Johnson Society Transactions* (1976): 21.

8. In the hypothetical college Johnson and Boswell conceived while in Scotland, Percy was assigned the task of teaching "British Antiquities" (*Tour*, pp. 78–79).

9. As a final word on Johnson's relationship with some of the antiquarians of his day, it is of interest to quote from Noel Turner's account in a December 1818 letter to the *New Monthly Magazine* (p. 388) of Johnson's visit to Cambridge in 1765. Upon meeting Richard Farmer, Johnson said, "Mr. Farmer, I understand you have a large collection of very rare and curious books. . . . Will you favour me with a specimen, Sir?" Farmer then pulled down Gervase Markham's "Booke of Armorie" (1595). Johnson responded, "Come, now I'll give you a test; now I'll try who is a true antiquary amongst you. Has any one of this company ever met with the History of Glorianus and Gloriana?" As Turner recounted the event, "Farmer, drawing the pipe out of his mouth, followed by a cloud of smoke, instantly said, 'I've got the book.' 'Gi' me your hand, gi' me your hand,' said Johnson, 'you are the man after my own heart.'" Hill-Powell feels the story is not to be trusted "in some details," but Edward Hart believes it is only Turner's dating of the visit that warrants question (*Life*, I, 518; Hart, *Minor Lives*, p. 39).

10. See chapter one for some of the antiquarian volumes Johnson knew, owned, and used in his work. In addition, as Thomas Curley indicates, Johnson was familiar with the "seminal antiquarian studies of Jacob Spon and George Wheler in the 1680s, the enthusiastic descriptions of classical and biblical ruins by Robert Wood and Alexander Drummond in the 1750s, and the nostalgic account of ancient Greece by Richard Chandler in 1776" (Curley, *Age of Travel*, p. 25). See as well further antiquarian entries in Fleeman, *Sale Catalogue*.

11. See Susie Tucker, "Dr. Johnson, Mediaevalist," *Notes and Queries*, N.S. 5 (1958): 20–24. See as well Edward Tomarken, " 'The Fictions of Romantick Chivalry': Samuel Johnson's Attitudes to the Middle Ages," *Studies in Medievalism* 1, no. 1 (1979): 5–13.

12. *Works*, XII, 192–193.

13. McAdam, "Dr. Johnson as Bibliographer and Book Collector," in Hilles, ed., *New Light*, p. 173.

14. For further background on the king's library and Barnard's bibliographical responsibilities see John Brooke, "The Library of King George III," *Yale University Library Gazette* 52 (1977): 33–45.

15. *Journey*, pp. 52, 134–135, 142 and *Tour*, pp. 190, 260–261.

16. *Rambler* 156, V, 70; *Adventurer* 131, pp. 486–487; and *Rasselas*, p. 113.

17. Donald Greene believes Johnson does not intrude "his own views and prejudices" in this abridgment of *Monarchy Asserted* (*Political Writings*, p. 78), but the thoughts on customs are his whether he paraphrased them from his source or created them anew.

18. Curley, *Age of Travel*, p. 209.

19. Johnson's imagination was undoubtedly stimulated, however, by the pyramids, the "most pompous monument of Egyptian greatness and one of the most bulky works of manual industry." As Imlac notes, the pyramids were fabrics "raised before the time of history and of which the earliest narratives afford us only uncertain traditions. . . . A concussion that should shatter the Pyramid would threaten the dissolution of the continent" (*Rasselas*, pp. 119, 120).

20. See *Ramblers* 82, 142, 161 and *Idler* 94.

21. This passage replaced the now famous "Cancel": "Let us not however make too much haste to despise our neighbours. There is now, as I have heard, a body of men, not less decent or virtuous than the Scottish council, longing to melt the lead of an English cathedral [Lichfield's]. What they shall melt, it were just that they should swallow" (*Journey*, p. xxxiv).

22. Curley, *Age of Travel*, p. 192. Further commentary on Johnson's *Journey* is extensive, but one might especially note the following essays: Jeffrey Hart, "Johnson's *A Journey to the Western Islands:* History as Art," *Essays in Criticism* 10 (1960): 44–59; Arthur Sherbo, "Johnson's Intent in the *Journey to the Western Islands of Scotland*," *Essays in Criticism* 16 (1966): 382–397; Francis R. Hart, "Johnson as Philosophical Traveler: The Perfecting of an Idea," *ELH* 36 (1969): 679–695; Richard B. Schwartz, "Johnson's *Journey*," *JEGP* 69 (1970): 292–303; and Donald T. Siebert, Jr., "Johnson as Satirical Traveler: *A Journey to the Western Islands of Scotland*," *TSL* 19 (1974): 137–147.

23. Ketton-Cremer, "Antiquarian World," pp. 6–7.

24. Accordingly, Johnson thought little of the subject matter of Thomas Browne's *Urn Burial:* it was "like other treatises of antiquity, rather for curiosity than use; for it is of small importance to know which nation buried their dead in the ground, which threw them into the sea" (*Works*, XV, 65–66).

25. For another perspective on *Rambler* 83 see Schwartz, *New Science*, pp. 112–115.

26. David P. Jordan, *Gibbon and His Roman Empire* (Urbana: University of Illinois Press, 1971), pp. 44–51.

27. "These are the men to whom we must always be indebted for the complete knowledge of our institutions." These remarks are attributed to Johnson by McAdam, *English Law*, p. 99.

28. A. F. Falconer, ed., *The Correspondence of Thomas Percy and George Paton* (New Haven: Yale University Press, 1961), p. 157. I thank Bertram H. Davis for directing my attention to Percy's recollection.

Chapter Four

1. From Hume, *The History of England under the House of Tudor* (1759) and Robertson, *The History of Scotland during the Reign of Queen Mary and of King James VI* (1759).

2. *Life*, II, 153.

3. Moore, "Dr. Johnson and Roman History," *Huntington Library Quarterly* 12 (1949): 311–314.

4. Johnson wrote George Horne that Warton's *History* set "a noble example" (*Letters*, I, 405). For Warton's emphasis on the "machinery" of the Middle Ages see *History of English Poetry* (London: J. Dodsley, 1774–1781), vol. 2, pp. 462–463.

5. Hagstrum, *Samuel Johnson's Literary Criticism* (1952; reprinted Chicago: University of Chicago Press, 1967), p. 23.

6. Damrosch, *The Uses of Johnson's Criticism* (Charlottesville: University of Virginia Press, 1976), p. 161.

7. Novak, "Johnson, Dryden, and the Wild Vicissitudes of Taste," in Burke and Kay, eds., *The Unknown Samuel Johnson*, pp. 54–75.

8. Horace Walpole wrote William Mason in regard to the second volume of Warton's *History:* "antiquary as I am, it was a tough achievement. He has dipped into an incredible ocean of dry and obsolete authors of the dark ages, and has brought up more rubbish than riches. . . . it is very fatiguing to wade through the muddy poetry of three or four centuries that never had a poet" (W. S. Lewis, ed., *The Correspondence of Horace Walpole* [New Haven: Yale University Press, 1937–1983], vol. 28, pp. 381, 385).

9. Novak, "Vicissitudes of Taste," pp. 71–72.

10. Folkenflik, *Biographer*, pp. 30–31, 176–180.

11. Modern biographies are of course expected to examine the historical milieu of the subject and devote considerable space to the important names and events that left their mark on the age as well as on the individual. But whether the work be a biography of Cromwell by Antonia Fraser or a life of Robert Kennedy

by Arthur Schlesinger, Jr., we must not forget that in such cases the authors are just as much historians as they are biographers.

12. As Walter Jackson Bate points out, this life does not go far beyond an abridged translation of Le Courayer's *Vie* (*Samuel Johnson*, p. 240), but Johnson chose what and how he wished to abridge. The concentration on historical matters could easily have been modified by someone with lesser historical interests.

13. As in the *Life of Drake*, this biography, as Bate writes, is so "heavily indebted to sources as to come close *at times* to mere paraphrase" (*Samuel Johnson*, p. 219; italics mine). Again, Johnson decided what details he included or what passages he came close to paraphrasing.

14. Later in the life Johnson becomes the naturalist and offers a paragraph on flying fish (p. 252).

15. Johnson took his information mainly from Anthony Wood's histories of the Oxford area.

16. Greene, *Samuel Johnson* (New York: Twayne Publishers, 1970), p. 101.

17. Curley, "Johnson's Secret Collaboration," in Burke and Kay, eds., *The Unknown Samuel Johnson*, pp. 91–112. Curley is at present editing the Vinerian lectures and writing Chambers's life.

18. During the period in which he was collaborating with Chambers, Johnson wrote to Frederick Augusta Barnard the following remarks on the collection of law volumes: "But the feudal and civil Law I cannot but wish to see complete. The feudal Constitution is the original of the law of property over all the civilised part of Europe, and the civil Law, as it is generally understood to include the law of Nations, may be called with great propriety a regal study." The letter is dated 28 May 1768; see *Letters*, I, 216.

19. McAdam, *English Law*, p. 85. All quotations from the lectures will come from this text.

20. Curley writes, "The difficult task of going beyond McAdam's assertions and investigating all the Vinerian lectures for a thorough evaluation of the problem [of authorship] remains to be done. . . . The precise nature of the collaboration, especially in its later stages, remains open to question. . . . Surely restraint and care must guide any investigation of their collaboration" ("Secret Collaboration," pp. 95, 98, 108).

21. Ibid., p. 103.

22. Ibid., p. 103.

Chapter Five

1. See Greene's remarks on the *Literary Magazine* in *Political Writings*, pp. 126–128 and those of James Clifford in *Dictionary Johnson* (New York: McGraw-Hill Book Company, 1979), pp. 165–187.

2. See Greene's commentary in *Political Writings*, pp. 151–155.

3. Greene's attribution of this piece to Johnson is not universally accepted.

4. Clifford asserts that in the *Observations* Johnson "allowed his moral indignation to have full rein" (*Dictionary Johnson*, p. 172).

5. Consult Donald Greene, "Samuel Johnson and the Great War for Empire," in John H. Middendorf, ed., *English Writers of the Eighteenth Century* (New York: Columbia University Press, 1971), pp. 37–65.

6. See Greene's introduction in *Political Writings,* pp. 213–217.

7. Greene, *Political Writings,* p. 127; Clifford, *Dictionary Johnson,* pp. 171–172.

8. There is debate about Johnson's authorship of these pieces. See Donald Greene, "The Development of the Johnson Canon," in Carroll Camden, ed., *Restoration and Eighteenth-Century Literature* (Chicago: University of Chicago Press, 1963), pp. 407–427.

9. See Clifford, *Dictionary Johnson,* pp. 225–226.

10. Sousa, *The Portugues Asia* (English translation, 1695) and Lafitau, *Histoire des découvertes et conquestes des Portugais* (1733).

11. Johnson may have already considered another island's military and social significance in the "History of Minorca," which some scholars believe he edited or wrote parts of for the *Literary Magazine* in 1756 (Clifford, *Dictionary Johnson,* pp. 173–174).

12. Anson, *A Voyage Round the World in the Years 1740, 1, 2, 3, 4.*

13. For response to the pamphlet during the 1982 war, see Donald Greene's summary account in *Johnsonian News Letter* 42, no. 2 (1982): 1–3.

14. Tomarken, "Travels into the Unknown: 'Rasselas' and 'A Journey to the Western Islands of Scotland,' " in Burke and Kay, eds., *The Unknown Samuel Johnson,* p. 161.

15. As one indication of Johnson's interest in the subject, Boswell relates that while riding in a coach on the way to Harwich in the summer of 1763 Johnson "seemed very intent" in reading "ancient geography" (*Life,* I, 465).

16. Tomarken writes that Johnson "discovered at select residences an inverse relationship between the harshness outside and the elegance within. He came to understand that civilization developed not by smoothing the rough rocks but by using their roughness as protection" ("Travels," p. 162).

17. Ibid., p. 163.

Chapter Six

1. See Johnson's letter to Hester Thrale of July 1775: "Therefore wherever you are, and whatever you see, talk not of the Punick war." Arthur Murphy noted furthermore that Johnson would be rude to the man or woman who talked of the event (*Letters,* II, 57; *Misc,* I, 452).

2. J. Y. T. Greig, ed., *The Letters of David Hume,* 2 vols. (Oxford: Clarendon Press, 1932), vol. 2, p. 196.

3. This unpublished manuscript is now in the Hyde Collection (Somerville, New Jersey).

4. Johnson noted in *Rambler* 145 that it was more important to understand contemporary events than to know historical occurrences.

5. *Account of the Harleian Library*, in *Works*, XII, 95.

6. Burke, *The Renaissance Sense of the Past* (New York: St. Martin's Press, 1969), p. 105.

7. George H. Nadel, "Philosophy of History before Historicism," reprinted in Nadel, ed., *Studies in the Philosophy of History* (New York: Harper and Row, Publishers, 1965), p. 73.

8. See Isaac Kramnick's introduction to *Lord Bolingbroke: Historical Writings* (Chicago: University of Chicago Press, 1972), p. xvii; and Nadel, "Philosophy of History," p. 53.

9. See Nadel, "Philosophy of History," pp. 64–67; Kramnick, *Lord Bolingbroke*, p. xx; and Whalley, *Essay on the Manner of Writing History*, ed. Keith Stewart, Augustan Reprint Society Publication number 80 (Los Angeles: William Andrews Clark Memorial Library, 1960), p. 4.

10. Gibbon, *Miscellaneous Works* (London: John Murray, 1814), vol. 3, p. 126.

11. Fussell, *The Rhetorical World of Augustan Humanism* (Oxford: Clarendon Press, 1965), pp. 6–7.

12. *Rambler* 49, III, 267 and Sermon 24, *Sermons*, p. 249.

13. Sermon 23, *Sermons*, p. 247. For further examples of such wording see *Rambler* 50, III, 270; 148, V, 25; *Adventurer* 45, p. 358; and Sermon 23, *Sermons*, p. 244.

14. Gibbon, *Decline and Fall of the Roman Empire*, 3 vols. (New York: Modern Library, 1932), vol. 1, pp. 453–454.

15. *Rambler* 60, III, 319 and *Idler* 84, p. 262. See similar comments in *Rambler* 17, III, 96 and 202, V, 289.

16. Keast, "Intellectual History," p. 256.

17. Stromberg, "History in the Eighteenth Century," *JHI* 12 (1951): 301.

18. See Harry Elmer Barnes, *A History of Historical Writing*, 2nd revised edition (New York: Dover Publications, Inc., 1963), p. 149 and Kramnick, *Lord Bolingbroke*, pp. xxviii–xxxix.

19. Barnes, *Historical Writing*, pp. 147–176. Other handy background sources would include Nadel's "Philosophy of History"; Stromberg's "History"; Denys Hay, *Annalists and Historians* (London: Methuen and Co. Ltd., 1977), pp. 133–185; Thomas K. Preston, "Historiography as an Art in Eighteenth-Century England," *TSLL* 11 (1969–1970): 1209–1221; Sherman B. Barnes, "The Age of Enlightenment," in M. A. Fitzsimons, A. G. Pundt, and C. E. Nowell, eds., *The Development of Historiography* (Harrisburg: The Stackpole Company, 1954), pp. 147–161; F. Smith Fussner, *The Historical Revolution: English Historical Writing and Thought* (London: Routledge and Kegan Paul, 1962); and J. G. A. Pocock, *The Ancient Constitution and the Feudal Law: A Study of English Historical Theory in*

the Seventeenth Century (Cambridge: University Press, 1957). To these one might add the "History" sections in the Oxford History of English Literature series: James Sutherland, *The Late Seventeenth Century;* Bonamy Dobrée, *The Early Eighteenth Century;* and Butt and Carnall, *The Mid-Eighteenth Century.* A good theoretical study with commentary on eighteenth-century historiography would be Edward Hallet Carr, *What Is History?* (New York: Vintage Books, 1961).

20. Blair, *Lectures on Rhetoric and Belles Lettres* (1783), no. 36. Quoted in Butt and Carnall, *Mid-Eighteenth Century,* p. 221.

21. Whereas the work of Hume and Gibbon probably had little if any influence on his own theory, Johnson found a kindred spirit in Voltaire the historian. In addition to calling the Frenchman's *History of Charles XII,* "one of the finest pieces of historical writing in the language" (*Misc,* II, 306), Johnson argued that Hume merely imitated the greater writer. It appears likely that Johnson knew fairly well Voltaire's *Essai sur les moeurs et l'esprit des nations.* For further commentary on this matter see Donald Greene, "Voltaire and Johnson," in Alfred J. Bingham and Virgil Topazio, eds., *Enlightenment Essays Presented to Lester G. Crocker* (Oxford: Voltaire Foundation, 1979), pp. 111–131. Regarding Montesquieu, another important voice in the field and one of Gibbon's major influences, Greene believes Johnson had been reading *Considérations sur les causes de la grandeur des Romains et leur décadence* within a few years after its publication in 1734 (*Political Writings,* p. 58). Although not history per se, Montesquieu's widely read *L'Esprit de lois* (1748), which Johnson also knew (*Political Writings,* p. 427), emphasized the importance of manners, climate, and institutions to an understanding of society.

22. Vico, *Principles of a New Science of the Nature of Nations* (1725).

23. T. E. Page et al., eds., *The Works of Lucian* (Cambridge: Harvard University Press, 1959), vol. 6, p. 55.

24. Whalley, *Essay,* pp. 9, 11.

25. Greig, *Letters,* vol. 1, p. 210.

26. Introductory essay to the *Universal Chronicle* (1758) in Hazen, p. 211.

27. See, for example, II, 433–434; III, 229–230, 373; and IV, 305. In the review of Sarah Churchill's memoirs, Johnson writes of "that ardent love of truth, which nature has kindled in the breast of man, and which remains even where every laudable passion is extinguished" (*Works,* XIII, 163). For more on Johnson and the truth see W. J. Bate, *The Achievement of Samuel Johnson* (New York: Oxford University Press, 1955), pp. 129–176.

28. In the "Life of Milton," Johnson sees Burnet's assertion that the blind poet was forgotten during the Restoration as another instance "which may confirm [John] Dalrymple's observation . . . 'that whenever Burnet's narrations are examined, he appears to be mistaken' " (*Poets,* I, 128).

29. Kramnick, *Lord Bolingbroke,* p. xxx. For more on the tradition of skepticism see David Fate Norton and Richard H. Popkin, eds., *David Hume: Philosophical Historian* (Indianapolis: Bobbs-Merrill Company, 1965), pp. IX–L; Rich-

ard H. Popkin, "David Hume: His Pyrrhonism and His Critique of Pyrrhonism," *Philosophical Quarterly* 1 (1951): 385–407; Popkin, *The History of Skepticism from Erasmus to Descartes* (New York: Humanities Press, 1964); and Popkin, "The High Road to Pyrrhonism," *American Philosophical Quarterly* 2 (1965): 1–15.

30. McAdam, *English Law*, p. 92 and Greene, *Politics*, p. 193.

31. Page, *Works of Lucian*, vol. 6, p. 57.

32. Kramnick, *Lord Bolingbroke*, pp. xxxvi–xxxvii; Jordan, *Gibbon and His Roman Empire*, pp. 89–91.

33. Barnes, *Historical Writing*, pp. 155, 159. Denys Hay writes that there was "a whiff" of "the gifted amateur about Hume" (Hay, *Annalists*, p. 179), and David Jordan notes that regardless of his scholarly talents and instincts Gibbon "showed little interest in the technical aspects of great scholarship" (Jordan, *Gibbon and His Roman Empire*, p. 67).

34. Hay calls the history a "piece of hack work" (Hay, *Annalists*, p. 138).

35. Stromberg, "History," p. 298.

36. For some idea of the complexity of the issue see Tom L. Beauchamp and Alexander Rosenberg, *Hume and the Problem of Causation* (New York: Oxford University Press, 1981). Hume's interest in causation was not restricted to the purely historical realm, as his *Treatise of Human Nature* and *Enquiry Concerning Human Understanding* more than indicate. For the purposes of this study, however, I have greatly simplified the term to embrace those easily defined reasons for important historical decisions, battles, movements of people, shifts of thought, and so on.

37. McAdam attributes this remark to Johnson in *English Law*, p. 92.

38. White, "The Fictions of Factual Representation," in Angus Fletcher, ed., *The Literature of Fact: Selected Papers from the English Institute* (New York: Columbia University Press, 1976), pp. 23–24.

39. See the introduction by J. C. Hilson to Moor, *An Essay on Historical Composition* (1759), Augustan Reprint Society Publication number 187 (Los Angeles: William Andrews Clark Memorial Library, 1978), pp. i–vi. For a modern perspective on this issue, see William R. Siebenschuh, *Fictional Techniques and Factual Works* (Athens: University of Georgia Press, 1983).

40. Moor, *Essay*, p. 127.

41. Jordan, *Gibbon and His Roman Empire*, pp. 90–91, 102–103. Gibbon's position has had many advocates. For example, Geoffrey Barraclough has argued that the history we read, "though based on facts, is, strictly speaking, not factual at all, but a series of accepted judgments" (Barraclough, *History in a Changing World* [London: Basil Blackwell and Mott, 1955], p. 14).

42. Greig, *Letters*, vol. 1, pp. 170–171.

43. Boulton, *The Critical Heritage*, p. 428.

44. Wexler, "David Hume's Discovery of a New Scene of Historical Thought," *ECS* 10 (1976–1977): 200.

45. See Charles Russell, "Johnson, Gibbon and Boswell," *Fortnightly Review*

119 (1926): 629–635; W. H. J., "Gibbon and Johnson," *Notes and Queries* 173 (1937): 97; and Low, "Edward Gibbon and the Johnsonian Circle," pp. 2–14.

46. As Boswell learned from Lord Eliot, when Johnson remarked in company that any educated man would rather be called a "rascal" than be accused of "deficiency in *the graces*," Gibbon turned to a lady "who knew Johnson well," tapped his snuff box, looked at Johnson, and said, "Don't you think Madam, . . . that among *all* your acquaintance, you could find *one* exception?" (*Life*, III, 54).

47. Quoted in Low, "Edward Gibbon and the Johnsonian Circle," p. 2.

48. The first volume appeared in February 1776.

49. Interestingly, Johnson owned a copy of young Henry Davis's brash *Examination* of Gibbon's treatment of Christianity in the *Decline and Fall*. See Greene, *Library*, p. 53 and *Life*, IV, 151.

50. Greig, *Letters*, vol. 1, p. 210.

51. Charles McC. Weis and Frederick A. Pottle, eds., *Boswell in Extremes, 1776–1778* (New York: McGraw-Hill Book Company, 1970), p. 13.

52. See *Life*, I, 444; IV, 194; and *Tour*, pp. 17, 239.

53. Katharine C. Balderston, ed., *Thraliana: The Diary of Mrs. Hester Lynch Thrale*, 2 vols. (Oxford: Clarendon Press, 1942), vol. 1, p. 191. Johnson's attitude toward Hume remains problematic, however, because he had no reservations about praising the historical work of another "modern infidel"—Voltaire.

54. Hay, *Annalists*, p. 179.

55. Six years later Johnson remarked in the same vein that "Robertson paints; but the misfortune is, you are sure he does not know the people whom he paints; so you cannot suppose a likeness" (*Life*, III, 404).

56. In the *Miscellanies* Johnson is quoted as wanting to hear "no more of the tinsel of Robertson" (II, 10), but this remark too was in response to a Scot's praise of his country's "great writers."

57. Dero A. Saunders, ed., *The Autobiography of Edward Gibbon* (New York: Meridian Books, 1961), p. 67.

58. Davies, "Dr. Johnson on History," p. 5.

59. *Life*, I, 451–452 and Charles Ryskamp and Frederick A. Pottle, eds., *Boswell: The Ominous Years, 1774–1776* (New York: McGraw-Hill Book Company, 1963), p. 113. Boswell admitted that Hailes had a significant influence on his initial desire to meet Johnson (*Life*, I, 432).

60. Wimsatt, *The Prose Style*, p. 97.

Chapter Seven

1. See Peter Burke, "Tradition and Experience: The Idea of Decline from Bruni to Gibbon," *Daedalus* 105, no. 3 (1976): 137–152.

2. Preface to *The Preceptor* in Hazen, p. 182.

3. Kramnick, *Lord Bolingbroke,* pp. 7–8.

4. Accordingly, Johnson was disappointed to find few long-standing trees in Scotland: "From the bank of the Tweed to St. Andrews I had never seen a single tree, which I did not believe to have grown up far within the present century." He held that planting and preserving trees was a useful and convenient way to encourage permanence, for, left unmolested, a tree might thrive for many lifetimes: "To drop a seed into the ground," he wrote, "can cost nothing," and it "requires little and no skill" (*Journey,* pp. 9, 10, 139). For more on Johnson and trees see John B. Radner, "The Significance of Johnson's Changing Views of the Hebrides," in Burke and Kay, eds., *The Unknown Samuel Johnson,* pp. 131–149.

5. *Tour,* p. 118 and *Essay on Epitaphs,* in *Works,* XII, 193.

6. For the best insight into Johnson's mental anguish see Bate, *Samuel Johnson,* especially pp. 115–129, 231–239, 273–276, 371–389.

7. Cooke, "The Life of Samuel Johnson," in O M Brack, Jr. and Robert E. Kelley, eds., *The Early Biographies of Samuel Johnson* (Iowa City: University of Iowa Press, 1974), p. 128.

Index

Account of the Harleian Library, 60
Adair, James, 23
Adventurer, 40, 160; no. 95, 31, 144; no. 99, 37–39, 41, 139
Agrippa, Marcus Vipsanius, 40
Alexander the Great, 37–38, 39, 40, 42, 43, 59, 88, 130
Aleyn, Charles, 23
Alfred, king of England, 33, 40, 44, 66, 109, 176
Anne, queen of England, 3, 10, 11, 40, 44, 52–53, 85, 105, 106, 127, 128, 186 (n. 29)
Anson, George, 124
Antony, Marc, 88
Archimedes, 63
Armstrong, John, 23
Ascham, Roger, 45, 99–101
Astle, Daniel, 23, 167, 168
Astle, Thomas, 64, 66
Augustus (Roman emperor), 43

Bacon, Francis, 6, 21, 22, 142, 153, 162
Bailey, John, 162
Bailey, Nathan, 21
Bajazet (Bayazid I), 43
Banks, John, 59
Baretti, Giuseppe, 165
Barnard, Frederick Augusta, 68, 73, 188 (n. 14), 190 (n. 18)
Barraclough, Geoffrey, 194 (n. 41)
Barrington, Daines, 64
Barry, James, 145

Bate, Walter Jackson, 10, 181 (n. 9), 190 (n. 12), 190 (n. 13)
Baxter, Richard, 61
Baxter, William, 7
Bayle, Pierre, 6, 149, 150, 152, 174
Beauclerk, Topham, 42, 184 (n. 8)
Becket, Thomas à, 183 (n. 36)
Bede, the Venerable, 7, 142
Benzo (Gerolamo Benzoni), 23, 136
Bernard, Frederick V., 184 (n. 4)
Birch, Thomas, 12, 13, 17, 22, 23, 64, 84
Blackwell, Thomas, 23, 84, 87, 88–89. *See also* Review, Blackwell's *Memoirs of the Court of Augustus*
Blair, Hugh, 139, 146, 157
Blake, Robert, 61, 96–98, 99. *See also Life of Blake*
Boece, Hector, 23, 148
Boleyn, Anne, 40
Bolingbroke, Henry St. John, Lord, 6, 10, 66, 138, 142, 143, 146, 149, 150, 151, 152, 161, 176, 179
Borlase, William, 84
Boswell, James, 1, 7, 10, 13, 20, 28, 29, 40–55 passim, 65, 67, 71, 75, 78, 79, 87, 88, 135, 136, 140, 147, 162–71 passim, 175, 177, 178, 185 (n. 14), 187 (n. 8), 191 (n. 15), 195 (n. 46), 195 (n. 59); *Life of Samuel Johnson*, 40, 42, 47, 49, 52, 53, 139, 142, 148, 160, 165, 167, 170, 171, 177, 179, 185 (n. 14)
Bowles, William, 59

Boyer, Abel, 6
Brent, Nathaniel, 12, 158
Brooke, Robert Greville, Lord, 25
Brown, John, 145
Browne, Patrick, 84
Browne, Thomas, 188 (n. 24)
Brutus, Marcus, 88, 89
Bryant, Jacob, 64
Buck, Samuel, 78
Burke, Peter, 141
Burnet, Gilbert, 6, 7, 23, 53, 59, 142,
    148, 151, 158, 162, 182 (n. 1), 193
    (n. 28)
Butler, Samuel, 49
Byron, "Foul-weather Jack," 125

Caesar, Julius, 7, 37, 39, 40, 42, 43,
    59, 87, 88, 89, 123, 130, 134
Caius, John, 22
Caligula, 40
Cambridge University, 20, 100, 183
    (n. 34)
Camden, William, 7, 21, 22, 142
Campbell, Thomas, 163
Carew, Richard, 21
Carinus, Marcus Aurelius, 7
Carte, Thomas, 23, 168
Cassius, Gaius, 88, 89
Catiline, Lucius Sergius, 37, 39, 40,
    42, 139
Catiline Conspiracy, 138, 139
Cato the Elder, 9
Cave, Edward, 12, 13, 14, 17, 135,
    158
Cave, William, 24
Chambers, Robert, 64, 65, 67, 84,
    107, 111, 134, 146, 186 (n. 45), 190
    (n. 18)
Chambers, William, 64
Chandler, Richard, 187 (n. 10)
Chapin, Chester, 10
Charlemagne, 7
Charles I, king of England, 10, 40,

44, 48–49, 54, 55, 89, 117, 127,
    128, 185 (n. 17), 185 (n. 24), 186
    (n. 31)
Charles II, king of England, 10, 42,
    46–47, 49–50, 52, 58, 85, 118,
    127, 184 (n. 8), 185 (n. 21),
    185 (n. 24)
Charles V, emperor and king of
    Spain, 40
Charles VI, emperor, 101, 102
Charles VII, emperor, 34, 102
Charles XII, king of Sweden, 34–43
    passim, 59, 103, 184 (n. 3)
Chaucer, Geoffrey, 93
Cheke, John, 100
Cheynel, Francis, 99
Churchill, Sarah (duchess of
    Marlborough), 13, 49, 52, 84–86,
    158, 185 (n. 24), 185 (n. 29). See
    also Review of *The Account of the
    Conduct of the Duchess of
    Marlborough*
Cicero, 5, 9, 40, 63, 82, 141, 147
Cincinnatus, L. Quintius, 40
Clarendon, Edward Hyde, Lord, 6,
    8, 9, 13, 21, 23, 34, 53, 59, 96,
    104, 142, 150, 151, 152, 158, 167–
    68, 182 (n. 1)
Cleopatra, 40
Clephane, John, 161
Clifford, James, 10, 13, 19, 25, 191
    (n. 4)
Colbert, Jean-Baptiste, 50, 118
Collier, Jeremy, 6
Columba, Saint, 29
Columbus, Christopher, 38, 120, 130
Constantine, 40
Cooke, William, 179
Cotton, Robert, 43, 185 (n. 19)
Cousin, Louis, 7
Cowley, Abraham, 49
Coxeter, Thomas, 64
Cranmer, Thomas, 40

Croesus, king of Lydia, 34
Cromwell, Oliver, 10, 16–17, 25, 27, 28, 40, 42, 54, 55, 56, 58–60, 63, 76, 104, 105, 118, 130, 132, 186 (n. 30), 186 (n. 44), 189 (n. 11)
Cromwell, Richard, 104
Cromwellian Interregnum, 11, 17, 44
Crouch, Nathaniel, 59
Crusades, 38, 90, 91, 135
Curley, Thomas M., 2, 24, 64, 73, 80, 107, 111, 187 (n. 10), 190 (n. 17), 190 (n. 20)
Curtius, Quintus, 23

Dalrymple, John, 23, 154, 193 (n. 28)
Damrosch, Leopold, Jr., 93
Daniel, Sanuel, 21
Darius, king of Persia, 42, 43
Darnley, Henry Stuart, Lord, 45, 87
Davies, Godfrey, 2, 168
Davies, Thomas, 46, 49, 50, 51, 53
Davis, Bertram H., 65, 189 (n. 28)
Davis, Henry, 195 (n. 49)
Davis, John, 123
Debate Between the Committee of the House of Commons and Oliver Cromwell, 16–17, 18, 59, 72
Dedication to Kennedy's *Chronology,* 84
Dedication to Lennox's *Sully's Memoirs,* 84
Dedication to Lindsay's *Evangelical History,* 84
Dedication to Percy's *Reliques,* 84
Defoe, Daniel, 6
Denham, John, 49
Dennis, John, 91
Derby, William Stanley, earl of, 9
De Thou, Jacques Auguste, 23, 135, 142
Dictionary, 20, 21–22, 69, 93, 166, 167, 178
Dio Cassius, Cocceianus, 7

Dionysius of Halicarnassus, 141, 143
D'Israeli, Isaac, 13
Dixie, Sir Wolstan, 183 (n. 33)
Dodsley, Robert, 20, 65
Drake, Francis, 40, 44, 98–99. *See also Life of Drake*
Drummond, Alexander, 187 (n. 10)
Drummond, William, 166
Du Fresnoy, Lenglet, 8, 23, 84, 142, 143
Dugdale, William, 62
Dupin, Louis, 23, 24
Dyott, John ("Dumb"), 25

Earbury, William, 99
Echard, Laurence, 6, 59
Edward I, king of England, 27
Edward III, king of England, 32, 33, 39, 44, 48, 66, 176
Edward IV, king of England, 19
Edward VI, king of England, 45, 100
Edward the Black Prince, 33
Edward the Confessor, 135
Eliot, Edward, Lord, 24, 195 (n. 46)
Elizabeth I, queen of England, 3, 8, 32, 33, 40, 44–46, 63, 86, 87, 91, 98, 99, 115, 124, 127, 154, 184 (n. 11)
English Civil War, 3, 4, 6, 8, 10, 11, 16, 20, 25, 26, 27, 28, 31, 39, 44, 48, 53–61, 78, 84, 96, 99, 104, 117, 135, 167, 173, 174, 176
Essay on Epitaphs, 67
"Essay on the Origin and Importance of Small Tracts and Fugitive Pieces," 20
Essays on "Foreign History," 115
Eusebius, bishop of Caesarea, 8, 142
Eutropius, 168

False Alarm, 127–28, 139
Faria y Sousa, Manuel de, 23, 120, 122

Index

Farmer, Richard, 64, 187 (n. 9)
Fawkes, Guy, 40
Ferdinand V, king of Castile, 40
Fergusson, Adam, 145
Fleeman, J. D., 6
Florus, Lucius Annaeus, 23, 168
Fludger, John, 11
Folkenflik, Robert, 95
Fontenelle, Bernard le Bovier de, 6, 175
Foote, Samuel, 62
Ford, Cornelius, 10
Ford, Phoebe, 162
Fox, Charles James, 138
Foxe, John, 35
Fraser, Antonia, 189 (n. 11)
Frederick the Great, king of Prussia, 18, 40, 42, 59, 101–3, 115, 135. See also *Life of Frederick of Prussia*
Frederick William I, king of Prussia, 101
Fussell, Paul, 143

Galileo, 34
Geddes, Michael, 11
Genghis Khan, 40, 58
Gentleman's Magazine, 12, 13, 16, 18, 84, 96, 115, 160
Geoffrey of Monmouth, 22
George I, king of England, 14, 15
George II, king of England, 14, 15, 53, 183 (n. 33)
George III, king of England, 46, 50, 53, 128
Gibbon, Edward, 22, 83, 135, 138, 142–64 passim, 168, 173, 175, 179, 193 (n. 21), 194 (n. 33), 194 (n. 41), 195 (n. 46), 195 (n. 49)
Glorious Revolution, 6, 10, 44, 50, 53
Godolphin, Sidney, earl of, 10
Gold, Joel, 182 (n. 11)
Goldsmith, Oliver, 7, 23, 165, 168, 176
Grafton, Richard, 7

Greene, Donald, 1, 2, 6, 8, 11, 16, 18, 19, 47, 51, 54, 103, 115, 122, 127, 129, 181 (n. 1), 185 (n. 16), 188 (n. 17), 191 (n. 3), 193 (n. 21)
Guthrie, William, 13, 17, 18
Gwynne, Nell, 184 (n. 8)

Hadrian, Publius Aelius (Roman emperor), 7
Hagstrum, Jean, 93
Hailes, David Dalrymple, Lord, 7, 23, 137, 140, 158, 162, 168–70, 195 (n. 59)
Hale, Matthew, 21, 23
Hall, Edward, 7, 22, 90
Hampden, John, 104, 127
Hannibal, 40, 42, 139
Harleian Collection, 19–20, 24, 53, 60, 64, 66, 68, 95
Harley, Robert, 10, 34, 105, 106
Harold, king of England, 27
Harrison, Thomas, 60
Hart, Edward L., 64, 187 (n. 9)
Harte, Walter, 8
Haselrig, Arthur, 127
Hawkins, John, 8, 11, 51, 146
Hawkins, John (Admiral), 44
Hay, Denys, 194 (n. 33), 194 (n. 34)
Hazen, Allen T., 123
Hearne, Thomas, 24, 33, 62, 82
Heath, James, 59
Helvicus, Christopher, 24
Henault, Charles, 23, 140, 142
Henry I, king of England, 19
Henry II, king of England, 42
Henry IV, king of England, 90
Henry IV, king of France, 96
Henry V, king of England, 25, 33, 39, 44, 48, 66, 176
Henry VII, king of England, 25, 63
Henry VIII, king of England, 26, 27, 35, 40, 41, 45, 57, 76, 100, 183 (n. 36)

Henry, Robert, 23, 147, 167
Henry the Navigator, Prince, 120, 122
Herodian, 136
Herodotus, 141
Hesiod, 9
Heylyn, Peter, 22
Hickes, George, 62
Hickey, Thomas, 46
Hill, Christopher, 58
Hill, George Birkbeck, 18, 135, 164
"History of Minorca," 191 (n. 11)
Holder, William, 24
Holinshed, Raphael, 8, 9, 22, 35, 90, 142
Hollis, Denzil, 127
Hooke, Nathaniel, 23
Hoover, Benjamin, 19
Horace, 9
Horne, George, 189 (n. 4)
Hubert, Nicholas, 46
Hume, David, 19, 22, 59, 69, 87, 110, 135, 138–65 passim, 174, 175, 176, 179, 184 (n. 11), 193 (n. 21), 194 (n. 33), 194 (n. 36), 195 (n. 53)
Hundred Years' War, 33
Hunt, Anthony, 125
Hunter, John, 9
Hurd, Richard, 92
Hutchinson, Lucy, 59

Idler, 40, 160, 164, 170, 171; no. 10, 40; no. 45, 60; no. 84, 171
Imlac (in *Rasselas*), 74, 83, 173, 174, 188 (n. 19)
Introduction to the Political State of Great Britain, 50, 52, 59, 115–19, 135, 146, 177
Introduction to *The World Displayed,* 120–23
Irene, 11
Isaacson, Henry, 24

Jacobite Rebellion of 1715, 10, 174
Jacobite Rebellion of 1745, 136, 166, 174
James I, king of England, 47–48, 52, 90, 96, 100, 116, 117, 127, 185 (n. 17), 185 (n. 19)
James II, king of England, 10, 46, 50–51, 52, 128, 185 (n. 24)
James, king of England, 63
Jesus Christ, 56, 183 (n. 36)
John, king of England, 42
Johnson, Michael, 9
Johnson, Samuel: antiquarian friendships, 64–66; biographical writings, history in, 94–107; books, rare, 67–69; broadened scope of history, 145–47; causation, 4, 16, 37, 120, 130, 155–57; colonization, discovery, migration, 12, 98, 99, 108, 113–15, 116, 117, 118, 119–27, 129–32, 134; customs, 70–73; exemplary history, 11–12, 34–40, 55, 58, 61, 142–45, 173; facts, chronology, specifics of history, 4, 90, 100–101, 120–21, 133, 138–41, 147; heritage, 8, 24–26; historians, 161–70; independence as historical thinker, 53, 118, 124, 127, 132; intellectual history, 21, 22, 92, 93, 100–101, 136, 146; knowledge, historical, development of, 7–13, 19–20, 21, 22–24; literature, historical approach to, 22, 91–94; local history, 64–65, 73; London, early years in, 12–22; medieval period, 32–34, 38, 39, 66–67, 107–111, 135; monarchs, English, 14–15, 44–53, 104, 116; oral tradition, 69–70, 133; permanence, 177–79; progress, 42, 111, 174–76; projects, historical, 14, 135–37; Renaissance period, 3, 32, 35–36, 91–92, 100–

Johnson, Samuel (*continued*)
101, 115–16; research, 85, 110,
153–55; Roman history, 35, 37–
38, 39, 40, 41, 87–89; romanticized
history, 31–32, 33, 38, 39, 41–42,
43, 45, 59, 70, 86–87, 117, 154,
175–76; ruins, 28–29, 74–80, 132;
skepticism, 11, 37, 38, 86, 87, 110,
148–53; style, historian's, 102,
157–60; travel, 8, 24–30; truth in
history, 38, 55, 69, 85, 86–87, 110,
119, 124, 125, 147–53. *See also
individual works*
Jordan, David, 194 (n. 33)
Journey to the Western Islands, 3, 75,
76, 80, 132, 134, 137, 177. *See also*
Johnson, Samuel, ruins; Scotland
Justinian (Byzantine emperor), 40
Justinus, Junianus, 7

Kames, Henry Home, Lord, 75, 145,
156, 157
Keast, William R., 2, 143
Kennedy, John, 8, 23, 84
Kennedy, Robert, 189 (n. 11)
Kennet, White, 6, 62
Kennett, Basil, 7, 10
Kett, Robert, 127, 128
Ketton-Cremer, R. W., 80
Kimber, Isaac, 59
Knolles, Richard, 11, 21, 158, 167
Knox, John, 28, 57, 76, 77, 78, 132
Kramnick, Isaac, 149
Krutch, Joseph Wood, 1

Lafitau, J. F., 23, 120, 121, 122
Langton, Bennet, 42, 43
Langton, Stephen, 42
Le Clerc, Jean, 24
Le Courayer, Pierre François, 12, 190
(n. 12)
Le Grand, Joachim, 11
Leland, Thomas, 23

Le Moyne, Pierre, 143
Lennox, Charlotte, 84
Leopold, prince of Anhalt Dessau,
102
Le Vayer, La Mothe, 6, 149
Lichfield, 8, 9, 10, 24, 25, 26, 40, 53,
55, 64, 67, 70, 73, 74
"Life of Addison," 103
Life of Ascham, 45, 99–101, 146
Life of Blake, 59, 96–98, 99, 102, 167
"Life of Boerhaave," 95
"Life of Burman," 95
"Life of Butler," 7, 57, 58, 61, 167
Life of Cheynel, 56, 99, 169
"Life of Cowley," 103, 167
"Life of Denham," 103
Life of Drake, 96, 98–99, 100, 121
"Life of Dryden," 94, 103
Life of Frederick of Prussia, 59, 101–3,
135, 148, 153
"Life of Halifax," 103
"Life of Milton," 60, 103, 104, 160,
164, 167, 173, 177, 193 (n. 28)
"Life of Morin," 95
"Life of Prior," 52, 103, 104, 105
"Life of Rochester," 103
"Life of Roscommon," 103
Life of Sarpi (and aborted translation
of Sarpi's *History of the Council of
Trent*), 12–13, 95–96, 100
Life of Savage, 154
"Life of Sprat," 103
"Life of Swift," 103, 104, 105–6
"Life of Sydenham," 95
"Life of Waller," 48, 60, 104–5, 167
Lindsay, John, 84
Lipsius, Justus, 7
Literary Magazine, 19, 101, 112, 115,
160, 183 (n. 22), 190 (n. 1), 191
(n. 11)
Lives of the Poets, 20, 49, 50, 53, 64,
92–93, 94, 95, 99, 103–6, 137,
177. *See also individual lives*

Index

Livy, 10, 141, 143
Lobo, Father Jerome, 10, 11
London, 12, 13, 26, 166
London, 32–34, 45, 175, 176
Lort, Michael, 64, 187 (n. 3)
Louis XIV, king of France, 50, 103, 119, 128
Low, D.M., 1
Lucian of Samosata, 141, 143, 147, 151
Lucretius, 7
Ludlow, Edmund, 58
Ludolf, Hiob, 8, 11
Lye, Edward, 64
Lyttelton, George, Lord, 23, 162

McAdam, E. L., Jr., 7, 68, 107, 108, 111, 146, 186 (n. 45)
Macaulay, Catharine, 7, 23, 59, 162, 164
Macaulay, Kenneth, 23
Macaulay, Thomas Babington, 1, 138, 161, 162, 167, 168, 179, 181 (n. 1)
Macbean, Alexander, 84
Machiavelli, 23, 37, 136, 142, 143
Macpherson, John, 23
Malone, Edmond, 73
Maria Theresa, queen of Hungary, 102, 148
Markham, Gervase, 187 (n. 9)
Marlborough, John Churchill, duke of, 10, 34, 42, 44, 106, 119
Marmor Norfolciense, 14–16, 62
Marshall, Benjamin, 8
Martin, Martin, 23, 79
Mary I, queen of England, 45, 100
Mary II, queen of England, 185 (n. 24)
Mary, queen of England, 63
Mary Queen of Scots, 23, 27, 28, 43, 45–46, 47, 63, 84, 86–87, 163, 184 (n. 10)

Mason, William, 189 (n. 8)
Mauduit, Israel, 23
Maxwell, William, 137
Mézeray, François, 8
Miltiades, 40
Milton, John, 60, 104. *See also* "Life of Milton"
Miscellaneous Observations on Macbeth, 90
Monboddo, James Burnett, Lord, 145, 146, 175
Montesquieu, 142, 193 (n. 21)
Moody, John, 46
Moor, James, 157, 158, 159, 160
Moore, John Robert, 88
More, Thomas, 22
Murphy, Arthur, 155, 167, 179, 191 (n. 1)

Nadel, George, 142
Nadir Shah (Kuli Khan), 184 (n. 4)
Nero (Roman emperor), 40
Newton, Isaac, 8
Nicephorus, Xanthopoulos, 6
Nicetas, Acominatus, 6
Nichols, John, 64, 65, 66, 73
Nicolson, William, 7
Northumberland, Elizabeth, countess of, 65
Novak, Maximillian E., 94, 103

"Observations" in *Universal Chronicle,* 115
Observations on a Letter from a French Refugee in America, 113
Observations on the Present State of Affairs, 113–15, 119
O'Connor, Charles, 64, 67, 137, 178
Ogg, David, 51
Oglethorpe, James, 41, 42, 50
Oldmixon, John, 6
Oldys, William, 19, 64

*"O.N." On the Fireworks for the Peace
   of Aix-la-Chapelle,* 78
On the Russian and Hessian Treaties, 113
Ovid, 9
Oxford, Edward, earl of, 20
Oxford University and area, 10, 11,
   20, 25, 26, 56, 65, 74, 77, 99, 163,
   190 (n. 15)

Paoli, Pasquale, 40
Parliamentary Debates, 16, 18–19, 112
The Patriot, 128–29
Patten, Thomas, 66
Paul V, Pope, 95, 96
Pennant, Thomas, 23, 79
Percy, Henry (Hotspur), 25
Percy, Thomas, 65, 66, 83, 84, 148,
   187 (n. 8)
Perrers, Alice, 32
Petavius, Dionysius, 24
Peter the Great, czar of Russia, 36,
   37, 38, 39, 42, 43, 103
Philip II, king of Spain, 124
Phillips, John, 56
Pindar, 9
Pinkerton, John, 64
Plutarch, 22
Polybius, 7, 141, 142, 147, 151, 155
Pompey (Pompeius Gnaeus), 40, 42,
   43
Pope, Alexander, 32, 33, 62
Popish Plot, 10
Preface, Du Fresnoy's *Chronological
   Tables,* 84, 140–41
Preface, Macbean's *Dictionary of
   Ancient Geography,* 84
Preface to *The Preceptor,* 23–24, 141,
   156, 160
Prior, Matthew, 105
Pufendorf, Samuel, 23
Punic Wars, 9, 138, 139, 191 (n. 1)
Pym, John, 104, 127
Pyrrhus, king of Epirus, 40

Raleigh, Walter, 6, 21, 159, 162
Rambler, 20, 142, 160, 161, 169, 170,
   171, 177; no. 4, 49; no. 49, 39–40;
   no. 60, 139, 171; no. 71, 82;
   no. 82, 63; no. 83, 81–82; no. 122,
   21, 158–59, 160–61, 167; no. 127,
   139; no. 145, 192 (n. 4); no. 154, 5;
   no. 161, 63; no. 177, 26, 64
Ranke, Leopold von, 145
Rapin Thoyras, Paul de, 142, 143,
   147
Rasselas, 20, 80, 136, 146, 169, 177.
   See also Imlac
Rawlinson, Richard, 24
Remarks on the Militia Bill, 113
Restoration, 20, 49, 90, 94, 186
   (n. 31), 193 (n. 28)
Review of *Account of the Conduct of
   the Duchess of Marlborough,* 49, 52,
   84–86, 148, 158, 160, 193 (n. 27)
Review of Birch's *History of the Royal
   Society,* 84
Review of Blackwell's *Memoirs of the
   Court of Augustus,* 84, 87, 88–89,
   139, 158, 159, 160
Review of Borlase's *History of the Isles
   of Sicily,* 84
Review of Browne's *History of
   Jamaica,* 84
Review of Tytler's *Historical and
   Critical Enquiry,* 45–46, 84, 86–87,
   100, 163, 166
Reviews of the Byngh Pamphlets,
   115
Reynolds, Joshua, 64
Richard I, king of England, 135
Richard II, king of England, 27
Richard III, king of England, 25
Richard, king of England, 63
Ridpath, George, 7
Robert of Gloucester, 7, 142
Robertson, William, 7, 8, 22, 23, 87,
   135, 138, 142, 143, 145, 146, 155,

157, 161, 162, 163, 164–67, 170,
195 (n. 55), 195 (n. 56)
Robespierre, 58
Rollin, Charles, 23, 142, 143
Ross, John Leslie, bishop of, 46
Rupert, Prince, 25, 96
Rymer, Thomas, 91

Sacheverell, Henry, 10
Sacheverell, William, 23, 79
Saint-Evremond, Charles de
Marquetel de Saint-Denis, 6, 149
Sallust, 7, 23, 139, 151
Sarpi, Father Paul, 12, 95–96, 142,
158
Scaliger, Joseph Justus, 24, 142
Schlesinger, Arthur, Jr., 190 (n. 11)
Schwartz, Richard B., 26, 183 (n. 36)
Scipio Africanus, Publius Cornelius,
40, 42
Scotland, 20, 27–30, 47, 57, 68–80
passim, 117, 132–34, 147, 153, 154,
166, 168, 169, 171, 175, 196 (n. 4)
Scott, Walter, 43
Sedley, Catherine, 34
Sermon 7, 56–57
Sermon 23, 54, 58, 144
Seven Years' War, 42, 101, 103, 112,
114, 115, 116, 118, 119, 135
Shaftesbury, Anthony
Ashley-Cooper, earl of, 10
Shakespeare edition and preface, 22,
80, 87, 90–92, 93, 94, 100, 146,
164, 167
Shakespeare, William, 22, 33, 35, 44,
57, 88, 89, 90–92, 93
Sheridan, Charles, 23, 168
Sheridan, Thomas, 48
Sidney, Algernon, 58–59
Smith, Adam, 145, 155, 157
Smith, Thomas, 100
Smollett, Tobias, 19, 182 (n. 22)
Socrates, 41

Solon, 40
South Sea Bubble, 10, 40
Spelman, John, 33
Spenser, Edmund, 44
Spon, Jacob, 187 (n. 10)
Steevens, George, 64
Stow, John, 7, 23
Strahan, William, 137, 166, 168
Strauch, Aegidius, 24
Strode, William, 127
Stromberg, R. N., 145
Strype, John, 6
Stuart, Gilbert, 7, 145, 175
Stuart, House of. *See* Anne, Charles
I, Charles II, James I, James II,
Mary Queen of Scots, William III
Stukeley, William, 62, 187 (n. 1)
Suetonius Tranquillus, Gaius, 7, 10
Sully, Maximilien de Béthune, duke
of, 8, 23
Swift, Jonathan, 14, 18, 106

Tacitus, Cornelius, 7, 141, 143
Tamerlane (Timur the Lame), 40, 42,
43
Tasker, William, 64
Taxation No Tyranny, 129–32, 177
Taylor, John, 27, 36, 54, 61
Temple, William, 23
Theocritus, 9
Thomson, James, 32, 33
*Thoughts on the Late Transactions
Respecting Falkland's Islands,* 123–27,
144, 156, 177
Thrale, Hester, 9, 29, 43, 74, 138,
139, 140, 141, 142, 160, 164, 171,
179, 184 (n. 38), 184 (n. 9), 191
(n. 1)
Thrale, Queeney, 43
Thucydides, 7, 19, 23, 141, 147
Thurloe, John, 13
Tomarken, Edward, 132, 134, 191
(n. 16)

Tully. *See* Cicero
Turner, Noel, 187 (n. 9)
Tyler, Wat, 127, 128
Tytler, William, 23, 45, 84, 86–87

Utrecht, Peace (Treaty) of, 10, 40, 105

Vallancey, Charles, 64
Vane, Anne, 34, 35
Vanity of Human Wishes, 20, 34–36, 144, 177
Velleius Paterculus, Marcus, 7
Vergil, Polydore, 22, 90, 142
Vertot, René, 23, 168
Vico, Giambattista, 142, 146
Villiers, George, 1st duke of Buckingham, 34
Vinerian Law Lectures, 64, 66–67, 84, 107–11, 134, 190 (n. 20)
Virgil, 9
Voltaire, 8, 36, 39, 91, 142, 145, 146, 148, 154, 156, 163, 193 (n. 21), 195 (n. 53)
Von Dalin, Olaf, 23

Wain, John, 2
Wales, 20, 27, 75
Waller, Edmund, 104–5
Walmesley, Gilbert, 10, 11, 40
Walpole, Horace, 164, 189 (n. 8)
Walpole, Robert, 10, 14, 18, 63
War of Jenkins's Ear, 18, 96
War of the Austrian Succession, 18, 35, 101–3, 114, 135

War of the Spanish Succession, 10, 105, 106
Wars of the Roses, 28
Warton, Joseph, 136
Warton, Thomas, 26, 32, 33, 62, 65, 66, 67, 75, 92, 94, 135, 136, 163, 189 (n. 4)
Watson, Robert, 23, 137, 168
Wentworth, Thomas, 34
Wexler, Victor, 162
Whalley, Peter, 143, 147, 153, 161
Wharton, Henry, 7, 62
Wheare, Degory, 24, 143
Wheler, George, 187 (n. 10)
White, Hayden, 157
Whitlock, Bulstrode, 13, 96, 104
Wilcox, [J.], 184 (n. 4)
Wilcox, Thomas, 12
Wilkes, John, 127, 128
William I, king of England, 15, 40
William II, king of England, 40
William III, king of England, 10, 14, 40, 44, 47, 51–52, 85, 119, 128, 133, 185 (n. 24)
Wilson, Thomas, 8, 66
Wimsatt, W. K., 1
Wolsey, Cardinal, 34, 35–36
Wood, Anthony à, 13, 23, 62, 190 (n. 15)
Wood, Robert, 187 (n. 10)

Xenophon, 7
Xerxes, 34, 37–38, 39, 40, 41

Zonaras, Joannes, 6